W9-BZM-910

"This masterful book will be a much-debated and welcomed addition to graduate and undergraduate courses in religion, philosophy, and social and political culture. I suspect readers will spend many hours pondering the powerful arguments that Poplin advances."

Carol M. Swain, professor of political science and law, Vanderbilt University

"This is a thorough and remarkably informative critique of what is wrong with today's predominant worldview, that is, secularism. The many atheists, humanists and materialists controlling so much of what is read in our colleges and presented in the media should put it on their informal but effective list of 'forbidden books.' Of course, Poplin's book should go on the list of required books for all Christians trying to survive the politically correct rejection of God and Christ now nervously maintained by our governing elite."

Paul C. Vitz, professor, Institute for the Psychological Sciences; professor emeritus, New York University; author of *Faith of the Fatherless: The Psychology of Atheism*

"Mary Poplin has lived out many of the ideologies of the past fifty years—secular humanism, ivory-tower Marxism, radical feminism, New Age spirituality, you name it. *Is Reality Secular?* is her penetrating analysis of these ideologies and a brilliant exposition of the profound truths of the Christian faith. A terrific book for undergraduates, grad students and all those who want to be really educated—that is, aware of the sweep of intellectual history, what it has been and is now, and where it should be headed."

James W. Sire, author of *The Universe Next Door*

"This is a serious book by a serious thinker. What's most appealing is its authenticity. Mary Poplin guides readers through the pitfalls of the same secular beliefs she held personally for many years until finally discovering the truth of Christianity at the age of forty. Her analysis reflects the insight of someone who has lived out secular philosophies and knows from the inside how destructive and dehumanizing they are. She makes the case that Christianity is not just a better theory, it is reality."

Nancy R. Pearcey, director, Francis Schaeffer Center for Worldview and Culture; professor and scholar in residence, Houston Baptist University

"This clearly written and wide-ranging book shows Mary Poplin to be an important Christian intellectual voice. The cumulative force of her best evidence provides a compelling case, one all the more relevant because of her personal story."

Craig Keener, professor of New Testament, Asbury Theological Seminary

"It is unusual these days for a book to be both provocative and reflective, but that is precisely what Professor Poplin has accomplished in *Is Reality Secular?* The roots of her reflection are clearly in what began as a personal quest for meaning and truth, but she has produced an extended essay that addresses a universal longing and therefore speaks to us all. Her fellow Christians will find the book edifying. I myself certainly did. But others, too, will find value in it. Even at its most provocative, it is never merely polemical. It provokes, rather, by engaging the reader where he is and challenging him to join her in thinking ever more deeply about ultimate things."

Robert P. George, McCormick Professor of Jurisprudence, Princeton University

"Truth, a wise man said, is valuable because it is what allows us to navigate reality. Mary Poplin has done us a great service—she helps us explore where truth lies and how it guides. This is fair-minded, clear-seeing and deeply informed."

John Ortberg, senior pastor of Menlo Park Presbyterian Church and author of *Who Is This Man?*

IS REALITY SECULAR?

TESTING THE ASSUMPTIONS OF
FOUR GLOBAL WORLDVIEWS

MARY POPLIN

An imprint of InterVarsity Press
Downers Grove, Illinois

InterVarsity Press
P.O. Box 1400, Downers Grove, IL 60515-1426
World Wide Web: www.ivpress.com
Email: email@ivpress.com

InterVarsity Press® is the book-publishing division of InterVarsity Christian Fellowship/USA®, a movement of students and faculty active on campus at hundreds of universities, colleges and schools of nursing in the United States of America, and a member movement of the International Fellowship of Evangelical Students. For information about local and regional activities, write Public Relations Dept., InterVarsity Christian Fellowship/USA, 6400 Schroeder Rd., P.O. Box 7895, Madison, WI 53707-7895, or visit the IVCF website at www.intervarsity.org.

Scripture quotations, unless otherwise noted, are from The Holy Bible, English Standard Version, copyright © 2001 by Crossway Bibles, a division of Good News Publishers. Used by permission. All rights reserved.

While all stories in this book are true, some names and identifying information in this book have been changed to protect the privacy of the individuals involved.

Cover design: David Fassett
Interior design: Beth Hagenberg
Images: Small globe: © ken roberts/iStockphoto
   Water surface wave: © kedsanee/iStockphoto

ISBN 978-0-8308-4406-7 (print)
ISBN 978-0-8308-7189-6 (digital)

Printed in the United States of America ∞

Library of Congress Cataloging-in-Publication Data

A catalog record for this book is available from the Library of Congress.

P	19	18	17	16	15	14	13	12	11	10	9	8	7	6	5	4	3	2	1
Y	30	29	28	27	26	25	24	23	22	21	20	19	18	17	16	15	14		

Stand by the roads, and look,

and ask for the ancient paths,

where the good way is; and walk in it,

and find rest for your souls.

JEREMIAH 6:16

In grateful appreciation to John Rivera,

a consistent reminder of "living water"

As the Scripture has said, "Out of his heart

will flow rivers of living water."

JOHN 7:38

CONTENTS

FOREWORD

I am glad to call attention to this book by Mary Poplin of Claremont
Graduate University. *Is Reality Secular?* is a challenge, by an insider,
to the secularism that is now assumed, with no significant evaluation, to
be the height of intellectual respectability and that dominates the most
elevated and most inclusive levels of higher education. From there it
pervades professional, social and official life in our world, with effects
that severely diminish human aspirations of the type that have traditionally been upheld for humanity by education in the Western world.

Mary is a person of excellent standing in her own professional field,
but also one with an established voice in the discussions of Christ and
culture now going on in America. She is a powerful (and much used)
speaker who is already well published. The line of argument she de-
velops in this book is vital for the future of education today and tomorrow, both for secularists and for Christians. For secularists, because
just being secular does not provide positive guidance in learning or in
learning how to live. It is, fundamentally, a negative stance. For Christians, because they have largely been publicly defined out of the
"knowledge" business into the "faith" business. Even in their own view,
they do not see their beliefs and practices as contributing to the human
need for publicly available knowledge necessary for human existence.
Thus they do not compete head on, as they should, with what is con-
veyed by the academy.

Mary breaks the impasse between secularists and Christians by intelligently reframing the questions that must be asked and answered for thoughtful and honest living today.

Dallas Willard

Part 1

IS REALITY SECULAR?

Is reality secular?
Is adequate knowledge secular?
And is that something that has been established
as a fact by thorough and unbiased inquiry? Is this
something that today's secular universities
thoroughly and freely discuss in
a disciplined way?

DALLAS WILLARD,
KNOWING CHRIST TODAY

1

TRUTH AND CONSEQUENCES

*Don't you believe that there is in man
a deep so profound as to be hidden
even to him in whom it is?*

Augustine of Hippo

*It can be very dangerous to see things
from somebody else's point of view
without the proper training.*

Douglas Adams,
The Hitchhiker's Guide to the Galaxy

In a seminar one evening in 2012 the class was discussing texts on secularism, the doctrine that rejects all religious principles in civic life.[1] I had posed the questions, Is reality secular? Is it true? One of the seventeen PhD students began a defense of secularism by saying, "Well, setting aside the idea of truth . . ." I venture to guess that there may have been only a couple of other people in the room that realized the gravity of what had just been said.

Though I said nothing at the time, this comment revealed in an instant how secularism has taken hold, how far it has gone and what have been its consequences. Truth has become an idea rather than a de-

scription of reality, and it can be set aside even though seeking truth is
or once was the sole reason for the university. Not so many years before,
this same phrase might have come from my own lips as I indoctrinated
my students into these same *ideas*.

Historian Charles Taylor claims that secularism has been the hegemonic master narrative for the last several hundred years in the West.[2]
Unpacking this popular academic phrase, the term *master narrative* or
metanarrative means the "grand story" around which we build our lives,
individually and culturally. These stories may differ by culture, language
and individual as well as across time. In the last few decades, metanarratives are believed to be social constructions made by human beings
rather than truths to be discovered and believed. Taylor explains that the
metanarrative that shaped the West in its ascendency was the Judeo-
Christian story of God, man and nature, but that story has been replaced
with the "metanarrative of secularism." It is hegemonic because we are
all forced to submit to this reality in public life, whether or not we believe
it, and regardless of the fact that it may not be true or in our best interest.[3]

In place of the Judeo-Christian story, the current metanarrative pro-
mulgated largely by the Western academy and media goes something
like the following. After the Enlightenment, and particularly in the twentieth century, we humans finally matured and no longer needed to socially construct God or gods or any supernatural entities to understand
our lives or guide our behaviors. We have now evolved enough to go it
on our own, armed only with human reason and scientific evidence to
steer the course of progress and break away from limiting rules and
regulations.

To hold secular worldviews is considered normal, more "progressive"
and "safer" because such worldviews transcend specific faith commitments. These are superior to "religious" worldviews—which are "pre-
scientific" or "pre-political" justifications based on faith.[4] Robert Bellah,
the late respected sociologist of religion, explains the phenomenon:
"The meta-narrative that is really the only one intelligible to all well-
educated people everywhere in the world is the meta-narrative of evolution."[5] He uses the term *evolution* in the broad sense of the evolution
of ideas, cultures and religious beliefs.

Secularists have a number of reasonable arguments for avoiding religious worldviews. For example, religious worldview holders believe in a spiritual world not verified by science; they often disagree with one another; they hold to particular universal unchanging moral codes; and they do not limit their understandings of reality to important but insufficient scientific facts about the natural world. Secularism is believed to be the necessary foundation on which to build a peaceful one-world global order—a world that will be run solely on the lessons of science and human reason.

David Bentley Hart articulates the original hope of our secular faith:

> Part of the enthralling promise of an age of reason was, at least at first, the prospect of a genuinely rational ethics, not bound to the local or tribal customs of this people or that, not limited to the moral precepts of any particular creed, but available to all reasoning minds regardless of culture and—when recognized—immediately compelling to the rational will.[6]

Regardless of elite Western culture's contemporary aversion to faith, all four global worldviews (material naturalism,[7] secular humanism,[8] pantheism and monotheism) begin with a faith commitment—a belief outside the reach of scientific verifiability. They are simply different faiths. A naturalist's faith is that all things ultimately can be reduced to material phenomena, including, for example, religious beliefs, the mind, the soul and consciousness. Secular humanists place their faith solely in human reason as the bedrock upon which to build "progressive" consensual social, moral, cultural and intellectual foundations. Pantheist faith lies in an ultimate spiritual reality (e.g., Brahman or Nirvana) that is the substance of all phenomena embedded in an ever-evolving cycle of rebirths or levels of consciousness.

In the same seminar a few weeks later we had read both the "new atheists" and some form of Christian apologetic. A student exclaimed in a worried tone, "You aren't going to suggest that Christianity is true, are you? What about Hinduism?" The only honest answer to that question is, if Hinduism is true, we should all become Hindu.

This exclamation perfectly reveals the second part of the new Western metanarrative, which addresses religious worldviews directly, both pantheism and monotheism. This new narrative contends that if for some reason individuals want or need some other support system for their lives (outside of secular descriptions of reality), they are relatively free to choose privately from among the various existing religions or construct their own understandings of the "spiritual" outside of specific religious commitments, that is, become spiritual and not religious. These various spiritual options are basically similar; they lead more or less to the same place. More important, these are personal choices for our private lives, not to be raised in contemporary public spaces such as government, law, business, education, arts and entertainment, or public media; nor are they to be entertained when running our businesses and going about our public work. They are optional embellishments that may be important to particular individuals, or historically or sociologically interesting, but they are not candidates for knowledge or truth.

On the other hand, the grand story or metanarrative of the West from the early Middle Ages well into the Enlightenment is the Judeo-Christian story, which was believed to be universally true (and still is for approximately one-third of the world). It is the story of God and "man," who was specially made in the image of God—"male and female" (Genesis 1:27). It was from this place that Western culture began to flourish—intellectually, socially, economically, technologically and morally. It was here that the great traditions of science, literature, art, music and architecture of the Middle Ages and Renaissance Europe were born. The narrative of this grand story was introduced by the Jews to the world around 1500 B.C. (the time of Moses). The revelations were transmitted orally for many generations before being written as the books of Moses—the Torah, known to Christians as the first five books of the Bible. The biblical revelations depict God's character as living and active, inviting us to know him and to know ourselves through him. Also in this central narrative are revelations about the natural world, early human history, the uniqueness of human beings (triumphal and fallen), and God's special provision to redeem humanity and the earth through Christ. Because of the emphasis in Christianity on *knowing* God, man and nature, monasteries established schools, universities and hospitals[9] to understand and apply the true principles around which the universe operates (natural, human and spiritual) and work alongside God to tend the earth and its inhabitants—to become our brothers' and sisters' keepers.

Rather than being one another's keeper, the tenor of the twenty-first century often feels to many like one of great strife, confusion and contestation. Well-meaning people all over the globe are deeply concerned about our many contentious disagreements and our inability to find common ground, but few understand the differences in worldviews that undergird these clashes in civilizations and families. Harvard political scientist Samuel Huntington, in his popular book *The Clash of Civilizations,* writes that "the twentieth-century conflict between liberal democracy and Marxist-Leninism is only a fleeting and superficial historical phenomenon compared to the continuing and deeply conflictual relation between Islam and Christianity."[10] The new metanarrative about religion, especially prominent since 9/11, is that religion is the primary source of violence in today's world. Theologian William Cavanaugh challenges this:

> The myth of religious violence helps create a blind spot about the violence of the putatively secular nation-state. We like to believe that the liberal state arose to make peace between warring religious factions. Today, the Western liberal state is charged with the burden of creating peace in the face of the cruel religious fanaticism of the Muslim world. The myth of religious violence promotes a dichotomy between *us* in the secular West who are rational and peacemaking and *them,* the hordes of violent religious fanatics in the Muslim world. *Their* violence is religious, and therefore irrational and divisive. *Our* violence, on the other hand, is rational, peacemaking, and necessary. Regrettably, we find ourselves forced to bomb them into the higher rationality.[11]

Oddly enough, radical Islamic terrorists were not attacking Christianity on September 11, 2001; rather, they were assailing the proliferation and mass dispensation of secular economic and moral norms in Western culture to the rest of the world. Their targets were the World Trade Center towers, the Pentagon and the White House, not the National Cathedral.[12] One of the major conundrums of secularism is its naive assumption of neutrality, an un-self-reflective position that makes its superiority seem plausible. But secularism is no more neutral than global Christianity, and it has no fewer contestations inside itself or with the outside world. These two, radical Islam and radical secularism, share a good deal in common—radical intolerance of all other worldviews. As award-winning British journalist Melanie Phillips writes, "The correspondences between Western progressives and Islamists are really quite remarkable. Both are attempting to create utopias to redeem past sins; both permit no dissent from the one revealed truth. . . . Both are giving expression to a totalitarian instinct that involves a wholesale repudiation of reason."[13]

Strangely unnoticed in many analyses is the fact that much of the contemporary upheaval around the world occurs within nation-states. These conflicts often arise from attempts by citizens to import Western ideals of egalitarianism, freedom, justice, democracy, human rights, freedom of conscience, and freedom of religion, speech and assembly, all of which grew out of Judeo-Christianity.[14] Part of the secular strategy, conscious or unconscious, has been to rewrite the history of Western civilization without reference to these contributions. Such was the case in the development of the new European Union. Eminent German philosopher Jürgen Habermas came to the defense of Pope John Paul II and Cardinal Ratzinger's objections to the omission of Christianity in the European documents. Though an atheist, Habermas has written:

> For the normative self-understanding of modernity, Christianity has functioned as more than just a precursor or catalyst. Universalistic egalitarianism, from which sprang the ideals of freedom and a collective life in solidarity, the autonomous conduct of life and emancipation, the individual morality of conscience, human rights and democracy, is the direct legacy of the Judaic ethic of justice and the Christian ethic of love. This legacy, substantially unchanged, has been the object of a continual critical re-appropriation and reinterpretation. Up to this very day there is no alternative to it. And in light of the current challenges of a post-national constellation, we must draw sustenance now, as in the past, from this substance. . . . Everything else is idle postmodern talk.[15]

I have a friend who occasionally remarks, "I don't let that [person, idea, thought] rent no space in my head." Would that we all knew what it is that rents space in our heads and whether, when we understood it and its alternatives, we would still believe it. If we consciously knew, we could live more awake in the world. James Sire, author of one of the most popular books on worldviews, suggests that "for any of us to be fully conscious intellectually we should not only be able to detect the worldviews of others but be aware of our own—why it is ours and why in the light of so many options we think it is true."[16]

Understanding the relatively straightforward assumptions of the four major worldviews around the globe—naturalism, secular humanism, pantheism and monotheism (represented here primarily by Judeo-Christianity)—makes us less susceptible to the strong ideologies (left and right) of the media, education and government of which we are often not consciously aware. Unfortunately, in today's culture there is often more indoctrination than education in its broadest sense.[17]

As a professor in a secular university who once fearlessly indoctrinated my students (to the left), I am now convinced that for people all around the globe to be well educated they must be acquainted with all the frameworks available from which to think, live and work. No reasonable worldview should be withheld, automatically discounted or ignored; all four major worldviews need to be made explicit. For serious seekers, the truth will vindicate itself. No matter what worldview(s) we may hold or seek to understand, "ideas have consequences," sometimes colossal and devastating ones, sometimes brilliant and life-enhancing ones.[18]

The fundamental concern here is whether one of these worldviews is actually true. Or does some combination of these worldviews more adequately describe what is real? Or should we look for another? Two of the four worldviews currently dominate the West; they are the secular worldviews of secular humanism and material naturalism. The first question before us then will be, is reality secular?

Philosopher Dallas Willard asks the first of the two most critical questions of the twenty-first century:

> Is reality secular? Is adequate knowledge secular? And is that something that has been established as a fact by thorough and unbiased inquiry? Is this something that today's secular universities thoroughly and freely

discuss in a disciplined way? Certainly not! Nowhere does that happen. It is now simply assumed that every field of knowledge or practice is perfectly complete without any reference to God. It may be logically possible that this assumption is true, but is it true?[19]

If there are doubts about reality being secular, the second question emerges: Is Judeo-Christianity or another religious worldview true? These are the guiding questions of this book as we test the assumptions of the four dominant worldviews on earth.

CONFESSIONS OF A PROFESSOR

*Every story of conversion
is the story of a blessed defeat.*

C. S. LEWIS, FOREWORD TO JOY DAVIDMAN'S
SMOKE ON THE MOUNTAIN

Before reading a book, it's helpful to know exactly where an author stands, how she reached that stance and what her path forward might be. This is now a prerequisite to feminist scholarship. So here is my confession. Though my parents took their four daughters to church nearly every Sunday, once I got to college I walked away, not really knowing exactly what I was leaving behind. The church we attended was already infected with a secularized gospel. My mind and soul were essentially formed by the more pervasive culture of television shows, movies, nightly news, books, magazines, schools and universities of the 1960s and 70s—all resolutely secular.

I grew up watching soap operas (the soft porn of my childhood) and learned to imagine my personal life within the parameters they set. What could be wrong with having affairs even with married men if they played on all three channels during the day and my mother was watching them? I learned that the most beautiful, bright and elite women were the most daring. These influences inflamed my own selfish and impure desires. Judaic principles claim that what we allow into our eyes and ears forms us.[1] Sitcoms depicted men as weak and ignorant, then and now, which reinforced my 1970s fascination with radical feminism. At the time, college environments were also strongly influenced by antiwar, free-love, open-marriage and Marxist movements. All these began to shape my mind and heart and thus the way I began to live my life. Until a few years ago, I saw nothing odd about this; I was a thoroughly postmodern woman.

Then for various reasons scattered throughout this book, in 1993, after having been awarded full tenure at my university six months earlier, I began to secretly explore and then later to clumsily attempt to follow Christ. Secretly—because I knew this was not going to gain me any status in the secular university that I loved. To be honest, at first my efforts to follow Christ were more of a trial. In my mind I always left open the possibility that this too might be just one more ultimately empty philosophy. I might in a couple of years find myself bored again, tired of it, and convinced that it also was too shallow to make any real difference. I had discarded many such philosophies before.

By the time I was forty, I was so confused that my panoply of thoughts and ideas often conflicted with one another. When I was conscious of the contradictions, I simply brushed them aside, not realizing (or caring) that there might be an alternative. In retrospect, by the time I was a fully tenured professor, I could not reliably think myself out of a paper bag. Perhaps worse, few people apparently noticed. One brave individual did try to tell me one day—he quipped that if I was half as open minded as I thought I was, my brains would fall out.

For most of my life, I believed the claims of secularists, and thus I intellectually worked out of the frameworks of secular humanism and material naturalism. I indoctrinated my students into these principles, drawing primarily on the various ever-changing theories emerging from secular humanism. I intentionally excluded any principles founded on religious frameworks except for slipping in a few "spiritual" principles I borrowed from time to time from pantheism. I was a material naturalist and secular humanist by day and a pantheist by night.

Within these frameworks, I also built my *personal* life. By the time I had become a professor I was regularly using drugs and alcohol (recreationally, of course), frequenting bars and discos (of all kinds), experiencing bouts of depression (sometimes serious), and watching pornography with my partners. In my better moments, I was serially monogamous. By the time I began to see and long for the life circumscribed by Christ, I had been married and divorced twice and had had two abortions.

Spiritually, I experimented with any number of pantheist methods, including Zen and Transcendental Meditation, and various manifestations of the New Age movement—feminist theology as well as holistic, whole earth, neo-pagan and Wiccan experiments. These forays revealed my rather desperate attempts to find peace and happiness, a desperation of which I was completely unaware. What I really wanted was power—intellectual, personal and spiritual power.

My *intellectual life* was tied up in the various "progressive education movements," such as radical feminism, post-structuralism, postmodernism, multiculturalism and Marxism (critical theory). My colleagues and I were Marxists by ideology, not by lifestyle. Most "Marxists" in the university are more like Marx and his contemporary apologist Bill Ayers, both of whom lived partially off their capitalist fathers' fortunes.[2] We also were living the good life; were we to be asked seriously to give up our own salaries to equalize things, we would have found another reason to revolt. As ivory tower Marxists, we were not serving the poor like Mother Teresa; we were admonishing the government to help the poor the way we wanted them to be helped (to become revolutionaries). We would of course lead the revolution because we were the intelligentsia.

Upon his election, Pope Francis echoed his predecessor, Pope Benedict XVI, in his resistance to secularism when he said to the cardinals at his first mass, "If we do not confess to Christ, what would we be? We would end up a compassionate NGO [nongovernmental organization]. What would happen would be like when children make sand castles and then it all falls down."[3] He is making the audacious claim that with Christ real things happen that do not happen when we simply help others without him. This would have been incomprehensible to me until I spent two months at Mother Teresa's homes in Calcutta.

In 1996, a year and a half before Mother Teresa passed away, I went on sabbatical to Calcutta to find out what she meant when she said, "Our work is not social work; it is religious work." My own research focuses on the inside of public school classrooms where the poor and handicapped are educated. I wondered what she might teach me now that I was exploring Christianity. In my mind the trip was a mix of research and adventure.

Upon my return, I experienced a profound intellectual crisis. I was beginning to speak and write about my experiences in Calcutta, but soon realized that the essence of Mother Teresa and the Missionaries of Charity was incomprehensible from any of the worldviews I had been living and teaching. I could explain what they did but not how or why they did it. I could only tell half the story with secular language; I could not adequately describe their core motivations and had no way to explain the peace and power that accompanied their works.

How was I going to explain to my world that Mother Teresa and the Missionaries of Charity did not believe the work we admired was their first work? Rather their first work was to belong to Jesus and to pray unceasingly. How was I going to explain that when they tended the most desperate and unlovable person, they believed they were tending Jesus in the distressing disguise of the poor?[4] How was I going to explain that her entire ministry was developed around three visions she had of Jesus who spoke to her from the cross?[5]

In time I overcame these worries and wrote a book as best I could from her worldview, but when the book was finished my crisis was not fully resolved.[6] I could see the outline of the problem but little else. I called the book *Finding Calcutta* because toward the end of my visit Mother Teresa impressed on me that God did not call everyone to work with the poor or to live like the poor as she and her sisters had been called, but God did call everyone to a "Calcutta." "You have to find yours," she commanded, shaking her finger at me. To work myself out of my intellectual crisis, I strategically began to study the worldviews in which I formerly had spent my life and the one for which I now longed. I had found my Calcutta; I was adamant to make sense of this new life as well as to understand better the lure of the old one.

Admittedly my conversion to Christianity has been a radical one. Biblical descriptions of conversions include the notion of turning one's mind around 180 degrees—*metanoia*. Unfortunately, *metanoia* is translated in English simply as "repentance." Repentance is an essential but incomplete description of what is involved in metanoia—completely turning around to face in God's direction.

Theologian Lesslie Newbigin describes the radical conversion as

> not only a conversion of the will and of the feelings but a conversion of the mind—a "paradigm shift" that leads to a new vision of how things are and, not at once but gradually, to the development of a new plausibility structure in which the most real of all realities is the living God whose character is "rendered" for us in the pages of Scripture.[7]

In the West we tend to analyze history in such a way that it looks as though we are always progressing. In the humanities and social sciences, the highest status is granted to those who are progressive (leftist). I prided myself on being among them. C. S. Lewis wisely noted, "If you have taken a wrong turning, then to go forward does not get you any nearer. If you are on the wrong road, progress means doing an about-turn and walking back to the right road; and in that case the man who turns back soonest is the most progressive."[8] I certainly win no prize for the one who turned back soonest; I was forty-one.

WORLDVIEWS AS
OPERATING SYSTEMS OF THE MIND

If little else, the brain is an educational toy. . . . While it may be a frus-
trating plaything, . . . [it] comes already assembled; you don't have to put
it together on Christmas morning. The problem with possessing such an
engaging toy is that other people want to play with it, too. Sometimes
they'd rather play with yours than theirs. Or they object if you play with
yours in a different manner from the way they play with theirs.

TOM ROBBINS, *EVEN COWGIRLS GET THE BLUES*

Worldviews are like operating systems on a computer except that
they are in our minds, which are far more powerful and efficient
than modern computers. Operating systems determine the particular
functions on a computer that can be accomplished and the ones that
cannot. Worldviews function in much the same way, determining the
range of thoughts we will entertain. Computer operating systems are
constantly being improved and their glitches fixed by downloading
new updates. It is the same with worldviews; we are constantly ac-
quiring new information and experiences that inform our beliefs and
can cause us to adjust or change our worldviews (operating systems)
altogether.[1]

Whatever worldview or worldviews we hold shape what we notice or ignore, how we interpret what we see and experience, how we process information, and ultimately what decisions we will make and how we will act. It is the lens through which we interpret reality and by which we reason. Our actions are stronger indicators of our actual worldviews than our thoughts, feelings or words.

Worldviews shape what we think is plausible and reject what does not seem plausible. We don't buy software that was designed for a Mac when we own a PC. Once we buy a machine and the operating system, we have limited our options. Limits are necessary; we all have them else we could not make decisions. We are constantly deciding—this is better than that, or I believe this and not that—though we are sometimes not aware of other options.

A contemporary example of how different worldviews influence our beliefs and actions is revealed in the debate over abortion. Some believe that the developing embryo is merely a mass of cells, nothing more than a clump of material that can be discarded when unwanted or no longer needed or used to help regenerate spinal cords, heal diseases or make better skin cream for the living (material naturalism). Others believe that the developing embryo is a baby human being, made in the image of God, with intrinsic value and purpose, whose life should be as well protected as any person would be under the law (Judeo-Christianity). Still others believe that abortion is wrong because it breaks the cycle of birth and rebirth; the soul's karmic journey is interrupted and must begin again (pantheism). Another group simply overlooks these existential issues and pragmatically defends the political position that, no matter what the fetus is, it is the right of the person in whose womb or test tube it lies to decide its future—life or death (existential secular humanism). In some countries the right to decide the fate of a fetus resides not with the mother but with the government (technocracy, another form of secular humanism). I used many of these secular positions to justify my two abortions; once I came to Christ, I began to grieve them.

Because of mass communication and individual differences, we find every worldview in the midst of every culture. There is as much diversity within a culture as between cultures. James Sire defines worldview in this way:

A worldview is a commitment, a fundamental orientation of the heart that can be expressed as a story or in a set of presuppositions (assumptions which may be true, partially true or entirely false) that we hold (consciously or subconsciously, consistently or inconsistently) about the basic constitution of reality, and that provides the foundation on which we live and move and have our being.[2]

Most of us hold some mixture of assumptions from two or more worldviews; on particular issues we lean to one or the other, even though they may be logically incompatible. For example, years ago I occasionally accompanied a colleague who had a special passion to investigate odd religious movements in Los Angeles; the city gave him endless opportunities. I remember we once ended up at an engineer's house where quite a number of logically exacting engineers were experimenting with various pantheist practices; some were bending spoons and others walking on coals.

The Four Dominant Worldviews

Different authors classify worldviews into various categories. Sources for a variety of approaches are provided in the notes.[3] I simply distill worldviews at their most basic level into four major global worldviews—material naturalism, secular humanism, pantheism and monotheism, represented here by Judeo-Christianity. (In chapter 25 is a brief discussion of the differences between Christianity and the monotheisms of Judaism and Islam.) It is generally possible to trace all philosophies, theories and even most practical actions back to one or more of these four worldviews.

When I stopped trying to write about Mother Teresa so that our secular culture might better appreciate her, I began to realize how differently she would be interpreted from each of the three non-Christian worldviews—material naturalism, secular humanism and pantheism.

Material naturalism is the belief that all that exists in the world is ultimately reducible to material phenomena. From this perspective, Mother Teresa was just a unique bundle of brain chemistry with particular psychoneural processes acting predictably, prompting her to do what she did. This chemistry fueled her thoughts, decisions, ethics and work.

Secular humanism is the belief that human beings are alone in the world and must act responsibly by forming their ethics solely from their human experience, human reason and science. From this perspective, Mother Teresa simply decided who she wanted to be and what she wanted to do and garnered the fortitude, determination and self-discipline necessary to do good works.

Both of these secular worldviews might have added the caveat that it was unfortunate that she clung to the myth of God, which was either an unnecessary genetic residue or neurochemical glitch destined eventually to devolve from human nature (material naturalism) or that she had created this God out of her own unmet needs and unfulfilled desires (Freudian secular humanism) or perhaps that she was just a poorly educated Albanian, in which case Mother Teresa's religious quirks could be tolerated and excused and, if exotic enough, maybe even celebrated (multicultural secular humanism). Less generously, Marxist secular humanists most likely would suggest, as popular atheist apologist Christopher Hitchens did, that Mother Teresa used Christianity strategically as an "opiate for the poor," a Marxist phrase meaning to make them happy with their condition.

Pantheism is the belief that everything in the universe is a manifestation of a universal spirit. From the perspective of this nonsecular worldview, Mother Teresa might be interpreted as a more highly enlightened or reincarnated soul who had a strong spiritual connection to the divine spirit inside all of nature, including human nature. According to pantheists, this spirit is an impersonal life force and not, as Mother Teresa believed, a transcendent personal God, external to her, living and acting in the world, as well as in and through her, hearing and answering her prayers.

But Mother Teresa was *Christian;* she believed that she and the Missionaries of Charity were, as she once said of herself, "pencil(s) in God's hand." Their first work was to belong to Jesus and to pray unceasingly; from this source they garnered the strength, wisdom and grace to conduct the work we saw and admired—serving the poorest of the poor.

That Jesus appeared to Mother Teresa in three visions and asked her to do precisely what she did when she left the safe cloister of the Loreto convent simply cannot be considered an admissible fact. It isn't plausible through the lenses of the secular worldviews. It isn't part of the Western secular plausibility structure (the set of meanings in a culture that qualify as being possible). Even Westernized Christians often find her visions incredible, acceptable only if interpreted as a personal psychological state, not as a reality.

Within the orthodox principles of the Judeo-Christian worldview, however, her visions of Christ and obedience to his request are wholly credible. My own conversion began with a very vivid and unshakable dream in which I remembered every detail—sights, sounds, colors, thoughts and feelings. To the pantheist, spiritual transactions such as visions and dreams are also credible, but they are either the result of an impersonal universal spirit or one of a host of deities, not the intentional communication of a personal, all-powerful Creator who hears and responds to prayers.

Characteristics of All Worldviews and Their Relation to Christianity

There are five characteristics of all worldviews. First and most consequential, *all worldviews begin with faith,* a metaphysical belief that cannot be verified using scientific methods. Robert Bellah points out that the Latin word for faith, *fides,* is more akin to the English term for *trust* rather than *belief.*[4] Though these faith statements can be argued philosophically, and from evidence we can inductively and deductively hypothesize, none can be proven empirically through scientific methods, including material naturalism. Every worldview begins with faith in something empirically or scientifically unknowable.

Second, *every non-Christian worldview holds within it some principles of the Judeo-Christian worldview.* Thus there is an overlap between principles of Judeo-Christianity and those of material naturalism, secular humanism and pantheism.

Third, there are also *principles held by each of these three worldviews that lie outside of the Judeo-Christian worldview,* such as the material-naturalist belief that everything that exists is ultimately a material or natural phenomenon. From a Judeo-Christian standpoint, these principles would be considered errors of commission.

Fourth, there are *principles of Judeo-Christianity that lie outside the purview of believers in these other three worldviews*. The absence of these principles in other worldviews would be considered by Christians as errors of omission.

Finally, none of these worldviews is more progressive or modern than the other. *They have all existed ever since recorded history*. The only real question is, are one or more of these an adequate description of reality?

TRACING HISTORY UP TO NOW

What has been is what will be,
and what has been done is what will be done,
and there is nothing new under the sun.

ECCLESIASTES 1:9

Imagine my surprise as I began to read ancient philosophy and religious texts and realized that ideas I thought were wildly progressive had been recorded thousands of years ago. The New Age, New Earth movements are nothing but Westernized ancient pantheist ideas that were better defined five hundred years before Christ than they were in the New Age works I was reading. Plato had suggested that children should be raised by the state, just as Marx and Engels had proposed in their *Communist Manifesto,* though for different reasons. Although the outward manifestations and consequences of the four global worldviews have differed across time and cultures, their basic principles are ancient.[1]

Early representatives of the two secular worldviews, the Sophists and the Skeptics were frequent opponents in the Socratic dialogues recorded by Plato (c. 500 B.C.).[2] The Sophists were a group of roving educators who apparently charged large sums of money to teach methods of argumentation to young Greek men—to learn to debate so persuasively that they could make even the worst appear best and the best worst. They prefigured the critical and postmodern theorists of our day who use similar language games, making the familiar appear strange and the strange familiar, in order to turn ideas, social norms and common cultural understandings on their head (secular humanism). Socrates criticized the Sophists for teaching their students to be merely independent thinkers rather than truth seekers. The most lasting idiom from the famous Sophist philosopher Protagoras is that "man is the measure of all things."[3]

The Skeptics, with whom Socrates and Plato also contended, were skeptical of all knowledge or truth claims based on logic or reason (secular humanism). Evidence drawn from the senses was the only allowable criteria for knowledge (material naturalism). Democritus proposed the existence of atoms and that all reality could be reduced to them; thus as early as 400 B.C. we see the emergence of material naturalism.

The early Hebrew Scriptures (emerging in the second century B.C., though originating almost six thousand years ago and passed on orally from generation to generation) were the first to clearly differentiate mythological gods and various spirits from the one true and living God of creation. The Jews introduced the world to the God who creates and reveals himself to human beings as living and active—not a passive, abstract, mythological deity or simply a series of good teachers, but literally as the ultimate being and substance—"I AM."

The Hebrew Scriptures also abound with evidence of monotheistic, pantheistic and atheistic worldviews. Whole people groups, kings and priests bowed down to false gods and idols and consulted mediums, magicians and fortunetellers. Sometimes even Israel's kings mocked God and worshiped other deities. Frequently the early Israelites were warned that the minds of those who turned to other gods would gradually be darkened and that though they thought themselves wise they would become as fools (1000 B.C.).[4]

Paul's experience in first-century Athens after Christ's death and resurrection reveals a great deal about first-century worldviews.[5] Athens was a multinational and multiethnic city-state where traders and learned men shared knowledge and traded goods around the world; globalization is not new either. Paul writes, "Now all the Athenians and the foreigners who lived there would spend their time in nothing except telling or hearing something new."[6] This description is quite apt for today's universities, which fashion themselves as the ultimate marketplace of ideas and progenitors of all that is new.

Paul found the city full of idols. The Greeks had their gods and goddesses, and the foreigners had brought theirs. Monuments and statues had been built for all of them, including one to an "unknown god," revealing the Greeks' openness to new ideas. At first, the Athenians were eager to hear Paul because he brought "some strange things to [their] ears." Having been invited to teach, Paul used their altar to an "unknown god" to teach them about Christ as the fulfillment of God's revelation and prophecy given to the Jews. Once they heard that this God was not simply one choice among many and that his divine and human son had been crucified and raised from the dead, some were converted but others scoffed.[7] The disciples along with large crowds of people had seen and knew that Jesus had died; they had seen him in his resurrected body for forty days. Had he simply died and been buried, we would surely be making pilgrimages to the tomb.

The Athenians and others were already familiar with Judaism since through the various conquests and captivities the Jews had been scattered throughout Babylon, Rome and then Greece (the Jewish diaspora or dispersion). The Old Testament books of Daniel (600 B.C.), Joel (600 B.C.) and Zechariah (500 B.C.) had predicted the coming Greek encounters. Tertullian (c. A.D. 200), concerned about the co-optation of Judeo-Christianity to the Greek worldview, echoed the earlier biblical predictions and warnings when he asked, what has Athens to do with Jerusalem?[8]

In Athens, Paul encountered both Stoic and Epicurean philosophers. Stoics were rigorous and systematic materialists: the god of the Stoics was involved in all of life yet unknowable; life was driven by fate.[9] However, they believed that through a highly disciplined life lived according to nature and logic, one could attain perfection. In order to do this, one's life had to be lived without passions, as the Stoics believed emotions were malfunctions of reason.

The Epicureans also believed, like the early Skeptics and today's material naturalists, that knowledge can only be derived from the senses and that the world is made of only atoms. Pleasure (the absence of pain) was the chief purpose of life, which ended with death. They were not quite as hedonistic as the term now implies; they did place high value on simplicity and friendships. Nevertheless, they also lived in morally freewheeling communes seeking the pleasures of a life that they believed was finite. While some believed in gods, they maintained that these gods did not intervene in the world and that man could not have any clear knowledge of them.[10]

From the fourth century until the mid-nineteenth and early twentieth centuries,[11] Europeans and later Americans interpreted the world and their place in it more or less through the grand metanarrative of the Judeo-Christian story.[12] Beginning around A.D. 350, schools, hospitals and even civic works began to emerge from European monasteries. Out of the monastic schools emerged the early university with its emphasis on theology and science.[13]

A History of Secularism in the Academy

From A.D. 1100 to the 1800s, Roman Catholics and later Protestants founded most Western universities. In the late 1800s the secular German research university model emerged with its primary emphasis on the application of the sciences to all research. Historian George Marsden details the shift in the nineteenth-century elite Protestant universities in the United States from their denominational heritage to nonsectarian status.[14] Until the twentieth century, Christians were founders, presidents, board members and other university leaders. Frequently, presidents were either clergy or theologians, and some even taught the first or last classes of the university curriculum, courses built on the integration of knowledge, theology and the cultivation of right virtues.[15] The universities were open to non-Christian faculty, students and theories. Until the late 1800s, most universities, even many of the early state universities, had mottoes, seals and buildings embellished with biblical texts.[16] Most universities had regular chapel requirements as late as the 1950s, and graduation ceremonies were essentially religious events.

Gradually religion was isolated into a separate discipline, no longer the foundation of the university and no longer integrated into discussions across disciplines. Universities became resolutely secular as Marsden describes.

> Eventually, the logic of the nonsectarian ideals, which the Protestant establishment had successfully promoted in public life, dictated that liberal Protestantism itself should be moved to the periphery to which other religious perspectives had been relegated for some time. The result was an *inclusive higher education that resolved the problems of pluralism by virtually excluding all religious perspectives from the nation's highest academic life.* . . . [Thus] they tend to exclude or discriminate against relating explicit religious perspectives to intellectual life. In other words, the free exercise of religion does not extend to the dominant intellectual centers of our culture.[17]

A similar but perhaps less extreme version of this secularization took place in Roman Catholic universities.[18] Catholic colleges and universities have always sought to maintain a strong "Catholic identity," though that identity has changed over the centuries of secularizing religious knowledge as well. Pope Benedict XVI repeatedly warned the Roman Catholic academy, the clergy and the larger world about the dangers of "aggressive secularism" of the West.[19] A century before, Cardinal John Henry Newman had explained the necessity of God in the university.

> Religious doctrine is knowledge, in as full a sense as Newton's doctrine is knowledge. . . . Truth is the object of Knowledge of whatever kind. . . . Truth means facts and their relations. . . . All that exists, as contemplated by the human mind, forms one large system or complex fact. . . . If there be Religious Truth at all, we cannot shut our eyes to it without prejudice to every kind, physical, metaphysical, historical and moral; for it bears upon all truth. . . . All branches of knowledge are connected together, because the subject-matter of knowledge is intimately united itself, as being the acts and the work of the Creator.[20]

Alasdair MacIntyre elaborates,

> Subtract the knowledge of God from our knowledge, either by denying

God's existence or by insisting that we can know nothing of him and what you have is an assortment of different kinds of knowledge, but no way of relating them to each other. We are condemned to think in terms of the disunity of the sciences.[21]

Julie Reuben, in an excellent history of the university, notes that throughout the various (secular) intellectual transformations in the Western university, the topic of morality gradually became separated from its religious foundations. She documents the marginalization of the moral conversation as it moved from the central-most place in the university—the president's office and core curriculum—to theology schools, to liberalized schools of religion, to moral philosophy and ethics, then to science, to sociology and to the humanities; last, it landed, if at all, on the desk of the dean of students. Finally, she says, "the separation of knowledge and morality in American universities" was complete.[22] The contemporary trend to inter- or transdisciplinary studies is the secular university's first attempt to respond to this crisis.

After the Enlightenment, the place for religious knowledge was increasingly constrained in the university and thus also in public life. The sciences gradually took the honored seat in the university from theology. Science overtook the humanities, and even philosophy began to lose its hold on metaphysics, becoming increasingly restricted to analytic philosophy alone. Theology began to move away from orthodox beliefs and soon became, in theologian Lesslie Newbigin's words,

a kind of anthropology . . . the study of an aspect of human experience. . . . It dictated that while the crucifixion of Jesus could be accepted as a fact of real history, his resurrection was a psychological experience of the disciples. . . . Intellectual integrity [after the Enlightenment] required that the Bible must be understood in terms of what is possible for the modern person to believe.[23]

Christian theologians in major university seminaries led the way to secularizing Christianity itself. German theologian Rudolf Bultmann was influential in Western theology with his efforts to "demythologize" the life of Christ. Beginning in the 1920s, Bultmann accomplished this by applying the methods of historical criticism.[24] He believed that demythologizing Jesus would make him more acceptable to the modern secular mind, to better match the plausibility structure of the contemporary academy. Eta Linnemann was a student of Bultmann's. After her conversion in 1977 to orthodox Christianity, which essentially ended her academic career, she could no longer support his method and tried to remove her books from the market. Unsuccessful at this, Linnemann eventually wrote a book against the method she had formerly embraced.[25] At the end of a day of conversation in 2006 in Leer, Germany, she told me "Mary, never forget this. When I was a theologian, I thought I was a Christian. I was not." This was not the first time I had been warned that it was not possible to be a Christian in mind alone. Mother Teresa, in her own way, had charged me a few days before I left Calcutta, "You fall more in love with Jesus every day."

Dallas Willard also traces how the university effectively divorced Judeo-Christian truths from the domain of knowledge, leaving morality to reside in politics rather than philosophy and theology.[26] Judeo-Christian principles were softened and reinterpreted as secular humanism; by necessity this required the elimination and distortion of a good deal of Judeo-Christian knowledge. The scientific method began to claim that it was the sole path to know reality (just as the Skeptics, Epicureans and Stoics had claimed). Truth became limited to those facts that could be scientifically verified. Even the fields of psychology, sociology and anthropology moved themselves out of philosophy and adopted the scientific method to study human social behavior, creating the social sciences.[27]

By the twentieth century many were predicting the end of religion—the claims of modernity would replace belief in God.[28] However, there is little evidence that this is the case even in the most highly technological cultures.[29] Even many countries in Europe are experiencing increases in orthodox Christianity and other religions.[30] Eta Linnemann told me in 2006 that if I were to go into any town of any size in Germany I could easily find on-fire evangelical churches.[31] The robustness of religion around the world has led philosopher Jürgen Habermas to call our age "post-secular."[32] Still, secularists are overrepresented in popular culture, government, law, media and higher education. Even the religious in these fields have been trained to leave their religious knowledge at home.

Secularism in Today's University

According to the latest Religious Landscape Survey administered by the Pew Forum on Religion & Public Life, over 82 percent of Americans are religious (78 percent are Christian). Another 6 percent say they are religious but unaffiliated, bringing the religious total to 88 percent. Four percent say they are atheists or agnostics, and another 6 percent say they are secularists.[33] Despite this, two studies found that only 52 percent of university faculty report that they believe in God and 23 percent identify as atheist or agnostic.[34] At the same time, university students are reportedly more interested in spirituality and religion than at any time previously measured.[35]

Outside of having a religion department, the only public nod to the religious at the secular graduate university where I have taught for thirty years is an invocation given each year at the annual graduation ceremonies. I presume it has gone on since the college's founding in 1925. Most of the time, the invocation ranges from a sort of simple reflection to a nondescript prayer given by someone from the chaplain's office, generally a rabbi, priest or pastor.

In 2011, the acting Protestant chaplain, who was himself a graduate student in the university and an African American pastor, was invited to give the invocation. He began in his big booming voice belting out, "Almighty God . . ." and ended with an equally strong, "Amen."[36] There was no reference to Jesus. However, this year, for the first time in my thirty-plus years of attending graduations, about half of the audience spontaneously applauded the invocation; some even cheered. After the audience's apparently rebellious act of applause, it took only a few hours until the faculty and administration received an email from one of our colleagues. The email read:

> Just wondering if anyone else out there finds it surprising that our commencement ceremony opens with a prayer to God. As far as I'm aware, we are not a religious institution, and we respect the right of our faculty, staff, and students to believe as they see fit—which might include the belief in

no god at all, in many gods, or in something/someone else I haven't thought of. Am I the only one who thinks this shouldn't be happening?

Within a few days, his email incited thirty-four responses (out of a faculty of fewer than one hundred), most siding to one degree or another with the initial secular inquisitor. One of my colleagues pointed out that this drew more email responses than the several attempts to hold an online discussion thread on the reorganization of the entire university. The president stepped in within a few days with a thoughtfully constructed email to the entire community:

> Diversity, inclusion and fairness have been the values that CGU espouses. We stand for integrity, collegiality and mutual respect too. Though we work and live under circumstances of uncertainty and imperfectness, these are the goals and principles after which we build our university and for which we refine ourselves. In your emails of a diversity of opinions, I have heard your concerns for our university. We are a university that has zero tolerance toward any sort of discrimination including, but not limited to, religion, race or color, and national origin. As your President, I will continue to work with you on both the underlying issues and the questions you have raised in the emails.[37]

The quandary in which we all find ourselves becomes obvious here. For example, does zero tolerance apply to the atheist or to the religious? Was the prayer a form of discrimination or an example of diversity? Would allowing or disallowing it have shown collegiality and mutual respect?

The following year the same pastor gave a vague invocation, which was simply a reflection on the graduates—no prayer, no objections and no applause. In the twenty-first century, we are experiencing secularism in its strongest form thus far in the United States. It seems in the new forms of secularism we are finding it very difficult to tolerate everything.

There are burgeoning critiques challenging secularism's relatively unquestioned public authority in the last three decades. These critiques come from several sources—scholars who are religious (primarily Christians),[38] scholars who are interested in "spirituality"[39] and high-profile secular scholars.[40] Political scientist Steven Smith uses Max Weber's metaphor to describe our current state:

> Max Weber famously described the change [from religious to secular worldviews] as the "disenchantment of the world"; he sometimes spoke of modernity as an "iron cage," in which life is lived and discourse is conducted according to the stern constraints of secular rationalism. It is that cage—the cage of secular discourse—within which public conversation and especially judicial and academic discourse occurs today.
>
> It may turn out that in our pluralistic society, the sort of thin, desiccated public discourse we have today—a discourse haphazardly policed in politics and more rigorously regimented in the academy by the constraints of secularism—is the best we can do. But we will only know if we open up the cage and see what happens.[41]

If the Judeo-Christian worldview had nothing to offer the culture today, understandably its principles would demand about the same attention as we give the ancient Epicureans. However, even by the admission of prominent secular European philosophers and cultural commentators such as Jürgen Habermas, Marcello Pera and Melanie Phillips, the Judeo-Christian worldview has been the most significant force in building and advancing the best of Western culture—egalitarianism, science, humanism and free democratic republics.[42] Researchers comparing international cultures have found a strong relationship between Christianity and the presence of less corruption, higher economic health, more democracy and more freedom in a nation.[43] Famous British historian Niall Ferguson noted, "after much hesitation, at least some of China's communist leaders now appear to recognize Christianity as one of the West's greatest sources of strength."[44]

The university is just one small example of the challenges posed to the Judeo-Christian worldview and to Christians and Jews. However, my concern here is not so much that Judeo-Christian voices are marginalized, diminished, misunderstood and misrepresented in the secular culture (partly out of ignorance and partly for political intent). Nor is my goal to confront the radical new atheists; many have superbly done this.[45] While they might be irritating and often polemical, atheists have been useful in making the issues plain and bringing the conversation to the forefront at a most opportune time. They force us all to realize we urgently need to investigate and understand worldviews, both those we hold (consciously or unconsciously) and those of others. However, none of these political issues is the most profound dilemma of our global culture. They are secondary consequences of a much weightier problem.

The most consequential issue is not who gets privileged or marginalized but the question, *what is true?* This is the question to which Western culture, in particular, needs desperately to return. Dallas Willard says simply, "Truth describes reality, and reality is what you run into when you are wrong."[46] Truth takes no sides and does not bend to human beliefs or desires. Reality simply is what it is; it functions with or without our agreement.

My position from study, observation and life experience is that the Judeo-Christian worldview encourages more freedom, supports more diversity, and is safer and healthier than secular or other religious worldviews. Indeed I will propose that the Judeo-Christian worldview includes all the true and productive principles found in the other three worldviews, fills the gaps between them and offers much more. I believe it can be demonstrated that it is a more accurate description of reality. A second theme running throughout is that in the absence of a higher commitment to truth, secularism has created a new era that might be termed the *political age.* Here decisions are made on the basis of who has the most power in democratic or totalitarian governments. This political power trumps truth claims, which are seen as the partisan ones. Thus religion, in particular Christianity, must be suppressed because the political state can stand no competitors for our affections and allegiance. My job will be to present the evidence.

Part 2

MATERIAL NATURALISM

What is real? . . . If you're talking about what you can feel,
what you can smell, what you can taste and see, then real is
simply electrical signals interpreted by your brain.

MORPHEUS IN THE MOVIE *THE MATRIX*

EVERYTHING IS A THING

Even more purposeless, more void of meaning, is the world, which Science presents for our belief. Amid such a world, if anywhere, our ideals henceforward must find a home. That Man is the product of causes which had no prevision of the end they were achieving; his origin, his growth, his hopes and fears, his loves and his beliefs, are but the outcome of accidental collocations of atoms . . . destined to extinction in the vast death of the solar system, and that the whole temple of Man's achievement must inevitably be buried beneath the debris of a universe in ruins. . . . Only within the scaffolding of these truths, only on the firm foundation of unyielding despair, can the soul's habitation henceforth be safely built.

BERTRAND RUSSELL, *MYSTICISM AND LOGIC*

In these few sentences, Bertrand Russell spells out a fundamental perspective of radical scientific naturalism and philosophic materialism. In Russell's words we are accidental collocations of atoms all the way down. A more nuanced form of material naturalism simply holds that only scientifically verifiable statements can present us with valid truth claims. Like all worldviews, naturalism and materialism in science and philosophy are predicated on a faith, a metaphysical assumption beyond scientific verifiability. Theirs is the belief that all that exists in the natural and human world is ultimately reducible to matter, energy and physical laws and processes, including human consciousness and religious belief. This is obviously a faith statement because there is simply no way for science to prove that all that exists is natural phenomena since the accepted methodology of science begins only after the identification of natural phenomena and thus can only state facts about those observations. It is then logically impossible for a material naturalist to discard any hypotheses that lie outside the boundaries of the existing physical matter and its mechanical processes without reverting to metaphysical theories and statements (the study of things beyond the physical, such as the soul, spirit, God, good and evil), which they a priori reject.

Philosopher Alvin Plantinga describes the dominance of the material-naturalist position:

> According to a semi-established consensus among the intellectual elite in the West, there is no such person as God or any other supernatural being. Life on our planet arose by way of ill-understood but completely naturalistic processes involving only the working of natural law. Given life, natural selection has taken over, and produced all the enormous variety that we find in the living world. Human beings, like the rest of the world, are material objects through and through; they have no soul or ego or self of any immaterial sort. At bottom, what there is in our world are the elementary particles described in physics, together with things composed of these particles. I say that this is a semi-established consensus, but of course there are some people, scientists and others, who disagree.... Still, by and large those are the views of academics and intellectuals in America now.[1]

Eminent philosopher Thomas Nagel calls this perspective *materialist naturalism*, representing both naturalism in science and materialism in philosophy[2]; I will use the term *material naturalism* to indicate both. Nagel is an atheist but not a materialist; he claims that materialist naturalism is reductionist, that it "attempts to reduce the true extent of reality to a common basis that is not rich enough for that purpose" and that the mind, in particular, is not merely physical. Thus our understanding of the mind "must be supplemented by something else to account for the missing elements." He adds, "If evolutionary biology is a physical theory—as it is generally taken to be—then it cannot account for the appearance of consciousness and of other phenomena that are not physically reducible. . . . The possibility opens up for mak[ing] the mind central, rather than a side effect of physical law."[3]

Material naturalism is not science. While naturalists are ardent advocates of science, not all of science's strongest advocates are materialists. Naturalism in science is *scientism*—the belief that science is the sole arbiter of truth in the modern world[4] and that such issues as ethics, free will and religion are also ultimately the result of natural material in the human body or that these subjective issues must simply be set apart from scientific knowledge as they cannot be known. Science is the only thing that is objective, real and true.[5]

Likewise, materialism is not fundamental to philosophy; religious or not, many philosophers are not materialists. A number of philosophers of science, such as Thomas Nagel, Richard Swinburne, Alvin Plantinga and Jerry Fodor,[6] make powerful arguments against material naturalism in philosophy and science. Philosophers who are religious are clearly among the nonmaterialists.[7]

Advocates of scientism often suggest that science and religion are set in some sort of unresolvable contest. Nothing could be further from the truth. Setting aside this popular folklore, Plantinga explains there is no conflict between Judeo-Christianity and science: "Given that naturalism is at least a quasi-religion, there is indeed a science/religion conflict, all right, but it is not between science and religion: it is between science and naturalism. That's where the conflict really lies."[8]

Sociologist Elaine Ecklund found in her research that 36 percent of scientists in American universities report that they believe in God,[9] a belief incompatible with strict naturalism.[10] Thirty-four percent report being atheist, which, like the percentage of all professors who report being atheist, is much higher than the 4 percent of the general American public who make that claim.[11] Interestingly, she found that 12 percent of self-identified atheist scientists also call themselves "spiritual." Ecklund also reported that many of the nonreligious scientists reported concern over the increase in the number of their students who are religious and suggested that some scientists and students of science who believe may remain "closeted" so as to avoid discrimination in the field. Gross and

Simmons have found that professors' religious belief is higher at non-elite secular universities. Atheism is highest among biology and psychology professors and lowest among professors in nursing, elementary education, accounting, finance, marketing, art and criminal justice.[12]

The Material-Naturalist Universe

Stephen Hawking's latest book with colleague Leonard Mlodinow, *The Grand Design,* suggests that we do not need the God hypothesis because the universe or multiple universes are "self-creating." Oxford mathematician and philosopher of science John Lennox says of this proposal,

> Hawking, insofar as he is interpreting and applying science to ultimate questions like the existence of God is doing metaphysics. . . . Here he confuses two very different things: physical law and personal agency. . . . This is a classical category error. His call for us to choose between physics and God is as manifestly absurd as demanding that we choose either the laws of physics or aeronautical engineer Sir Frank Whittle in order to explain the jet engine. Both explanations are necessary: they do not conflict, but complement one another.[13]

A naturalist, like Hawking, may make statements regarding these topics, but it's important for his readers to understand that these hypotheses lie outside his own methodological and epistemological commitments and expertise.[14] Indeed, some of what we "know" intuitively from common sense and experience lies outside of scientific verification.

The Material-Naturalist Mind

Prolific naturalist philosopher of science Daniel Dennett uses empirical methods to model the functions of the mind. Some of his recent work involves developing algorithms for robots to eventually "replace the thinker" by mimicking the human mind.[15] Because single computers are unable to approximate the speed of human brain processing, Dennett links series of high-speed parallel computers together. Philosopher and cognitive scientist Jerry Fodor points out that despite a growing number of cognitive science explanations of the brain using these computational models, these reductionist models are very far from mimicking the human mind.[16] The human mind can drive, be aware of surrounding traffic, follow a book on tape and refresh itself with a sip of water all at the same time.

The material-naturalist logic behind using computer models and biochemical ones to explain cognition, reasoning and decision making presumes that the brain (indeed all of nature) is very much like a machine and that the machine metaphor is fully adequate. Thus the functions of the mind are entirely determined by its physical/material architecture (chemical, electrical, neural); these material aspects of our physical being drive not just our senses but also our thoughts, feelings, beliefs, consciousness and, ultimately, decisions to act.

Plantinga describes the logical fissure in the material naturalists' faith:

> Human persons are material objects; they are not immaterial selves or souls or substances joined to a body, and they don't contain any immaterial substance as a part. From this point of view, our beliefs would be dependent on neurophysiology, and (no doubt) a belief would just be a neurological structure of some complex kind. Now the neurophysiology on which our beliefs depend will doubtless be adaptive; but why think for a moment that the beliefs dependent on or caused by that neurophysiology will be mostly true? Why think our cognitive faculties are reliable?[17]

In another publication, Plantinga questions the material metaphor further:

> Suppose you are a naturalist: you think that there is no such person as God, and that we and our cognitive faculties have been cobbled together by natural selection. Can you then sensibly think that our cognitive faculties are for the most part reliable? . . . There is no particular reason to think they would be: natural selection is interested, not in truth, but in appropriate behavior.[18]

How then are we able to discern a reliable thought from an unreliable one, a properly functioning consciousness from a deranged one? What tells us one particular cognitive activity is any better than another? Perhaps more critically, how then can we tell what is good or true?

Emeritus Oxford philosopher Richard Swinburne directly challenges materialism by painstakingly demonstrating that our minds are more than our biological brains, that our minds can cause brain events, not just the reverse. As a result, Swinburne argues that human beings have free will; not all our actions are predetermined by either biology or God, thus rendering human beings morally responsible.[19]

Getting Better and Better

Most material naturalists believe that we are developing toward a grander human species and able to speed up this process with new technologies; and most, like Russell, believe ultimately the human race is headed for certain physical extinction.[20] The material naturalist believes that the universe (or multiple universes, if they are found to exist) is purposeless, and yet all living things are in a state of constant evolution through the unguided processes of natural selection. [21]

Material naturalists suggest that gradually, through science, we have the ability to advance a more perfect world than evolution alone would grant us. Jonathan Moreno, professor of biomedical ethics, summarizes, "Much of the history of bioethics might be read as a 40-year conversation about the prospects for changing human nature through startling developments in the life-sciences."[22] Some of the recent advances in genetic knowledge suggest that we will ultimately be able to expand the brain's capacity even to inhibit fear, enhance memory, read minds and work for days without sleep. We already have a nose spray that increases trust, generosity and cooperativeness in laboratory experiments.[23] Who determines the mass application of such technologies, and what about the fact that there are some things we should fear and not trust? Courage is a virtue when used for good intents, but it can be used for evil.

"Post-human projects," as they are called, provide examples of the cutting edge of evolutionary science. Biological enhancements can be as simple as physical transformations, such as breast implants and Botox injections, as well as medical advances such as hearing aids, mechanical cochlea and artificial limbs. More radical human enhancements are now being explored, such as mechanical implants in the brain to supplement memory[24] and a project under consideration by NASA to genetically alter the DNA of astronauts to make them able and fit to travel to and work on Mars without being destroyed by its intense radiation.[25]

Science, Judeo-Christianity and Scientism

> *I am against religion because it teaches us to be*
> *satisfied with not understanding the world.*
>
> RICHARD DAWKINS,
> *THE GOD DELUSION*

> *Come now,*
> *let us reason together,*
> *says the* LORD.
>
> ISAIAH 1:18

Contrary to Dawkins's sentiments about the religious being satisfied with not understanding the world, both the Scriptures and the inseparable history of Christianity and science reveal quite the opposite reality.[26] In both the Hebrew and Greek Scriptures, God is always telling man to look, see, taste, hear, open our eyes, examine him and test him, and to seek wisdom, knowledge and understanding. "It is the glory of God to conceal things, but the glory of kings is to search things out."[27] Evangelicals, for example, graduate from college at the same rate as most other groups of Americans.[28] In fact, a 2012 study of more than seven thousand people in Britain revealed that religious believers are more likely to have obtained post high school degrees than either their nonreligious or "spiritual but not religious" peers.[29]

The early Christian church was the primary site of early scientific inquiries.[30] The Vatican has a Pontifical Academy of Sciences that officially began in 1603; today it is an international, multiethnic body of eighty scientists and includes an active observatory in Arizona.[31] Regardless of all the folklore about Galileo Galilei and his persecution by the church, Galileo discovered what he did because the Church had a powerful telescope for study and sponsored all of his work, before and after his trial. Nancy Frankenberry, in her book on atheist and believing scientists, concludes after an exhaustive search of the primary documents in the Galileo case:

The more complex picture that now emerges in the work of contemporary historians of science depicts a Galileo who was generally committed to the Church and a Church that was traditionally committed to natural philosophy as a rational, independent route to truth. In other words, Galileo was far more inclined to a conservative religious position and the Church much better disposed to the new astronomical data than is commonly believed.[32]

Scientists and mathematicians such as Galileo, Copernicus, Louis Pasteur, Isaac Newton, Francis Bacon, Blaise Pascal, George Mendel, Robert Boyle, Michael Faraday and Johann Kepler were all Christians, as are many contemporary scientists, including Francis Collins, the prestigious first director of the human genome project who now heads the National Institutes of Health in the United States.[33]

The Material-Naturalist Worldview in Contemporary Culture

For decades, secular education and media have shaped us to think to a large degree as material-naturalists. Most of us can still remember watching popular astronomer Carl Sagan standing in front of a picture of the universe, always beginning his long-running *Cosmos* television series proclaiming, "The cosmos is all that is or ever was or ever will be!" Even preschoolers are taught the same material-naturalist sentiments when they encounter the Berenstain Bears proclaiming, "Nature is all that is or was or ever will be."[34] Recently I saw a T-shirt emblazoned with an extreme sentiment of naturalism: "I used to care but I take a pill for that now."

When something is wrong inside us, we often first seek a medication to alter our body chemistry. Only secondarily do most of us stop to consider that what might be wrong could have originated first in our soul or spirit (the ultimate site of transformation). When I suffered from depression, medication was the only remedy I wanted. However, the origin of my depression was an intense inward focus, self-absorption, which was only exacerbated by secular counseling that encouraged wallowing in my pride, which was oddly diagnosed as low self-esteem—two sides of the same coin. Medication can be a tremendous aid as one struggles to right one's thought life, just as a bandage can help a wound heal more effectively even though it is the work of the material inside one's cells that actually accomplishes the healing.

In the final analysis, the strict material naturalist believes that a person's potential to become Mother Teresa or Adolf Hitler is predetermined by the biochemical and neurological matter acting upon and creating that person's unique reasoning and subsequent actions.[35] To the material naturalist, both Hitler and Mother Teresa were human beings with unique brain chemistry, who acted according to their neurology, which drove their human reason and experience.

To a material naturalist, Mother Teresa's work was inspired by her biology, and even her religious devotion was not a conscious "mindful" choice guided by her relationship with a personal God and her free will, but the result of a "God gene" or a "moral molecule" in her "spiritual brain."[36] The attempts to study the relationship between particular genes, neurochemicals and hormones, such as oxytocin, and religious beliefs are offered as evidence that it is chemistry and not God that spurs belief.

However, if God exists and both created and interacts with the world and human beings, it would be certain that God would have created us with a structural architecture to accommodate this ultimate reality. A God that desired a relationship with human beings would surely have created a capacity to connect, to use a machine metaphor, just as cell towers offer connectivity for cell phone users.

Naturalism and Religion

It would be rare indeed to find a true material naturalist who is not an atheist; however, not every atheist is a material naturalist, even those in the philosophy of science. Notable exceptions include Thomas Nagel and Jerry Fodor. Tom Bartlett, senior social science writer for the *Chronicle of Higher Education*, reviews a number of new books on the new science of religion in an article entitled "Dusting Off God." Bartlett writes,

> A growing body of research suggests that religion or religious ideas, in certain circumstances, in some people, can elicit the kind of behavior that is good for society: fairness, generosity, honesty. At the very least, when you read the literature, it becomes difficult to confidently assert that religion, despite the undeniable evil it has sometimes inspired, is entirely toxic.[37]

Given this fact, many scientists are eager to study the phenomenon of religion, even material naturalists, who tend to study religion as either a biochemical phenomenon or an evolutionary one, that is, religion survives because it is good for society.

A more recent argument suggests that evolution be broadened from pure individual natural selection to a group-selection theory, such as the one posited by the famous biologist and naturalist Edward O. Wilson in his book *The Social Conquest of Earth,* whereupon he also pits religion and science in an irreconcilable conflict—"their opposition defines the difference between science and religion, between trust in empiricism and belief in the supernatural." Both God and free will are brain illusions to Wilson who writes, "We cannot escape the question of free will, which some philosophers still argue sets us apart. It is a product of the subconscious decision-making center of the brain that gives the cerebral cortex the illusion of independent action."[38]

The new science of religion is not about God and human beings but largely about chemistry and evolution. Tom Bartlett writes of evolutionary biologist David Sloan Wilson's work that he insists that "trying to discover why we believe is more intriguing than the debate over whether anyone is up there looking down."[39] Thus these studies are disassociated from such questions as, Does God exist? How does knowing and relating to God influence human well-being? Rather these works are interested in the biology of belief and its utilitarian social advantages.

Summary

The Judeo-Christian critique of material naturalism *is not a critique of science but of scientism*, the insistence that science is the only source of knowledge about reality and that reality is entirely material.[40] Alvin Plantinga, perhaps the most articulate and able critic of the idea that religion and science are pitted in some inevitable battle, outlines the "deep concord between Christian theism and the deep roots of science."[41] Plantinga explains:

> Modern Western empirical science originated and flourished in the bosom of Christian theism and originated nowhere else. . . . The fact is it was Christian Europe that fostered, promoted, and nourished modern science.

All of the great names of early Western science, furthermore, Nicholas Copernicus, Galileo Galilei, Isaac Newton, Robert Boyle, John Wilkins, Roger Cotes and many others—all were serious believers in God. Indeed the twentieth-century physicist C. F. von Weizäcker goes so far as to say, "In this sense, I call modern science a legacy of Christianity."[42]

Atheist Thomas Nagel convincingly challenges the problems of material-naturalism in his book *Mind and Cosmos*. In his review of Plantinga's book, Nagel writes that while he cannot imagine believing in God,

> Plantinga's criticisms of naturalism are directed at the deepest problem with that view—how it can account for the appearance, through the operation of the laws of physics and chemistry, of conscious beings like ourselves, capable of discovering those laws and understanding the universe that they govern. Defenders of naturalism have not ignored this problem, but I believe that so far, even with the aid of evolutionary theory, they have not proposed a credible solution.[43]

Material naturalists and Christians agree that there is a physical material reality independent of our minds. That we can know and should learn as much as we can about physical material phenomena by applying the scientific method is equally agreed upon. There are no irreconcilable differences between good science and the Judeo-Christian worldview from which it flourished. There are only differences between scientists and philosophers of science, some who are strict material naturalists and others who are not.

SCIENCE AS THE ONLY TRUTH

The scientific method can shed light on every and any concept, even those that have troubled humans since the earliest stirrings of consciousness and continue to do so today. It can elucidate love, hope, and charity. It can elucidate those great inspirations to human achievement, the seven deadly sins of pride, envy, anger, greed, sloth, gluttony, and lust. In this book . . . I consider merely the great questions of being, questions that for millennia have been the inspiration of myth, and explore what science can say to illuminate them and dispel their mystery without diminishing their grandeur or reducing our wonder.

PETER ATKINS, *ON BEING*

A**ll scientists—those who** *are* and those who *are not* material naturalists—agree on and use the same scientific methods to study natural phenomena in physics, chemistry and biology. Material naturalists simply hold that facts derived in this way are the only things we can reliably know about the universe and human nature. Those who are not naturalists (religious or nonreligious) recognize that material explanations are necessary but inadequate; there are other ways to understand and discern what is real, good and true, other approaches to knowledge.

In 1620, Francis Bacon, a professing Christian, first proposed the scientific method that all scientists use. In his classic treatise *Novum*

Organum (new instrument), he began his explanation of the new method by critiquing Aristotle's long-established classic, *Organon,* which used largely deductive logic to argue from the universal to the particular. Bacon was convinced that inductive logic and systematic scientific inquiry and experimentation would be highly productive, and indeed it has been, resulting in countless inventions in the areas of medicine, technology and agriculture, from space travel to frozen foods. In fact, Bacon died of pneumonia while conducting an experiment in the snow to see if freezing chicken would preserve the meat.

Francis Bacon was a scientist and a Christian, but not a material naturalist; he was a sort of Renaissance man writing broadly in philosophy, law and poetry, even translating Psalms.[1] Bacon believed that God had imbued man with both the desire and the ability to understand and invent. In Bacon's thinking, God had given us two works from which we could know him and ourselves—the Scriptures and the study of nature. Bacon contended that scientific knowledge had to be positioned within a moral system, else it could become dangerous; he wrote in the preface to his *Instauratio Magna*:

> I humbly pray . . . that knowledge being now discharged of that venom which the serpent infused into it, and which makes the mind of man to swell, we may not be wise above measure and sobriety, but cultivate truth in charity. . . . Lastly, I would address one general admonition to all; that they consider what are the true ends of knowledge, and that they seek it not either for pleasure of the mind, or for contention, or for superiority to others, or for profit, or fame, or power, or any of these inferior things; but for the benefit and use of life; and that they perfect and govern it in charity. For it was from the lust of power that the angels fell, from lust of knowledge that man fell; but of charity there can be no excess, neither did angel or man ever come in danger by it.[2]

A Law-Governed Universe

The reason the scientific method is so reliable and productive is that we live in a law-governed universe rather than one that operates on random or changing laws. In addition, our minds, being made in the image of God, are specially fit to study and understand the world. To the theist this is another of the signposts of the existence of God. All scientists study and operate within these laws and use them to further knowledge. Plantinga describes the match between our minds and the pursuit of knowledge and understanding:

> God created both us and our world in such a way as there is a certain fit or match between the world and our cognitive faculties. The medievals had a phrase for it: *adequatio intellectus ad rem* (the adequation of the intellect to reality). The basic idea, here, is simply that there is a match between our cognitive or intellectual faculties and reality, thought of as including whatever exists, a match that enables us to know something, indeed a great deal about the world—and also about ourselves and God himself.[3]

While there can be no clear nonoverlapping division between them, we tend to classify the laws that form our reality into the physical, natural, moral and spiritual. Nevertheless these laws are a part of a unified whole and cannot be understood alone. Though we can study aspects of these laws independently, as we often do using the scientific method, they operate not in isolation but rather in unity with one another.

Physical laws govern the operations of physical material and energy and their processes, studied by physicists, chemists and astronomers. *Natural laws* govern the flourishing of nature—as studied by biologists, botanists, zoologists and chemists. Studying these laws of nature provides endless opportunities to observe phenomena that can give rise to new technologies, for example, birds as a model for airplanes and dragonflies and hummingbirds for helicopters.

There are also *human natural laws* that define those ways of being that most promote human flourishing (individually and collectively), such as those that undergird physical, psychological and social well-being. There are also *moral laws*, which result in optimal individual and social flourishing, such as the principles of ethics, politics, psychology, sociology, anthropology, health and even history. When a natural human law or a moral law is broken—for example, in physical health by alcoholism, in psychological health by a lack of forgiveness or in sociological health by sexual promiscuity—the consequences may not be as immediately apparent as when physical laws like gravity are broken. Nevertheless, there are consequences.

Though not recognized by material naturalists or secular humanists, there are also *spiritual laws,* which govern transactions in the unseen spiritual world. Missiologist Charles Kraft notes,

> Laws and principles in the spiritual realm are every bit as binding as those that operate in the physical realm. . . . If we consciously declare that we don't believe in the law of gravity and defy it, we soon find we are subject to it whether we want to be or not. The same is true of spiritual laws.[4]

Regarding the study of spiritual laws, scientific methods may be less useful because the origins and outcomes of particular spiritual transactions (1) do not engage identified natural phenomena, (2) engage the natural world at such an astronomical or infinitesimal level that the scientific method is incapable of capturing the whole picture within the parameters of scientific methods or (3) are secondarily useful because the consequences of spiritual transactions may be observed in the natural world, albeit after the fact. Spiritual transactions precede their natural manifestations. What we often view as physical or psychological causes may be first the results of spiritual transactions from broken human moral laws. For example, my depression was a consequence of a long history of wrong thoughts and actions, and thus my serotonin and other biochemical levels most likely went askew due to my actions and thoughts and not the reverse.

I have no doubt that many spiritual transactions ultimately can be detected using both science and metaphysical knowledge, including spiritual discernment. Reflecting on my thought patterns twenty years ago, I am certain that if I had been given any psychoneurological measurements prior to my conversion and then again a few years after my conversion, these measurements would have yielded very different results, not because the chemical and neurophysiological changes caused my conversion but the reverse. Gradually I developed an increased clarity that I had never experienced before, which over the years surely would have been detectable even by standard psychological measures. However, when material naturalists propose biochemistry as cause, when it may well be the result, our understanding of psychological, sociological and spiritual knowledge is limited.

Sigmund Koch, president of the American Psychological Association in 1981, described the material-naturalist methodological limits placed on psychology and the other social sciences when they moved themselves out of philosophy and into the sciences in the twentieth century. He argued that this move subjected the field to "ameaningful thinking" and diminished its capacity to define and study the bigger questions of life such as meaning, goodness, evil, suffering and purpose.[5]

A Material Naturalist's Proposal to Reconcile the Spiritual and the Physical World

In an attempt to reconcile scientists who do and do not believe in God, popular evolutionary biologist and historian Stephen Jay Gould suggested that religious thought not be excluded but relegated to a separate sphere because he believed science and religion could not speak on the same subjects. Gould suggested they occupied "nonoverlapping magisteria" (NOMA—different legitimate domains of authority that do not overlap). Gould writes:

> Religion is too important to too many people for any dismissal or denigration of the comfort still sought by many folks from theology. I may, for example, privately suspect that papal insistence on divine infusion of the soul represents a sop to our fears, a device for maintaining a belief in human superiority within an evolutionary world offering no privileged position to any creature. But I also know that souls represent a subject outside the magisterium of science. My world cannot prove or disprove such a notion, and the concept of souls cannot threaten or impact my domain. Moreover, while I cannot personally accept the Catholic view of souls, I surely honor the metaphorical value of such a concept both for grounding moral discussion and for expressing what we most value about human potentiality: our decency, care, and all the ethical and intellectual struggles that the evolution of consciousness imposed upon us.[6]

However, according to Judeo-Christian principles, the spiritual and physical not only coexist but are inextricable because both are present and interact in the formation and continuation of the universe. When separated, knowledge of both is diminished—natural and spiritual, religion and science. How could a universe exist where coexisting phenomena do not interact? Unity in diversity has always been foundational in the human search for truth; thus a major purpose of the development of the uni-versity.

Any well-educated, diligent scientist—material naturalist or not, atheist, Jew, Hindu, Muslim, Christian or Buddhist—can make many important discoveries working within the framework of the scientific method, exploring hypotheses in experiments on natural phenomena and processes. Religious and areligious scientists have equal opportunity to excel in answering well-designed questions about specific natural phenomena within specified conditions in time and space. While scientific evidence is a critical part of the data taken into consideration even when discerning spiritual phenomena, it is only one part of a much larger whole.

7

THE PURPOSELESS UNIVERSE
EMERGED FROM NOTHING

In the beginning the universe was created.
This has made a lot of people very angry and has
been widely regarded as a bad move.

Douglas Adams,
The Restaurant at the End of the Universe

No matter scientists' positions on the *agency question* (who or what agent caused the universe—God or spontaneously generating or preexisting/evolving material) or the *origins question* (why and how human beings came to be), most scientists, material naturalists or not, now agree that the universe in which we live had a beginning, that it continues to expand and that there will inevitably be an end. Lawrence Krauss proposes, as do a number of other material naturalists, that the laws of quantum mechanics were enough to create the universe.[1] Catching more of the media spotlight, Stephen Hawking and colleague Leonard Mlodinow in their most recent book theorized that "because there is a law such as gravity the Universe can and will create itself from nothing."[2] The *New York Times* review was titled "Many Kinds of Universes, and None Require God."[3]

Oxford mathematician and historian of science John Lennox responds,

Clearly, [Hawking] assumes that gravity exists. That is not nothing. So the universe is not created from nothing. Worse still, the statement "the universe can and will create itself from nothing" is self-contradictory. If I say, "X creates Y," this presupposes the existence of X in the first place in order to bring Y into existence. If I say, "X creates X," I presuppose the existence of X in order to account for the existence of X. To presuppose the existence of the universe to account for its existence is logically incoherent.[4]

Lennox explains further:

The world of strict naturalism in which clever mathematical laws all by themselves bring the universe and life into existence, is pure (science) fiction. Theories and laws do not bring matter/energy into existence. The view that they nevertheless somehow have that capacity seems a rather desperate refuge . . . from the alternative possibility. . . . Trying to avoid the clear evidence for the existence of a divine intelligence behind nature, atheist scientists are forced to ascribe creative powers to less and less credible candidates like mass/energy and the laws of nature.[5]

Atheist astronomer and mathematician Fred Hoyle ultimately believed that "a supercalculating intelligence had monkeyed with physics, as well as with chemistry and biology," as he discovered the extraordinary precision and design that exists in the universe. He wrote:

So try as I would, I couldn't convince myself that even the whole universe would be sufficient to find life by random processes—by what are called blind forces of nature. The thought occurred to me one day that the human chemical industry doesn't chance on its products by throwing chemicals at random in a stewpot. . . . Wasn't it even more ridiculous to suppose that the vastly more complicated systems of biology had been obtained by throwing chemicals at random into a wildly chaotic astronomical stewpot? By far the simplest way to arrive at the correct sequences of amino acids in the enzymes would be by thought, not random processes. . . . It would need a somewhat more superhuman scientist. . . . Rather than accept the fantastically small probability of life having arisen through blind forces of nature, it seemed better to suppose that the origin of life was a deliberate intellectual act. By "better" I mean less likely to be wrong.[6]

The intricate design of our universe, planet and life forms is sometimes referred to as the anthropic principle or the Goldilocks phenomenon, which describes the mind-boggling precision and fine-tuned nature of the earth and universe we occupy.[7] For example, if we were just slightly closer or further from the sun or moon we could not survive. Astrophysicist Guillermo Gonzalez and philosopher Jay Richards also note how uniquely the earth is positioned for observation of both the universe and our own galaxy.[8] Some atheists suggest that in the case of a different universe, natural selection would have simply selected different beings so suited; this obviously would still raise the same question.

Scott Hahn and Benjamin Wiker suggest that the new atheists go out of their way to avoid obvious conclusions from the evidence:

> In fact, [as Richard Dawkins says,] living things have every appearance of being designed by a supernatural intelligent being. That puts Dawkins in an interesting position, quite the reverse of the one implied. Since complicated biological things at least appear to be designed by an intelligent being, then it would be foolish (until one had better evidence) to believe that they were not.[9]

British philosopher Antony Flew served as one of the premier apologists for atheism and material naturalism for most of the last half of the twentieth century. Flew ultimately concluded, after careful philosophic analysis of scientific data, that he believed "that this universe's intricate laws manifest what scientists have called the Mind of God. I believe that life and reproduction originate in a divine Source." He explains:

> Why do I believe this, given that I expounded and defended atheism for more than a half a century? . . . Science spotlights three dimensions of nature that point to God. The first is the fact that nature obeys laws. The second is the dimension of life, of intelligently organized and purpose-driven beings, which arose from matter. The third is the very existence of nature.[10]

Flew said in an interview with Gary Habermas that he had simply followed the evidence wherever it led.[11] Flew was subsequently drawn to the intelligent design arguments and joined other academics to urge the British government schools to teach intelligent design as one theory.

Human Evolution

Far out in the uncharted backwaters of the unfashionable end of the western arm of the galaxy lies a small, unregarded yellow sun. Orbiting this at a distance of roughly ninety-two million miles is an utterly insignificant little blue-green planet whose ape-descended life forms are so amazingly primitive that they still think digital watches are a pretty neat idea. Many were increasingly of the opinion that they'd all made a big mistake in coming down from the trees in the first place. And some said that even the trees had been a bad move, and that no one should ever have left the oceans.

DOUGLAS ADAMS, *THE HITCHHIKER'S GUIDE TO THE GALAXY*

Douglas Adams's clever spoof on human nature highlights one of the more contentious ideological debates of our time—the origin of the human species. Though often depicted as a struggle between science and religion, it is actually a controversy between material naturalists and those who are not, religious or otherwise. Some of the more contemporary and able critics of the material-naturalist evolution theory are atheists. For example, atheist philosopher Thomas Nagel's new book *Mind and Cosmos* bears this subtitle: *Why the Materialist Neo-Darwinian Conception of Nature Is Almost Certainly False.*[12]

Popular media, public educational institutions and museums encourage us to believe there are only two options—naturalistic evolution and six twenty-four-hour-day creationism (only one of which is presented as scientific and reasonable). However, there are five very distinct views, which include (1) naturalistic evolution, (2) theistic evolution, (3) intelligent design, (4) old-earth special creation and (5) young-earth special creation. All but the young-earth-special-creation advocates agree on the age of the earth being approximately 4.5 billion years and the age of the universe being approximately 13.7 billion years.

Regardless of a scientist's commitment to one of these five major views, the actual daily practice of "doing science" on existing material does not differ based on one's a priori theoretical commitment to a particular position on the origin of human life. Thus a scientist who believes in six twenty-four-hour creation days or naturalistic evolution has the same potential for scientific discovery. Scientific methods are not dependent on a particular metaphysical belief about origins. Rather than wring our hands about which position students in our science classes hold and why, we should simply present them all and then proceed to engage their minds in the wonders of the universe from astronomy to cellular biology in order to encourage their pursuit of science, which is infinitely beautiful, complex and irresistible.

Jerry Fodor highlights the metaphysical nature of all the various positions.

> The problem with creationism, even if you are not a hard-core atheist as I am, is that anything is compatible with creationism. If God created the world, he could have created it anyway he liked. . . . Creationism isn't the only doctrine that's heavily into post-hoc explanation. Darwinism is too. If a creature develops the capacity to spin a web, you tell a story about why spinning a web was good in the context of evolution.[13]

Setting aside the memorable but hypothetical textbook drawings of apes straightening up to become human, indelibly written on our minds from our elementary science texts, which even evolutionary biologist Stephen Jay Gould criticized,[14] there are growing numbers of religious, agnostic and atheist scientists and philosophers who are skeptical of the standard evolution story.[15] Thomas Nagel writes of the Darwinist story,

> The more details we learn about the chemical basis of life and the intricacy of the genetic code, the more unbelievable the standard historical account becomes. . . . It seems to me, as it is usually presented, the current orthodoxy about the cosmic order is the product of governing assumptions that are unsupported, and that it flies in the face of common sense.[16]

There is an apocryphal story going around that illustrates the problem of origins of human beings. Upon completion of the map of the human genome, a group of scientists made a visit to God to inform him they had finished mapping the human genome and thus unlocked the secret of life. "Thank you, but we won't be needing your help any longer," they told him. God graciously thanked them for the information and then suggested they have a man-making contest before they left. Enthusiastically they agreed. God picked up a handful of dirt, and the lead scientist did the same. God stopped, looked at the scientist and said, "No, no, no; you get your own dirt."

Agreement on Evolution Within Species

Proponents of all five views on human origins agree that within a species, genetic material changes or evolves in response to environmental conditions over time such that the organism adjusts to new conditions, making it more likely to survive. White moths turned dark during industrialization; beaks of finches on the Galapagos Islands become harder during droughts; bacteria evolve to become drug resistant. However, these bacteria, finches and moths remain the same bacteria, finches and moths; they do not become substantially different organisms. Evolution does occur within a species over a long period of time, but, beyond this microevolution, scientists disagree on mechanisms accounting for the origins of higher levels of life (higher taxon-level disparity) and in particular disagree about the viability of the standard account of evolution to produce new species.[17]

Though no species has ever been observed to change into another (using the broad as opposed to narrow definitions of species), two of the five positions (naturalistic and theistic evolution) believe there is enough deductive and inductive evidence to propose evolution across species (the common ancestry of all species); three others do not believe there is adequate evidence. Four of the five views believe that God or some superior intelligence is the agent behind the creation of all life. All monotheists believe that human beings are uniquely and purposely made in the image of God (theistic evolution, intelligent design, old-earth creation and young-earth special creation).

All five of the positions on the origin of human life (naturalist or otherwise) rely on metaphysical assumptions that are difficult to verify using scientific methods. Although it is widely circulated through documentaries, textbooks and museums that Darwinian evolution is a value-neutral fact of science, all these positions are equally dependent on metaphysical assumptions.

The Five Positions

Naturalistic Darwinian evolution.

> *We admit that we are like apes,*
> *but we seldom realize that we are apes.*
>
> RICHARD DAWKINS,
> *A DEVIL'S CHAPLAIN*

Material naturalists maintain that humans evolved from lower animals, which began as single-cell organisms that had emerged from nonliving matter through an unknown process. This evolution from lower to higher animals is accomplished through nondirected processes such as mutation, natural selection, gene exchange and genetic drift,[18] without any supernatural intervention, forethought or purpose. A cardinal principle of all evolutionary theory is that all living things are related to one another and all descended from a single early form of life,[19] even though the process whereby nothing becomes inert material and inert material produces living matter is not known. Advances in living organisms are said to occur when genetic mutations sort themselves out through natural selection, the process whereby over generations certain genetic traits are selected for expression over others because of their utility in helping the organism better survive and reproduce. These processes are dependent on chance genetic mutations that produce advantages for survival.

Daniel Dennett, philosopher of science and able proponent of the naturalist's evolutionary position, believes that Darwinian evolution is perfectly capable of explaining the complexity of life. He suggests the more we know about undirected evolution, the more God is left with just a "ceremonial role to play."[20] In a Public Broadcasting System interview, Dennett explains, "After Darwin, God's role changes from being the designer of all creatures, great and small, to being the designer of the laws of nature, from which natural selection can unfold, to being just perhaps the chooser of the laws."[21]

Like Dennett, other material naturalists believe that science's vast accumulation of knowledge is gradually filling in the gaps in our knowledge that we have previously assigned to God.[22] This is often referred to as the God-of-the-gaps hypothesis, which suggests that Christians and other monotheists believe in God because of the things that are unknown, and thus attribute to God anything not yet understood. John Lennox provides an analogy to the argument that the more we know the less we can believe in God as creator. Lennox notes that just because we understand everything about the internal combustion engine does not mean that Henry Ford did not exist.[23]

Thomas Nagel, in reviewing Dawkins's *The God Delusion,* explains the confusion here.

> But God, whatever he may be, is not a complex physical inhabitant of the natural world. The explanation of his existence as a chance concatenation of atoms [via evolution] is not a possibility for which we must find an alternative, because this is not what anybody means by God. . . . The point of the [God] hypothesis is to claim that not all explanation is physical, and that there is . . . an explanation more fundamental than all the basic laws of physics, because it even explains them.[24]

Theistic evolution. Theistic evolutionists agree with most of the neo-Darwinian evolutionary hypotheses but add that this evolutionary process was intentionally designed, created, directed and sustained through God's supernatural intervention. They believe God set these materials and processes in motion, resulting in the development of the human species, intentionally created in his image and for relationship with him and with one another. The BioLogos Foundation defines the difference between material naturalists' and theists' accounts of evolution. The theist believes "that all life on earth came about by the God-ordained process of evolution with common descent [which] . . . is the means by which God providentially achieves his purposes in creation."[25] While recognizing that mutations are random, in that they are unpredictable, theistic evolutionists believe that natural selection is not random because there is a plan and purpose for the evolutionary processes established by God at creation.

Several prominent scientists and mathematicians who are not material naturalists count themselves in this group. These include Francis

Collins, Ard Louis, John Polkinghorne, David Vosburg, Darrel Falk and Karl Giberson. The Roman Catholic Church and some prominent Protestant theologians, such as N. T. Wright and Tim Keller, also support this position. From this position, Hahn and Wiker tell us,

> So, we can see that the disagreement between theists and Dawkins, then, is not about the universe being 13.5 billion years old or that evolution of some kind has occurred. Both are entirely compatible with a theistic account of the universe, and hence present no difficulty for Catholics. The problem with Dawkins is his against-all-odds insistence that chance be the blind god who brings everything about.[26]

Although it is often believed that should evolutionary theory be conclusively proven (if that could ever be) this would negate a God who stands beyond creation and purposefully plans and directs the substance and order of all things, it would not. There are many theists who believe in evolution but simply not as an unintended and undirected process. Rather to them the process of evolution is seen as part of God's design. Theistic evolutionist Francis Collins, who headed the human genome project and now leads the powerful National Institutes of Health, writes in his book *The Language of God*,

> Science is the only legitimate way to investigate the natural world. . . . Science can make mistakes. But the nature of science is self-correcting. . . . Nevertheless, science alone is not enough to answer all the important questions. . . . Science is not the only way of knowing. The spiritual worldview provides another way of finding truth. Scientists who deny this would be well advised to consider the limits of their own tools.[27]

The relationship outlined by Collins between science and religion is somewhat akin to Stephen Jay Gould's nonoverlapping magisteria; the two do not necessarily overlap, but complement one another.[28] For many it is difficult to justify that the acts of God in creation were not, in large part, also "spiritual." If this is true, it would take both kinds of reasoning to understand the design and operations of the universe.

The BioLogos Foundation serves as the center of intellectual activity where many theistic evolutionists come together, publish papers and blogs regarding theistic evolution and often contest other theistic positions, as well as nontheist evolutionists.[29] They tend to be particularly critical of intelligent-design advocates who contest evolutionary theory in general on scientific grounds.[30]

Scientific arguments against evolution across species. Some theists are not the only doubters of the theory of evolution across species; the theory is under intense challenges also by nontheists, such as philosophers of science Jerry Fodor and Thomas Nagel and biochemist and cognitive scientist Massimo Piattelli-Palmarini. Fodor and Piattelli-Palmarini write, "There is something wrong—quite possibly fatally wrong—with the theory of natural selection; and we are aware that, even among those who are not quite sure what it is, allegiance to Darwinism has become a litmus for deciding who does, and who does not, hold a 'properly scientific' world view."[31] Similarly, Nagel writes, "It seems to me that, as it is usually presented, the current orthodoxy about the cosmic order is the product of governing assumptions that are unsupported, and that it flies in the face of common sense. . . . It is prima facie highly improbable that life as we know it is the result of a sequence of physical accidents together with the mechanism of natural selection."[32]

There are three major challenges to the theory of evolution across species. First, Darwin himself noted that for his theory to be true, scientists would have to find remains of many *transitional beings*—forms that would indicate the transition from one species to another, for example, from an ape to a man. Despite the many bones displayed in museums all over the world, on close examination the bones on display are either still apes or humans.[33] Even the celebrated Lucy, Ardi and Java Man have not begun to fill the gap of beings supposed to exist between apes and man that Darwin predicted would be filled by paleontology (the study of prehistoric life).[34]

There have been various attempts of evolutionists to explain the lack of transitional forms. Stephen Jay Gould, atheist paleontologist and evolutionary biologist, proposed a way around the problem by hypothesizing that new species could have evolved very quickly from other species in particular places at particular times, thus not requiring a long line of transitional beings. He named the process "punctuated equilibrium." This poses problems for traditional Darwinists whose theory depends on *gradual change* over time through *natural selection.*

Second, the *"Cambrian explosion,"* estimated to have taken place 543 million years ago, presents another challenge to the idea that single-cell organisms gradually become more complex ones. During this period single-cell organisms did not slowly evolve into more complex ones; rather, many highly disparate complex living organisms suddenly appear in the fossil record without evidence of the theoretically necessary minor changes that should precede them if the theory is true.[35] Gould described the fissure here between theory and evidence:

> The peculiar character of this evidence has not matched Darwin's prediction of a continuous rise in complexity toward Cambrian life, and the problem of the Cambrian explosion has remained as stubborn as ever—if not more so, since our confusion now rests on knowledge, rather than ignorance, about the nature of Precambrian life.[36]

Third, and perhaps the most troubling scientific conundrum, is the claim that species evolve through natural selection via the process of *mutations.* Mutations generally involve either the rearrangement of existing genetic information or loss of genetic information. Overwhelmingly, science demonstrates that mutations are predominantly neutral or detrimental to the organism, and very rarely beneficial to life. Some scientists have attempted to create new species by forming genetic mutations in the earliest stages of development of less complex life forms—called evo-devo biology (evolutionary developmental). Regarding such experiments with fruit flies in the evo-devo labs, molecular biologist Jonathan Wells states, "no matter what we do to a fruit fly embryo, there are only three possible outcomes—a normal fruit fly, a defective fruit fly, or a dead fruit fly."[37] Michael Denton adds that transitional forms cannot breed.[38] Evolution to another species requires many mutations, increasing in complexity simultaneously, and they all must take place while the organism stays alive—"half-formed lungs won't work because the organism can't breathe."[39]

On the other hand, material naturalists counter the God hypothesis by pointing to *"functionless (vestigial) structures"* and "junk DNA," which appeared at first glance to serve no purpose, as evidence against God. Other scientists insist that these structures, such as our tailbone or appendix, do serve important functions; our tailbone connects muscles in our pelvis, and the appendix appears to aid in the generation of beneficial bacteria.[40] Why, they ask, would an all-knowing God have left such things lying around? Most recent studies are revealing that what was once called junk DNA turns out to serve critical functions, such as triggering various elements of DNA to turn off or on.[41]

More recently, evolutionists point to *genetic similarities* between species to bolster Darwinian views of evolution. It is widely reported that the human genome and that of the chimpanzee share about 95-98 percent similar DNA.[42] This is used by material naturalists to bolster their arguments against the exceptionality of human beings in nature. But why would we not expect God to use the same material for many different things? We use metal for children's toys, skyscrapers, mechanical limbs and bombs. Rather, the more obvious question is how much then can the physical genome actually explain? While there are some obvious physical similarities between apes and humans, there are vast differences in our behaviors, histories and abilities. This argument seems only to suggest that DNA studies may not be sufficient to describe the radical differences between the species.

Why if there are such similarities at a molecular level are there so many differences in nature? No chimpanzee, ape or similar animal has ever set up complex societies, built houses, produced works of art and music, developed an oral or written language, or studied itself. Where do these tremendous differences come from? Perhaps, as salmon scientist Ernie Brannon suggests, there is something more to the biblical explanation that God breathed his spirit into man and made him in his image than is thus far evident in the gene pool.[43]

Intelligent design. On sabbatical in 1993, Berkeley law professor Phillip Johnson began reading about the theory of evolution. From his position as a lawyer, he reasoned that the theory lacked evidence. He later wrote asking some troubling questions about Darwin's theory.[44] From this beginning, Johnson attracted other scientists with similar concerns. These now form a group of scientists and philosophers who collectively refer to themselves as intelligent design theorists and scientists.

Biochemist Michael Behe, famous for the study of the bacterial fla-
gellum, argues that certain biological systems would have to have
been assembled in one fell swoop in order to function. His argument
on "irreducible complexity" dovetails with the argument of philosopher William Dembski's notion of "specified complexity," revealing
the impossibility of particular complex systems to have emerged in
the manner described in neo-Darwinian evolutionary theory. Stephen
Meyer's work suggests that the complexity of the DNA genetic code is
evidence alone of a designing intelligence. Other ID advocates include
both religious and agnostic scholars Antony Flew, Michael Denton,
Jonathan Wells, Caroline Crocker, Richard Steinberger, Robert Marks,
Jeff Schwartz, Guillermo Gonzalez, Jay Richards, David Berlinski and
Phillip Johnson.[45]

ID proponents scientifically analyze systems in astronomy, biology,
physics and chemistry to determine whether the observed structures are
most likely products of unguided natural selection, intelligent design or
some combination. Like other scientists, they advance their propositions by inference to the best possible explanation and conduct experiments that arise from these hypotheses. They have discovered new
planets and worked on the finely tuned nature of the universe and earth,
the initial conditions necessary to support life, the origin of irreducibly
complex life including DNA transcription, the origin of major body
plans in the Cambrian explosion, biological disparity and species diversity, and the processes of mutation, such as those involved in bacterial drug resistance.

Intelligent design advocates hold prestigious degrees and have consid-
erable scientific accomplishments but are often marginalized and sometimes even excluded from the scientific establishment in elite universities
and other institutions.[46] For example, in August 2013 a university president announced that the theory of intelligent design could not be taught
in science classrooms.[47] Thus proponents who remain in universities work
largely under the radar and keep their skepticism of Darwinian evolution
and their metaphysical commitments hidden. Ben Stein's popular film
Expelled, though hotly criticized, revealed a reality that ID proponents face

often from the same people who paradoxically accuse the early Roman Catholic Church of persecuting Galileo for his doubts.[48]

In an attempt to discount the academic rigor of intelligent-design theorists and their work, material naturalists often label its advocates creationists. The term *creationist* has suffered so much derision in the media that it makes it easy to dismiss ID out of hand without engaging the advocates' scientific research and theory. Unlike young-earth creationism, ID draws its metaphysics not from arguments about the age of the earth or man but from empirical scientific data revealing the design components that would be unlikely to have formed as a result of a slow process of evolution.

Intelligent design advocates define themselves as a community of scientists, philosophers and other scholars seeking to understand the "prodigious evidence of design in nature."[49] The Discovery Institute serves as the primary gathering place and think tank for intelligent-design advocates.[50] They believe that the operations of the universe and the intricacies of living things are best explained by an intelligent, purposive design and reject theoretical propositions that solely material phenomena acting according to unguided processes brought the universe and nature into being.[51] Since 2001, over seven hundred scientists have signed Discovery's Statement of Dissent from Darwinism, which reads, "We are skeptical of claims for the ability of random mutation and natural selection to account for the complexity of life. Careful examination of the evidence for Darwinian theory should be encouraged."[52]

The reason that ID refers to an *intelligent designer* rather than God is that some members of its community of scholars are agnostics, Muslims or Buddhists in addition to Jews and Christians. Even atheists like Nagel support their work as a viable theory. Nevertheless, one of the criticisms is that most intelligent-design theorists, in fact, do believe in God or at least that God is probable. Philosopher of science and self-described "ex-Christian" Michael Ruse quips that their use of the words "intelligent designer" rather than God is "a terminological inexactitude."[53] Mathematician and philosopher David Berlinski, who calls himself a secular Jew, says of intelligent design theory, "I do not know whether any of this is true. I am certain that the scientific community does not know that it is false."[54]

Old-earth special creation. Old-earth creation proponents look at the seven-day story more in terms of geological epochs or as a narrative framework for interpreting the origins account as did many of the early church fathers.[55] They accept the traditional dating of the universe and earth but do not accept evolution as an adequate explanation for the origins of life.[56] Some point out that the fossil record does basically follow the same order as listed in the "generations of days of creation" in Genesis, while others will disregard the apparent chronology. These scholars use scientific evidence to argue for the existence of God and believe that scientific ideas are evident in the Bible but that not all these biblical passages are to be interpreted literally.

Old-earth creationist and Orthodox Jewish physicist Gerald Schroeder is a physicist, earth scientist and theologian whose science degrees are from Massachusetts Institute of Technology. His early scientific work centered primarily on the control of radioactivity. He is a popular and prolific writer on the "confluence of modern science and ancient biblical commentary."[57] He was influential in the conversion of famous philosopher Antony Flew.[58]

The most prominent old-earth creationist, astrophysicist Hugh Ross, has pulled together scholars across the scientific disciplines to develop the Reasons to Believe Institute.[59] RTB has a large number of scholars working to articulate the latest discoveries to a well-educated audience who may or may not be scientists. Their mission is to equip Christians "by demonstrating that sound reason and scientific research—including the very latest discoveries—consistently support, rather than erode, confidence in the truth of the Bible and faith in the personal, transcendent God revealed in both Scripture and nature."[60] Ross was the youngest person (at seventeen) to serve as director of observations for Vancouver's branch of the Royal Astronomical Society of Canada. He is a prolific writer articulating a biblical creation model that is testable, falsifiable and predictive.[61]

Young-earth creation. Young-earth or six twenty-four-hour-day creationists tend to argue from the Bible to science and back, interpreting scientific discoveries and knowledge through biblical texts, particularly the book of Genesis. Much of the general public's understanding of this form of creationism comes from the movie *Inherit the Wind*, in which the "creationists" are depicted as bumbling simpletons. The original movie was actually a critical commentary on the repression of intellectuals during the McCarthy era. Unlike the film's end, the actual trial upheld the teaching of creation.

Young-earth creationists believe that God created the earth in six twenty-four-hour days, that the universe is only about ten thousand years old and that fossils are primarily artifacts from the flood that Noah and his family survived. One of the major problems associated with this is the lack of clarity in the Bible regarding what a day constituted in the beginning and its multiple Hebraic definitions.[62]

Advocates of young-earth creationism include Henry Morris, who developed the Institute for Creation Research; Carl Baugh; Duane Gish; and Ken Ham, who founded Answers from Genesis.[63] Rather than conducting scientific studies themselves, they primarily interpret emerging scientific studies in the context of biblical revelation. Their website describes their purpose: "For over four decades, the Institute for Creation Research has equipped believers with evidence of the Bible's accuracy and authority through scientific research, educational programs, and media presentations, all conducted within a thoroughly biblical framework."[64] Their energies are most directly focused on finding scientific research that sheds doubt on the age of the earth and the theory of evolution.

God or Material Origins

John Lennox asks the ultimate question that theistic evolutionists, intelligent-design theorists and old- and young-earth creation theorists ask: given whatever the materials, processes and laws one believes caused the universe to exist, where did or do the basic building blocks of the material world come from, and, in particular, where did information (coded in DNA) come from? Lennox asks, "How much more likely, then, is the existence of an intelligent creator behind human DNA, the colossal biological database that contains no fewer than 3.5

billion 'letters'—the longest word yet discovered?"[65] DNA's storage density alone has been found to be six powers of ten denser than flash-drive technology.[66]

Once an apologist for atheism, Antony Flew advised us to follow the evidence where it leads. In science, as in all human endeavors, scientists cannot afford to hold on to a priori ideological commitments (secular or religious) that may become blinders for themselves or others. In all these theories, none is any more dependent on faith than any other. Most important, none of these five perspectives on origins and agency inhibits scientific inquiry or discovery. Quite the opposite, they all encourage it. Proponents of nontheistic evolution, theistic evolution, intelligent design, old-earth creation and young-earth creation all use the same scientific methods when they conduct actual studies.

These highly politicized metaphysical battles over five distinct scientific theories about the origin and agency of life on earth cannot be solved on one side or the other using the scientific method alone. Cambridge physicist, theologian and former chancellor John Polkinghorne, an esteemed scholar of both science and religion, reminds us that metaphysical claims need to be defended with metaphysical arguments.[67] Evolutionary biologist Michael Ruse admits the naturalist's Darwinian evolutionary bias has political intent:

> Evolution is promoted by its practitioners as more than mere science. Evolution is promulgated as an ideology, a secular religion—a full-fledged alternative to Christianity, with meaning and morality. I am an ardent evolutionist and an ex-Christian, but I must admit that in this one complaint the literalists are absolutely right. Evolution is a religion. This was true of evolution in the beginning, and it is true of evolution still today. . . . Evolution therefore came into being as a kind of secular ideology, an explicit substitute for Christianity.[68]

Oxford philosopher Richard Swinburne describes the theist logic:

> We find that the view that there is a God explains everything we observe, not just some narrow range of data. It explains the fact that there is a universe at all, that scientific laws operate within it, that it contains conscious animals and humans with very complex, intricately organized bodies, that

we have abundant opportunities for developing ourselves and the world, as well as the more particular data that humans report miracles and have religious experiences. In so far as scientific causes and laws explain some of these things (and in part they do), these very causes and laws need explaining, and God's action explains them. The very same criteria which scientists use to reach their own theories lead us to move beyond those theories to a creator God who sustains everything in existence.[69]

NO MIRACLES ALLOWED

There is not to be found in all history,
any miracle attested by a sufficient number of men,
of such unquestioned good sense, education and learning,
as to secure us against all delusion in themselves.

DAVID HUME, *AN ENQUIRY*
CONCERNING HUMAN UNDERSTANDING

Miracles are not contrary to nature,
but only contrary to what we know about nature.

AUGUSTINE OF HIPPO

The small book *Heaven Is for Real*, published in 2010, now has 6.5 million copies in print and a children's version with 500,000 in print.[1] It is an account of a family discovering that their young son, Colton, had an experience in heaven at age three while his life hung in the balance from a ruptured appendix. He talked about meeting Papa, a great-grandfather who had died long before Colton was born. He selected Papa's picture from his father's photos, insisting that Papa was not the older man his father showed him but Papa in his thirties. He described the angels singing, talks he had with Jesus and meeting Jesus' cousin named John. In heaven Colton met his own sister, who had been conceived before him but miscarried, another fact that he could not have known. His parents showed him many pictures of Jesus, but the only one he recognized was a picture painted by Akiane, an artistic prodigy who was seven when she painted a picture of Jesus, whom she had seen in a vision.[2]

For those of us educated in the modern world, which has increasingly restricted what can be believed through material naturalism, these accounts are always held with a mix of fascination, suspicion and even contempt. However, New Testament scholar Craig Keener recently has helped break the stubborn material-naturalist barricade that has existed since Hume. Keener's two-volume text on miracles is one of the most relentlessly referenced texts on the subject. Keener documents miraculous experiences around the world and concludes,

> Not only the Majority World today but also the history of Christianity, including in the West, is replete with supernaturalist claims. The modern Western prejudice against acknowledging or exploring miracle claims rests not on a total lack of evidence for such claims, even in Western history, but on an a priori insistence that they be screened from consideration. Yet such claims belong not only to earlier history or to non-Western cultures; countless examples can be offered today, including in the West.[3]

Religious studies professor Candy Gunther Brown has also studied the phenomenal growth of Pentecostal and charismatic Christianity around the world, with its accompanying miraculous signs. One such example is the ministry of Heidi and Roland Baker in Mozambique, where there are frequent reports of healings, deliverances and even the dead being raised.[4] Brown's recommendation is that scientists actively explore the benefits of prayer in healing, benefits that have been shown to be worthy of attention.[5] Psychological anthropologist T. M. Luhrmann at Stanford has studied the phenomena of evangelical reports of hearing God, and Tim Stafford, senior writer for *Christianity Today,* has examined contemporary reports of human experiences with God's power.[6] Prize-winning NPR reporter Barbara Bradley Hagerty has written a compelling book summarizing scientific evidence of the brain and spiritual experience. After years of study, she concluded, "Nothing I have learned [about the brain] has undercut the fundamentals of my Christian faith."[7]

The West, including Western theology, has long been influenced by philosopher David Hume's eighteenth-century writings that dismissed the miraculous as delusions of the poorly educated. As Keener notes, "If even a handful of miracle claims prove more probable than not, Hume's argument fails, removing the initial default setting against miracles."[8] He suggests those ministers and theologians trained to believe that the miracles of Jesus operated only for a period of time and are not effectual today might need to check their theological allegiance with actual data.

The miraculous is more frequently experienced in the Christian church outside of the West—in the Majority World of Africa, South America and Asia. This suggests that disbelief in the miraculous itself is a deterrent.[9] Jesus often emphasized the role of faith in the miraculous: "your faith has made you well."[10] Theologian and missiologist Charles Kraft suggests the reason for our lack of faith:

> It is interesting (and discouraging) to note that even though we are Christians, our basic assumptions are usually more like those of non-Christian Westerners around us than we like to admit. We have as Christians made certain modifications. But even though there is often a wide discrepancy between the teachings of Scripture and the common Western assumptions . . . we often find ourselves more Western than Scriptural. . . . This tension is especially acute if we seek to be more open in the area of spiritual power.[11]

The Naturalists' View of Miracles

Michael Ruse describes the naturalist view of the miraculous in Judeo-Christianity. He writes,

> But does not belief in miracles fly in the face of science? . . . It is true that back in the seventeenth century some—Newton himself, prominently— were prepared to allow God some kind of intervening and adjusting role in the universe's running, but at least since the nineteenth century this has not been permitted. . . . Science demands unbroken law, Christianity posits miracles, violations of law. Hence, science and Christianity are in

conflict. Even though Christianity may speak to science's unanswered questions, science cannot accept the legitimacy of Christian faith.[12]

Several things can be said here about the material-naturalistic view of the miraculous being illegitimate. First, Alvin Plantinga has pointed out that this view is dependent on the principle that the universe is a closed system, which has not been scientifically established. Plantinga writes, "With the advent of quantum mechanics it has become harder yet to find conflict between special divine action and current physics. . . . God is constantly acting specially in the world and the material universe is never causally closed."[13]

Second, not only has the hegemony of secular worldviews rendered miracles an almost inapproachable topic in public, but for the last century many mainline Western pastors have been educated in liberal seminaries that treat spiritual phenomena that cannot be expressed in naturalistic terms as mere human psychological experience. Lesslie Newbigin notes that here God becomes simply "a projection of the human ego on the cosmos."[14] When scientism became the only arbiter of truth, liberal theologians eliminated miracles because they were not consistent with what a modern person could believe.[15] The Bible read through the lenses of material naturalism is a very different book.

If God is real, he is much more than a constructed state of mind or a decision we make to believe or disbelieve. All that exists is wrapped up in his being, in his words "I AM." This would make the primary focus of our lives to know the One who created us and knows us. This may be one of the reasons that miracles are among the most excoriated tenets of Judeo-Christianity; they shift the focus of our lives and work from us to the most expansive, true and grand reality of all.

Third, many believe instances of divine intervention actually do involve natural laws, simply a divine acceleration of the natural laws. For example, during healing, a person's natural body defense and repair systems are simply dramatically sped up. C. S. Lewis and other scholars believe miracles are consistent with what we know about both the laws of nature and the life of Christ. Lewis wrote that miracles involve:

An interference with nature by the supernatural. . . . A miracle is emphatically not an event without a cause or without results. Its cause is the activity of God: Its results follow according to Natural law. . . . By definition, miracles must of course interrupt the usual course of Nature; but if they are real they must, in the very act of so doing, assert all the more the unity and self-consistency of the total reality at some deeper level.[16]

In 1908, G. K. Chesterton noted the paradox that it is liberals, greatly influenced by material naturalism, who deny miracles.

For some extraordinary reason, there is a fixed notion that it is more liberal to disbelieve in miracles than to believe in them. Why, I cannot imagine, nor can anybody tell me. For some inconceivable cause a "broad" or "liberal" clergyman always means a man who wishes at least to diminish the number of miracles; it never means a man who wishes to increase that number. . . . But in truth this notion that it is "free" to deny miracles has nothing to do with the evidence for or against them. It is a lifeless verbal prejudice of which the original life and beginning was not in the freedom of thought, but simply in the dogma, of materialism. . . . A miracle only means the liberty of God.[17]

It is important to note here that words like *supernatural* and *miraculous* actually never appear in the biblical text. They are inventions of the Western mind. Apparently to God, Jesus and his disciples, and indeed the early church, these phenomena were simply part and parcel of the world, a world whose laws were one—undivided between natural and supernatural. C. P. Snow's famous observation of the split between the sciences and the humanities might never have been an issue in the academy had we left intact knowledge of Judeo-Christian principles that easily hold together the metaphysical and the natural sciences and avoid the temptation to material naturalism.[18]

The Resurrection—The Ultimate Miracle

Michael Ruse describes the resurrection from a material-naturalist position:

Most probably Jesus did die, and his physical body rotted in the tomb. But the disciples felt his presence. By rights they should have been depressed and downtrodden. The very contrary was the case. They felt a surge of comfort and power. They knew that Jesus' death had not been in vain. He had conquered death in the only sense that was needed. They were thus emboldened to go forth and to preach the gospel. This is what happened and was all that needed to happen. That there may be a naturalistic explanation for all of this, something in terms of group psychology, is absolutely irrelevant. It is what you would expect. It was the meaning of it all that made for the miracle.[19]

This raises a number of important questions aside from the obvious question of why so many would have lied and been comforted if they knew he had died. If this feeling of the disciples was "the only sense that was needed" or "all that needed to happen," then why were virtually all the disciples willing to die proclaiming that he had been physically raised? What exactly was "the only sense that was needed"? Why did hundreds of people report they saw him? How did Paul have an encounter with Jesus well after not only his physical death but also after his ascension? How do people today have similar experiences? Further, why did the disciples not carefully mark and revere his tomb if they knew he had died, even if not in vain?

Lesslie Newbigin describes the radical challenge of Christ's resurrection to the secular plausibility structure of the West:

> The difference between the two plausibility structures is seen most sharply at the point where we have to come to terms with the Christian tradition about the resurrection of Jesus. The community of faith makes the confession that God raised Jesus from the dead and that the tomb was empty thereafter. Within the plausibility structure of the modern world, this will become something like the following: The disciples had a series of experiences that led them to the belief that, in some sense, Jesus was still alive and therefore to interpret the Cross as victory and not defeat. This experience can be accepted as a "fact." People do have such psychological experiences. If this is what is meant by the "Easter event" it qualifies for admission into the world of fact. *The former statement (i.e., that the tomb was empty) can be accepted as a fact only if the whole plausibility structure of contemporary Western culture is called into question.*[20]

The bottom line is this: if the resurrection happened and if Jesus is still alive and accessible to human beings all around the earth, as one-third of the world professes, and if there are miracles, even one, then material naturalism cannot be the full truth. Its principles offer at best a limited view of reality.

The principles of material naturalism that are true and overlap with Judeo-Christian beliefs—the ability of men to understand the natural world and improve it, the utility of the scientific method, the various facts about matter, energy and laws of physics, chemistry and biology—are not undermined by belief in miracles. Indeed, from the Judeo-Christian natural and spiritual vantage point, the natural world and its processes are even more comprehensible and beautiful. This is why Christianity is an eager proponent of science—science with a moral tether.

THE ETHICS OF THINGS UPON THINGS

We know that science can tell us much about morality. . . . Biology can throw considerable light on these issues—moral behavior is ultimately an adaptation put in place by natural selection to make us functioning social beings. And it goes without saying that, in understanding morality, cultural investigations also have a major role to play. We in the Western world think that female circumcision is a cruel mutilation of women and girls. People in Africa think differently. . . . We know no scientific justification can be given for moral beliefs. There is no metaethical foundation to be found in nature.

MICHAEL RUSE, *SCIENCE AND SPIRITUALITY*

Philosopher of science Michael Ruse explains the reality that there is no metaethical foundation internal to nature or to material naturalism—larger and stronger animals win over smaller ones, males over females, healthy over the infirm and the young over the old. Scientism yields largely utilitarian ethics. Because material naturalists are atheists, their moral reasoning is drawn from a combination of scientific data read in light of human reasoning, which is also to them ultimately nothing more than neurochemical material and its processes. A culture under the grips of material naturalism is at the mercy of the human reasoning of those in power to know what is scientifically possible, to decide what needs to be done (their human ethics) and to use their power to implement their "reasoned" policies.

It is good to remind ourselves that it was the scientific and academic community that undergirded Hitler in his quest for the perfect race. Intellectuals educated in German research universities helped design and execute the Final Solution. They were combining Darwinian concepts of evolution as applied in animal breeding and Nietzsche's theory of the potential of developing a superman or superior race (*Übermensch*). Hitler reasoned that because his Third Reich *could* develop what they believed would be a superior race, they were responsible to an enlightened society to do so. There was no recourse to a set of permanent God-given moral values that believed all human life sacred and that named the Jews as the apple of God's eye.[1]

According to strict Darwinian theory, this super race would have developed on its own without human intervention because it would be more advantageous to the species. Nevertheless, this would take a good deal of time because evolution is a very gradual process. So scientism stepped in to speed up the evolution of a superior race. Historian Richard Weikart writes,

> Darwinism by itself did not produce the Holocaust, but without Darwinism, especially in its social Darwinist and eugenics permutations, neither Hitler nor his Nazi followers would have the necessary scientific underpinnings to convince themselves and their collaborators that one of the world's greatest atrocities was really morally praiseworthy.[2]

Adolf Hitler, Friedrich Nietzsche and Charles Darwin all knew orthodox Judeo-Christian beliefs were their primary barrier. Clearly, they stubbornly block the path to utilitarian ethics. Nietzsche thought Judeo-Christian virtues such as "charity" encouraged a "slave morality." Darwin discussed how human empathy for the weak overrode the purely evolutionary laws governing lower life forms, though he knew it would be ultimately injurious to the evolution of humankind.

> With savages, the weak in body or mind are soon eliminated; and those that survive commonly exhibit a vigorous state of health. We civilized men, on the other hand, do our utmost to check the process of elimination. We

build asylums for the imbecile, the maimed and the sick; we institute poor-laws; and our medical men exert their utmost skill to save the life of every one to the last moment. . . . Thus the weak members of civilized societies propagate their kind. No one who has attended to the breeding of domestic animals will doubt that this must be highly injurious to the race of man.[3]

Nevertheless, Darwin also recognized Judeo-Christian principles upon which Western civilization was grounded:

The aid which we feel impelled to give to the helpless is mainly an inci-dental result of the instinct of sympathy, which was originally acquired as part of the social instincts, more tender and widely diffused. Nor could we check our sympathy, if so urged by hard reason, without deterioration of the noblest part of our nature. . . . Hence we must bear without com-plaining the undoubtedly bad effects of the weak surviving and propa-gating their kind; but there appears to be at least one check in steady action, namely the weaker and inferior members of society not marrying so freely as the sound; and this check might be indefinitely increased, though this is more to be hoped for than expected.[4]

Others who followed him have not been nearly so generous. Darwin's book, known to most of us simply as *The Origin of the Species,* was ac-tually titled *The Origin of the Species by Means of Natural Selection and the Preservation of Favoured Races in the Struggle for Life*—a fact that informs us about the history of racism and Aryanism.

Nietzsche widely announced that man had killed God, and thus we had set ourselves free from absolute moral authority, free to develop our selves, the world and our own utilitarian ethics. Even Nietzsche knew this would result in the use of sheer "will to power." Thus Pandora's box was wide open in the late 1800s for despots of the next century who saw no higher value than that of human reason aided by scientific knowledge. These secular killing machines of the twentieth century were not limited to the West; for example, Joseph Stalin in the Soviet Union, Mao Tse Tung in China, Pol Pot in Cambodia, Idi Amin of Uganda and the Kims of North Korea.

Today's Eugenics Impulse

The ultimate consequences of material-naturalist ethics are not only still with us but are gaining political ground in contemporary Western culture in the increased support for sterilization, abortion and euthanasia, as well as in new rules for doling out medical resources based on age and ability. Related to this, we also see the frightful beginnings of people being forced to do things that are against their own consciences.[5] Hannah Arendt demonstrated that historically regimes that require people to act in defiance of their conscience lead to unprecedented totalitarianism on the left or the right.[6] In the Judeo-Christian worldview, conscience and intuition are two of the ways through which the Spirit of God communicates to the human spirit.[7]

Naturalism's treatment of all that exists as simply material phenomena was quite useful in justifying my two abortions. In the doctor's office when I heard the news of my pregnancy, the nurse immediately assumed I would want an abortion and offered to refer me to a clinic with which they worked. I was told it was a simple, common and safe *procedure*; I immediately accepted their offer. She left the room and came back only a few minutes later, "How is Saturday at nine? Would that work for you?" I am not suggesting my decision was the nurse's responsibility; I am pointing out that I was happy to have the strict material-naturalist view of the pregnancy.

I was relieved that the morality of it was never raised; this "simple, common and safe medical procedure" circumvented any moral questions. I (and they) could end the life of a child with hardly a conscious thought. However, my lack of conscious reflection then on the real consequences of abortion on the child and my own body, soul and spirit was no guarantee that things would not be simmering inside me for years afterward. I became increasingly callous, and as a result my second abortion was an even easier decision than my first; I went to the doctor knowing what I wanted. A growing body of scientific research (often dismissed for ideological rather than scientific reasons) reveals that women who have abortions later suffer from higher levels of mental and physical ailments, including breast cancer, anxiety and depression, a fact rarely shared with women contemplating abortion.[8]

Contemporary terms for pregnancy are primarily naturalistic physical descriptions such as fetus, embryo, blastocyst, information speck, product-of-conception or a clump of stem cells. Biblical descriptions, on the other hand, simply proclaim the woman "is with child," conveying both a physical and moral state of both mother and child. Eric Metaxas notes the irony that even in the baby's first trimester, the son of Prince William and Duchess Kate Middleton was not called the Royal Fetus; rather the child was called a baby, third in line to the throne.[9]

For women of means, abortion has always been a choice; for poor women, it's also a market strategy staged by the euphemistically named Planned Parenthood organizations whose founder Margaret Sanger was a well-known supporter of eugenics (the movement that uses science and medicine to cull out the weakest in the human species in order to build a stronger human race, such as in dog breeding). Abby Johnson, who worked for Planned Parenthood, revealed the eugenic practices behind their work.[10] For those living in totalitarian nations, abortions may be required by the government. Sterilizations may even be performed without women's knowledge at the directive of the government, as I learned had happened in India with prompting and funding from the United States.[11]

The new eugenics movement has gained even more force with the concern over human ecological footprints (the sum of a person's drain on the environment and society over the course of their lives). The weakest are to be reduced so as to allow more resources for the young, strong and powerful to have larger ecological footprints. Eugenics movements target the frailest, the poorest, the handicapped, elderly and sometimes girls; sex-selective abortions are now estimated to be at 200 million worldwide.[12]

Mara Hvistendahl described the results of population control in this century; one such consequence has been the abortion of 160 million female babies. Now there are 20 percent more men in China than women, but this is not limited to China.[13] She suggests that this imbalance fuels the growing sex trade, bride buying, a rise in crime and cultural instability. Despite Hvistendahl's shocking findings, she abhors it when journalists use her results to criticize abortion-on-demand. Charles Colson suggested this is a "classic example of the postmodern impasse," and I would add the naturalistic ethics problem. He writes,

"In a society that worships self-autonomy over all else, when we get what we want, we discover we can't live with it."[14]

Because of the belief that all human life is sacred, abortion and other eugenic practices do not fall within orthodox Judeo-Christian principles. There are also particular experiments that scientists who are religious may not engage in, just as there are places where material naturalists might not tread. Some Christians, Jews, Buddhists, Hindus and Muslims do not work with embryonic stem cell research or participate in abortions because of their a priori beliefs in the sanctity of life, although they may eagerly work with adult stem cells. For example, Dr. Ming Wang and his colleague, Chris Adams, worked for years to discover how to use fetal wound-healing tissue without touching the baby; they discovered a technique that uses amniotic membrane for contact lens to avoid corneal scars and speed healing after eye injuries.[15]

Material-naturalist scientists may not choose to study miracles because of their a priori disbeliefs, nor work on extending the lives of the seriously handicapped or elderly, nor on fertility problems due to a pragmatic commitment to reduce the world population for social or ecological reasons.

Free Will or Biological Destiny

In 1993 Daniel Moynihan, sociologist and long-time senator from New York, published an essay in *The American Spectator* where he described how American culture is lowering the level at which an act is considered deviant or criminal, resulting in an increase in violent crimes often never prosecuted.[16] Sociologist Anne Hendershott describes the cold reception sociologists gave Moynihan for his observations in "defining deviancy down." In her own book, *The Politics of Deviance,* Hendershott suggests that today rather than hold people accountable for their behaviors, we label them as suffering from naturalistic medical conditions, leaving victims of crimes defenseless and perpetrators free. She says of this empowerment of deviance, "It is appealing because it holds promise for a biological solution to what we are no longer willing to treat as a moral problem."[17]

These arguments point to an even larger question—the presence or absence of free will. Some material naturalists now suggest that we have no free will,[18] and some suggest that this is evidence that we should not prosecute anyone.[19] In his much-acclaimed book on *The Social Conquest of Earth,* Edward O. Wilson writes that free will is

> a product of the subconscious decision-making center of the brain that gives the cerebral cortex the illusion of independent action. The more the physical processes of consciousness have been defined by scientific research, the less has been left to any phenomenon that can be intuitively labeled as free will. We are free as independent beings, but our decisions are not free of all organic processes that created our personal brains and minds. Free will therefore appears to be ultimately biological.[20]

Wilson similarly defines religious belief as an "evolutionary biological product," though here he suggests this biological function encourages ignorance, distracts people from the real world and leads them into disastrous actions.[21] Within five pages, Wilson then shifts his argument to suggest that "we are alone on this planet with whatever reason and understanding we can muster, and hence solely responsible for our actions as a species." Then he concludes that "out of an ethic of simple decency to one another, the unrelenting application of reason, and acceptance of what we truly are, our dreams will finally come home to stay." But he has just told us ethics and reason are biological functions, some good illusions, some bad illusions.

Now this puts him in the quandary suggested by Alvin Plantinga earlier. How does one biological function of the brain judge the other as either an illusion or disastrous? Given that these are all simply biological functions, why expect to be able to achieve our dreams, or even know what our dreams should be, through biologically induced illusions? Will one biological mechanism decide to disable another as soon as we understand its biological process? For example, would naturalists attempt to disable the biological processes behind religious belief, and would this qualify as what "the Brights"—Richard Dawkins, Daniel Dennett, Sam Harris and Christopher Hitchens—call bringing "principled actions to bear on matters of civic importance"?[22] Fellow atheist, but not naturalist, Thomas Nagel explains the problem: "If we came to believe that our capacity for objective theory [true beliefs] were the product of

natural selection, that would warrant skepticism about its results . . .
[and] would provide absolutely no confirmation of its capacity to get at
the truth."[23]

Utilitarian Ethics

Moral philosopher Peter Singer at Princeton is a popular and articulate
proponent of utilitarian ethics. Some of Singer's shocking claims include
that (1) parents of infants should take up to twenty-one days to decide
whether their child should live, (2) bestiality can be ethical and (3)
human infants are no more valuable than animals.[24] Singer frequently
argues that abortion is not right or wrong because the fetus is a human
(which he accepts) but that the decision should be made on adult preferences. The mother chooses her preference since the fetus, though human,
has no capacity to suffer or feel satisfaction and no preference because
the fetus cannot yet know what it is like to live.[25]

Within the Judeo-Christian worldview, the question is not whether
science is able to do something, or what one prefers. Rather, given that
something can be done, should it be done? God's moral laws and grace
allow us to live our lives above our simple biological urges, desires and
convenience. I thought I would be happier and live my life more conve-
niently without a child; thus I preferred the abortion. Science had determined an easy, safe and legal way for me to get what I wanted, and I
went for it. The bigger question was, Should I have? Was it right? In the
final analysis, are utilitarian ethics good for human beings and society?
Had abortion been illegal, I would not have done it.

In contrast to Singer's support of selective and elective euthanasia,
in Judeo-Christian thought all human beings are made in God's
image and even the "least" of us is critical in the larger scheme of
things (see 1 Corinthians 12). Professor Chris Gabbard wrote a particularly moving piece about his love for his severely handicapped
son, August:

> That is not to deny that August, along with my daughter and my wife, is
> the most amazing and wonderful thing that has ever happened to me, for
> he has allowed me an additional opportunity to profoundly love another
> human being. A person such as Peter Singer well may conclude, rea-

sonably, that I have become overpowered by parental sentiment. So be it. I can live with that. There are limits to reason.[26]

George Will wrote a delightful fortieth birthday tribute of his son Jon, who has Down syndrome. He writes, "Judging by Jon, the world would be improved by more people with Down syndrome, who are quite nice, as humans go." Will tells us,

> This year Jon will spend his birthday where every year he spends 81 spring, summer and autumn days and evenings, at Nationals Park, in his seat behind the home team's dugout. The Phillies will be in town, and Jon will be wishing them ruination, just another man, beer in hand, among equals in the republic of baseball.[27]

Perhaps 90 percent of prenatally diagnosed children conceived with Down syndrome are now aborted.[28] Ellen Hsu learned that her unborn baby would have Down syndrome, and though doctors suggested the couple terminate, they chose to let their son live. Ellen's heartrending and revealing account concludes,

> Elijah's first year was sometimes difficult and overwhelming, but life with Elijah has settled into its own routine. Taking care of him is not all that different from taking care of our typical child. And loving Elijah comes just as naturally to me as loving Josiah. I can't imagine life without Elijah anymore. He brings us so much joy.[29]

In theologian Lesslie Newbigin's terms, Gabbard, Will and Hsu are operating on a "higher rationality"—a rationality that transcends simple naturalistic analyses.

Utilitarian Ethics and Bureaucracy

German philosopher Jürgen Habermas is an ardent critic of the way the West uses science and technology as an ideology that "reduces practical questions about the good life to technical problems for experts, contemporary elites."[30] He warns of the dangers of "technocracy"—scientific experts working through government bureaucracies.[31] Emeritus Pope Benedict XVI warned of the dangers of a solely material-naturalist view of science in his address to professors in Madrid in 2011,

We know that when mere utility and pure pragmatism become the principal criteria, much is lost and the results can be tragic: from the abuses associated with a science that acknowledges no limits beyond itself, to the political totalitarianism which easily arises when one eliminates any higher reference than the mere calculus of power.[32]

In March 2012, *The Journal of Medical Ethics* published a paper defending infanticide of newborns, not only for "medical indications," such as abnormalities, but for "social indications." The journal's editor defended the publication because it had passed peer review and "because of the quality of the argument," even though he said he personally disagreed. As part of his defense, the editor pointed out that there have been "at least 100 articles . . . published on infanticide in the Journal over its history, with articles both for and many against it."[33]

Material naturalism can mask the gravity of life when knowledge trumps virtue. In 1949, C. S. Lewis discerned this spirit of separating the physical from the moral and spiritual:

> The extreme of this self-binding is seen in those who, like the rest of us, have consciousness, yet go about to study the human organism as if they did not know it was conscious. As long as this deliberate refusal to understand things from above, even where such understanding is possible, continues, it is idle to talk of any final victory over materialism. The critique of every experience from below, the voluntary ignoring of meaning and concentration on fact, will always have the same plausibility. There will always be evidence, and every month fresh evidence, to show that religion is only psychological, justice only self-protection, politics only economics, love only lust, and thought itself only cerebral biochemistry.[34]

COUNTERING GOD AS CREATOR

The heavens declare the glory of God,
and the sky above proclaims his handiwork.
Day to day pours out speech,
and night to night reveals knowledge.
There is no speech, nor are there words,
whose voice is not heard.
Their voice goes out through all the earth,
and their words to the end of the world.
In them he has set a tent for the sun,
which comes out like a bridegroom leaving his chamber,
and, like a strong man, runs its course with joy.
Its rising is from the end of the heavens,
and its circuit to the end of them,
and there is nothing hidden from its heat.

PSALM 19:1-6

E **ach of the worldviews outside** of Christianity primarily counters a different person of the Trinity—God, Holy Spirit or Christ—who act in perfect harmony with one another (the ultimate reality and the ultimate expression of unity in diversity). Material naturalists counter God as creator because they can allow nothing but material phenomena and its natural processes; nothing outside material can create or intervene in the universe, else their worldview fails. If there were a God, there would be other implications, including moral ones.

Whether one is a material naturalist or not, an atheist or religious, the universe is obviously brilliant, complex, orderly, exquisitely designed and endlessly fascinating. Our knowledge of the universe astronomically expands at both ends of the spectrum. With the Hubble technology, scientists focused on previously believed blank space and saw for the first time ten thousand galaxies unknown before, causing them to estimate that there are over a hundred billion galaxies in the universe, all speedily spreading away from one another.[1] We live on one planet inside one of these hundred billion galaxies. Scripture describes it this way:

> It is [God] who sits above the circle of the earth, . . .
> who stretches out the heavens like a curtain,
>   and spreads them like a tent to dwell in. (Isaiah 40:22)

With other technologies, scientists focus on the minutiae of a single molecule in our DNA, which is up to three meters long, all of which is contained alongside many other molecules inside the nucleus of a single human cell. As if this were not enough, the human being is so designed as to be able to study, observe and understand these things.

There are two grand metanarratives or stories to explain the existence and operation of the universe from galaxies to molecules. In the material-naturalist story there once was nothing. Then there was an explosion whose material origin is unknown, though the time of the origin is being investigated using sound waves. After this explosion, there was physical material (and presumably just before). This physical material alone, via another unknown process, suddenly produced one-cell living organisms, which then through the process of natural selection became multi-cell organisms, then increasingly complex plant and animal life, finally ending (at least for now) in the development of human beings. All these actions involve only material and the processes that govern material, deemed to be unintentional, purposeless and independent of any design or designer.

The second major metanarrative rejects both material naturalism and atheism but does not reject the fact that material was created or that it started suddenly, most likely through an explosive act, and that some of that material is solely physical matter, that some is living and that the living did indeed follow the nonliving creation. This narrative is embodied in the beginning of the Torah/Bible. In the first three verses, the Godhead is present acting in perfect harmony to create the universe and earth:

> In the beginning, God created the heavens and the earth. The earth was without form and void, and darkness was over the face of the deep. And the Spirit of God was hovering over the face of the waters. And God said, "Let there be light," and there was light. (Genesis 1:1-3)

God the Father created while the Spirit of God hovered over water and God's spoken Word (sound waves, which later became the incarnated Word, manifesting on earth as Jesus, the Christ, fully divine and fully human). This happened over six *days* (the word *days* has various meanings in Hebrew—epochs or ages, twenty-four-hour days, or a single day that is as long as a thousand years).[2] Over these six segments of time, God created, in order, light and darkness; the heavens, waters, land and seas; plants and trees yielding seed and fruit; the sun, moon and stars; living creatures in the waters and birds in the air; animals on the earth; and finally man, who was made in their image (the Godhead)— male and female. God called these *good* and man *very good*. Unlike the other animals that were created "according to their kind," God (more than two in Hebrew) made man in their image, and breathed his life into man. God gave man dominion over the earth and instructed the first man to multiply and fill the earth, be our brothers' keepers, as well as tend the earth.

In this metanarrative that has existed for almost six thousand years, there are no gaps; that is, the big bang is explained by the sound of God's voice, which explains the appearance of physical material and its laws. The gradual appearance of living things and ultimately the creation of man are all a part of the intentional and purposive actions of God. With each new discovery, we understand more about the mind and heart of God and our own.

Metanarratives in science and religion, like all origin hypotheses, must be deduced from the data at hand because there could conceivably be an infinite number of alternatives. So we have to use what we already know and the data at hand. First, what we know, even Richard Dawkins admits, is that we have a universe that gives the appearance of having been designed; thus there is little reason for us to think otherwise. Experience leads us to believe that things that are complex and orderly have a designer. Humans have no experience where things that are orderly appear suddenly on their own. There is no evidence (data) that would lead us to believe the universe is any different. Second, this order follows regular laws in its operation, suggesting it was intentionally designed. Third, humans can study and understand these laws and this order, suggesting there is a purpose for human beings. Fourth, human beings have regularly believed they have some connection to God (or spirit) across the millennia—they sense his presence, in some cases hear his voice, and in the case of Jesus saw and heard him teach on the earth.

Human beings appear to have been created for fellowship with the Godhead. Material naturalists are actually able to measure some of the results of this fellowship, such as the relationship between belief in God and mental and physical health. Nevertheless, they would deny their source, which stands beyond our capacity to physically document since God is spirit and not a physical inhabitant of our universe. As mind bending as this metanarrative might be to those who are not religious, hundreds of years of evidence show that the God hypothesis encourages the spirit of inquiry and has never been a deterrent to scientific investigation. Naturalist philosopher Michael Ruse, though an atheist, dismisses the notion that belief in Christianity precludes one being a scientist: "I do not say that you must be a Christian, but I do say that in the light of modern science you can be a Christian. We have seen no sound arguments to the contrary."[3]

Part of the urgency for material naturalists and philosophic materialists to convince the world of *undirected* evolutionary theory is that it directly contradicts God. It is also the major bulwark holding up secular humanism, which suggests that humans are advancing not only physically but in their ability to reason and act reasonably and responsibly (social Darwinism). While material naturalists propose we can move closer to utopia by applying science to transform and control human nature and the natural world, secular humanists (who may or may not also be material naturalists) propose we can develop a human utopia on earth or at least a workable global village by simply using our human reason and experience. This is why many secular humanists defend naturalistic evolution as fervently as do material naturalists. This brings us to the second secular worldview—secular humanism.

Part 3

SECULAR HUMANISM

If man, as the existentialist conceives him, is indefinable, it is because at first he is nothing. Only afterward will he be something, and he himself will have made what he will be. Thus, there is no human nature, since there is no God to conceive it. . . . Man is nothing else but what he makes of himself. Such is the first principle of existentialism. . . . Man is at the start a plan which is aware of itself; . . . nothing exists prior to this plan; there is nothing in heaven; man will be what he will have planned to be.
    . . . When we say that a man is responsible for himself, we do not only mean that he is responsible for his own individuality, but that he is responsible for all men.

JEAN-PAUL SARTRE, *ESSAYS IN EXISTENTIALISM*

MAN MAKES HIMSELF
AND HIS WORLD

Humanism is a democratic and ethical life stance, which affirms that human beings have the right and responsibility to give meaning and shape to their own lives. It stands for the building of a more humane society through an ethic based on human and other natural values in the spirit of reason and free inquiry through human capabilities. It is not theistic, and it does not accept supernatural views of reality.

INTERNATIONAL HUMANIST AND ETHICAL UNION

The single best visual picture of secular humanism is a cartoon published in the *Los Angeles Times* the day after the famous existential philosopher Jean-Paul Sartre died. Paul Conrad drew Sartre in the form of a statue bent over chiseling himself out of stone; he had almost reached his feet. The text carved at the base of the statue read, "Man makes himself." If another cartoon had depicted Sartre with a few of his friends carving the edges of the earth into the shape of man, it would have completed the picture of secular humanism.

The defining tenet of secular humanism is the belief that human reason is sufficiently reliable and just to guide the course of our lives—individually and collectively—without any consideration of divine authority, which is a priori rejected. God phenomena are either the result of biochemical or genetic material, like the naturalists believe, or socially constructed by human beings within the context of one's culture, language and desires. Secular humanists are optimistic about our abilities as a human community to come to consensus on civic and moral norms.

Secular humanists may or may not overlap with naturalists; those who do embrace naturalism believe that human reason with science is adequate for advancing humanity, nations and communities and defining our lives. However, some secular humanists are not naturalists and have concerns about empiricism as the only way to know. These may include advocates of humanistic psychology, the arts and humanities, and those whose frameworks are similar to the early romanticists or the later postmodernists; these would view science with some suspicion. Nevertheless, all secular humanists would hold that religious worldviews are either wrong or that religious beliefs are not to be brought into the public square; that is, they are not candidates for the knowledge we need to function. Man becomes the measure of all things, as Protagoras suggested. Of the four self-professed "horsemen of the anti-apocalypse," Christopher Hitchens was more the secular humanist.

Longtime spokesperson for secular humanism Paul Kurtz, who is also a naturalist, led the development of A Secular Humanist Declaration of 1980, which declares that while there are wide differences in opinions held by secular humanists, there is a "loose consensus around several propositions," which include religious skepticism; radical separation of church and state; the ideals of individual freedom and democracy; supremacy of free inquiry; ethics based solely on critical human intelligence, reason, science and technology; evolution; and a radically secularized and moral education.[1]

The cultural indoctrination of secular humanism is so pervasive that it is difficult to describe; here we are like fish trying to understand water. With rare exceptions, movies and television shows (including those rated G and PG), newscasts and newspapers (liberal and conservative ones), court decisions, public music, magazines, popular media, books and textbooks, and most public and private human services draw exclusively from the principles of secular humanism.

The History of Secular Humanism

Political scientist Hunter Baker writes,

> During the past several decades, the secularist reading of history and reality has bid with some success to become the reigning structure of plausibility. Part of the strategy in so doing has been to secularize Christian values into the values of a liberal democratic society and to fail to acknowledge the source. . . . Secularism itself acts like a reporter reserving the right to question without itself being questioned.[2]

Secular humanists' slow takeover of the European and American imaginations and institutions began most consciously after the Enlightenment. The introduction of French Revolutionary writings (late eighteenth century), the theory of Darwinian evolution (mid-nineteenth century), the emergence of existential philosophy and the rise of the German research university model (late nineteenth, early twentieth century) all fueled the secular humanist imagination with the celebration of man's accomplishments, the transference of the transcendent from God to man and the expansion of the doctrine of evolution into stages of history, human consciousness, intellectual and moral development.

The American Humanist Association was founded in 1941 by a group of professors at the University of Chicago who previously had formed the Humanist Fellowship.[3] A member of this group, the educator and philosopher John Dewey, gave a series of influential talks at Yale, which were published as *A Common Faith* in 1934. In these lectures Dewey describes a common faith as being beyond traditional religions that believed in the supernatural and yet not so far as a science. The new secular-humanist faith was placed in human imagination, experience, reason and action.[4]

Other organizations followed, including the International Humanist and Ethical Union founded in Amsterdam in 1952, the Council for Secular Humanism founded in 1980 and the European Humanist Federation convening in East Berlin in 1993. Together these various organizations and their leadership have produced and published three Secular Humanist Manifestos in 1933,[5] 1973[6] and 2000[7] and the Secular Humanist Declaration of 1980.[8] Today a virtual explosion of secularist initiatives has spawned hundreds of new books, journals, magazines and websites, as well as billboard and transit ads. There are also secularist/atheist/freethinker clubs on virtually every college campus.

An umbrella group in the United States was formed in 2002—The Secular Coalition for America. They met in October of 2010 in Los Angeles and reportedly faced dissension within their own ranks from a younger group who wanted to more aggressively challenge religious believers and take on today's cultural and political issues. According to both the *Los Angeles Times* and the *New York Times,* those for a more confrontational agenda won the day.[9] Founder and long-time head of the Council for Secular Humanism Paul Kurtz resigned in May of 2010 from the organization and journal he founded saying that he had been "shoved on an ice flow."[10] The organization he founded is now headed by younger, more aggressive Tom Flynn, who began his executive and editorial functions with an issue of their magazine, *Free Inquiry,* devoted to gay rights, thus entering today's political as well as philosophic debates.

According to Flynn, secular humanism is "a comprehensive nonreligious life stance that incorporates a naturalistic philosophy, a cosmic outlook rooted in science, and a consequentialist ethical system." Consequentialist ethics emerges from "hard-minded scientific realism tempered by the compassionate commitment to an ethics that welcomes being judged by its results."[11]

The Amsterdam Declaration of 2002, developed by a group of humanist organizations, is often considered the official statement of world humanism today. It declares that humanism is ethical and rational; supports democracy, human rights, personal liberty with social responsibility, science and the arts; and provides an alternative to "dogmatic religion." The declaration concludes, "Humanism is a lifestance aiming at the maximum possible fulfilment through the cultivation of ethical and creative living" offering "an ethical and rational means of addressing the challenges of our times."[12] David Bentley Hart warns there are two sides of human reason, "Either human reason reflects an objective order of divine truth, which awakens the will to its deepest purposes, . . . or human reason is merely the instrument and servant of the will, which is under no obligation to choose the path of mercy, or of 'rational self-interest,' or of sympathy or of peace."[13]

Salman Rushdie, author of *The Satanic Verses,* disagrees:

I tried to give a secular humanist vision of the birth of a great world religion. For this, apparently I should be tried. . . . The forces of inhumanity are on the march. "Battle lines are being drawn in India today," one of my characters remarks. "Secular versus religious, the light versus the dark. Better you choose which side you are on." Now that the battle has spread to Britain, I can only hope it will not be lost by default. It is time for us to choose.[14]

The secular-humanist vision of the birth of a great secular world religion is not new. John Dewey proposed it in the 1930s, and the Unitarians institutionalized it. The same ideas were around in Socrates's day. Political scientist Jean Bethke Elshtain challenges the idealism in secular humanism and suggests it shares the characteristics of religious belief.

For if we understand religion to be values of ultimate concern, the 20th century saw two world-threatening examples—Nazism in Germany, and communism in the Soviet Union—of the emergence of secular religions, or what might be called replacement religions, each violently intent on eliminating its society's traditional religious faiths (in effect, its competitor faiths), and each, when in power, ruthlessly indifferent to human dignity and basic human rights.[15]

Common contradictory accusations usually begin with the Crusades and the Inquisition. The Crusades (named after the fact) were secular governmental and Christian military actions that took place seven hundred to nine hundred years ago (A.D. 1090 to 1290) in an effort to protect Europe and Jerusalem from takeover by radical Muslim rule. Philip Jenkins reconstructs for us the history of the Middle East, which was Christian for centuries before the Crusades and succumbed ultimately to Mongols, Turks and radical Islam.[16] The Crusades were initiated after four hundred years of Muhammad's followers gradually taking over land in northern Africa and the Middle East (mostly Christian lands at the time) as well as moving into Spain, Italy and Jerusalem.[17] This struggle continues today, albeit in only slightly different forms and without the direct involvement of Christendom.

The Inquisition was a long process purported to be about cleansing the church of heretics and heretical teaching, but as Hart points out, history reveals that it was as much about cleansing the secular state of the rulers' enemies as about cleansing the church of heresy. Even the most gruesome of the Inquisitions—the Spanish Inquisition—was strongly supported by Ferdinand, who silenced Pope Sixtus IV when he contested the cruelty and sought to intervene. Ferdinand II of Aragon, not the church, appointed Torquemada and used him to consolidate power for national unity until Pope Alexander VI (1431–1503) finally stopped Torquemada's rule. Other officials of the church continued to encourage leniency, including Pope Innocent VIII and Ignatius of Loyola, the founder of the Jesuits.[18]

Independent historians (neither Spanish nor Christian) pored over the private Inquisition records kept between 1540 and 1700, putting them in a database. During the period when records are available, it was found that 846 were killed or about 10 per year between 1480 and 1700 in Spain. The church's primary goal in the Inquisition was the recantation and repentance of heretical teachings; torture was not considered by most as effective. The Christian church had no authority to execute a death penalty (just as the Jews did not during the time of Jesus); they could only turn condemned people over to the secular state and rarely did so.[19] During this same time, the church prisons were considered far more humane than public ones.

Hart also points out that witch trials were not "the final desperate expressions of an intellectual and religious tradition slowly fading into obsolescence before the advance of scientific and social enlightenment. . . . They were in a sense extreme manifestations of [secular modernity]."[20] Secular scholars such as Thomas Hobbes and Jean Bodin also argued that witches must be exterminated for the good of society.[21] As C. S. Lewis wrote,

> Surely the reason we do not execute witches is that we do not believe there are such things. If we did—if we really thought that there were people going about who had sold themselves to the devil and received super-natural powers from him in return and were using these powers to kill

their neighbors or drive them mad or bring bad weather—surely we would all agree that if anyone deserved the death penalty, then these filthy quislings did?[22]

This is not to excuse cruel acts that certainly accompanied these and all wars, but we need to put these arguments into a larger perspective. These events in which Christendom is partially implicated occurred hundreds up to almost a thousand years ago, not in the last century, and they dramatically pale in comparison to every secular war of the twentieth century.

Hart points out that these events are vastly exaggerated in the new atheist writings. For example, he says of Sam Harris's work:

> He makes his inevitable pilgrimage to the dungeons of the Spanish Inquisition, though without pausing to acquaint himself with the Inquisition's actual history or any of the recent scholarship on it. He more or less explicitly states that every episode of violence or injustice in Christian history is a natural consequence of Christianity's basic tenets (which is obviously false), and that Christianity's twenty centuries of unprecedented and still unmatched moral triumphs—its care of widows and orphans, its almshouses, hospitals, foundling homes, schools, shelters, relief organizations, soup kitchens, medical missions, charitable aid societies, and so on—are simply expressions of normal human kindness, with no necessary connection to Christian conviction (which is even more false).[23]

Christians Are Not Necessarily Better Than Secularists

When I give my view that there are no supernatural dimensions . . . I attract pitying looks and anxious questions. How, in that case, I am asked, do I find meaning and purpose in life? How does a mere and gross materialist, with no expectation of life to come, decide what, if anything, is worth caring about? . . . Since you don't believe in our god, what stops you from stealing and lying and raping and killing to your heart's content? The answer to the latter question is self-respect and the desire for the respect of others.

CHRISTOPHER HITCHENS, *HITCH-22*

Whether anyone ever said these things to Hitchens, I do not know, but actual Judeo-Christian principles suggest something very different. Judeo-Christian Scriptures do not suggest that atheists cannot perform righteous acts. The Bible presents many examples of men and women who lived outside of Judaism and Christianity and who acted more righteously than believers. Witness the kings Cyrus and Darius, the prostitute Rahab, and the good Samaritan. Christ's harshest criticism was of the religious spirit of the Pharisees. Of the five women listed in Jesus' earthly genealogy, Ruth was a Moabite, not a Jew; Rahab was a Canaanite and harlot; Tamar pretended to be a prostitute to trick Judah; and Bathsheba was the adulterous wife of Uriah, a Hittite, whom David had killed in war. Only Mary his mother would have been considered by scriptural standards to be both Jewish and righteous.

C. S. Lewis explained the operative principle in Judeo-Christianity: "If Christianity is true, then it ought to follow that any Christian will be nicer *than that same person* would be if he were not a Christian and that any man who becomes a Christian will be *nicer than he was before.*"[24] The excellence of Christianity lies in its principles, which contain knowledge that each of us who are seeking to follow Christ only partially understands and lives; no one is ever perfect.

In other words, Christopher Hitchens may in many cases have acted more ethically than believing Jews or Christians like myself. Clearly, Hitchens, like many secular humanists, was sincerely concerned with important social issues and was not afraid of public criticism. However, according to Judeo-Christian principles Hitchens would have become a more righteous, whole and effective person had he sought and accepted Christ. He even may have had available a measure of divine grace to break his addictions to alcohol and cigarettes that ultimately precipitated the early death (at sixty-two) of this talented public intellectual.

Good Works

With rare exceptions, people desire to do "good works." Secular humanists are obviously committed to this. Secular humanists, as well as naturalists and other religious people, believe some manner of Christ's second commandment: love your neighbor as yourself. However, Christ's first commandment makes this imminently more possible: love the Lord your God with all your heart, soul and mind.

There are any number of secular organizations, such as OxFam and United Way, that provide extraordinary humanitarian assistance. OxFam, a secular organization that concentrates on relief and environmental concerns, was begun in 1995 and spent 771 million dollars in 2008 with administrative costs of approximately 20 percent.[25] In 2009 the umbrella organization United Way spent 80 million dollars and only 11 percent on administrative and fundraising costs.[26] We are familiar with these organizations because of regular free public service announcements on television, airport, public transportation and radio ads.

Clearly it is admirable that Oprah Winfrey, Starbucks and other secular organizations are digging wells for clean water and building schools in Africa. But a former graduate student from northern Ghana put this in perspective when in a coffee shop he noted with a small laugh that five cents of our water purchase would go to digging clean water wells in developing nations. He told me that the Catholics have been digging clean water wells and educating his people in remote northern Ghana since the 1500s. They are still there today.

The fact is private secular efforts to provide aid to less economically prosperous nations and individuals fall behind private Christian efforts in both magnitude and timing. About one-half of the health care in Africa comes from Christian organizations; Catholics alone deliver one-quarter of the worldwide HIV/AIDS care.[27] Christians began working in poor communities and underdeveloped nations long before the Enlightenment and have continued ever since. Monasteries began to flourish in A.D. 300, providing agriculture, water works, hospitals, schools and aid for the poor, as well as employment to townspeople in the Middle Ages.[28]

The evangelical Christian organization World Vision was founded in 1950 and in 2009 aided more than 100 million people in over one hundred countries with a budget of 2.79 billion dollars and administrative costs of 11 percent.[29] Founded in the United States in 1910, Catholic Charities spent 26.5 million dollars in 2009 in the United States alone; they spent 11 percent of their budget on administration.[30] The overseas charity Catholic Relief Services, begun in 1943, spent 780 million dollars in 2010 and only 5 percent of their budget on administration; it is considered one of the most efficient organizations in the world.[31] The Christian Foundation for Children and the Aging directly sponsors families, children, youth, scholarships and small business ventures around the world. Founded in 1981, they are sponsoring 300 thousand people around the world. In 2011 they disbursed 94.9 million dollars with 6.3 percent of income going toward administrative and fundraising costs.[32]

Virtually every active Christian church anywhere in the world is contributing to their local communities, and most support worldwide aid as well. There are no free public service announcements for these organizations.

Studies find both the religious and the conservative surpass the non-religious and liberals in giving to charity. Arthur Brooks found that although liberal families' incomes average 6 percent higher than those of conservative families, conservative-headed households give, on average, 30 percent more to charity than does the average liberal-headed household ($1,600 per year versus $1,227). While the average charitable giving in the ten most liberal US states was 1.9 percent, the average in the ten most conservative states was 3.5 percent. Brooks reports that Christians not only give more than secularists to Christian-based charities, but they also give more to secular ones.[33]

While Christian organizations that deliver aid have often been accused of proselytizing because they share the Christian gospel with those they serve, nevertheless aid is not withheld from people who do not accept the gospel. On the other hand, the US and British governments recently attempted to make new demands on developing nations requiring them to adopt the same abortion and homosexual rights agenda as the Western political elite in order to receive aid. When the African nations exerted their rights to self-determination, the governments relented.[34]

RADICAL INDIVIDUAL FREEDOM

[We hold] a keen commitment to individualism . . . emancipating individuals from illicit controls of every type. . . . As secular humanists, we belong first to ourselves. We are our own gatekeepers when it comes to mediating the demands any communities might place on us—even communities we freely choose to join.

Tom Flynn, Council for Secular Humanism

When I became convinced that the Universe is natural—that all the ghosts and gods are myths, there entered into my brain, into my soul, into every drop of my blood, the sense, the feeling, the joy of freedom. The walls of my prison crumbled and fell. . . . I was no longer a servant, a serf or a slave. There was for me no master in all the wide world—not even in infinite space. I was free—free to think, to express my thoughts—free to live to my own ideal—free to live for myself and those I loved . . . free from devils, ghosts and gods. For the first time I was free. There were no prohibited places. . . . I was free. I stood erect and fearlessly, joyously, faced all worlds.

Robert Ingersoll, "Why I Am an Agnostic"

Robert Ingersoll was a great American orator who ministered briefly with Charles Finney, one of the most famous American revivalists. Later, Ingersoll became an agnostic or "freethinker." In this often-quoted passage, Ingersoll passionately articulates the desire for radical individual freedom. The Secular Humanist Declaration of 1980 declares a more balanced commitment to various freedoms:

> Free inquiry entails recognition of civil liberties as integral to its pursuit, that is, a free press, freedom of communication, the right to organize opposition parties and to join voluntary associations, and freedom to cultivate and publish the fruits of scientific, philosophical, artistic, literary, moral and religious freedom. Free inquiry requires that we tolerate diversity of opinion and that we respect the right of individuals to express their beliefs, however unpopular they may be, without social or legal prohibition or fear of sanctions.[1]

Both secular humanists and Christians value the freedoms listed above, although these ideals are cradled within different contexts. Secular humanists ground these beliefs in the assumptions that human beings have evolved enough and are good enough to let go of limiting religious dogma, that we have inalienable rights to these freedoms, and that human reason and science alone are sufficient to guide appropriate ethical actions. In Judeo-Christianity these commitments to individual freedom are based on the fact that God made each individual in his image and that he gave us free will, a rational mind and a set of guiding moral principles that define the manner in which human beings and nature flourish. These God-given moral principles provide guardrails to keep our social commitments to *progress* and our individual desires from careening down personal, moral, cultural and global precipices, taking others with us.

With our free will, we are given the choice to pursue an intentional relationship with God or not. We could have been made like the fictional Stepford wives, who were bioengineered to love and obey their husbands, but we were not. Our free will not only propels individual freedom but also injects into the world the possibility and reality of human evil. We are free to choose evil and to privilege our individual freedom over others. We are not solely our own gatekeeper, but also our brother's keeper, which eclipses radical individualism.

Judeo-Christian humanist principles tend to be both more liberal and more conservative than secular humanist ones. Political scientist Jon Shields notes,

> The commitment to love one's neighbor encourages Christians to transcend the thinner democratic requirements of toleration and civility. However short they fall off this aim, the project itself is one that attempts to cultivate the kind of civic generosity that many find so admirable and wanting in public life.[2]

The commandment to love one's enemies takes this principle to a wholly different level.

The Conundrum of Conflicting Freedoms

> *The problem of leading a Christian life in a non-Christian society is now very present to us. . . . It is the problem constituted by our implication in a network of institutions from which we cannot dissociate ourselves: institutions the operation of which appears no longer neutral, but non-Christian. And as for the Christian who is not conscious of his dilemma— and he is the majority—he is becoming more and more de-Christianized by all sorts of unconscious pressure: paganism holds all the most valuable advertising space. . . . When the Christian is treated as an enemy of the State, his course is very much harder.*

T. S. ELIOT, *CHRISTIANITY AND CULTURE*, 1942

Law professor Steven Smith points out the ultimate conundrum of radical individual freedom:

> Freedom is a term that inspires respect, even reverence. In the abstract, everyone admires it. . . . [However,] an expansion of one person's freedom often means a contraction of other people's freedom: if we recognize and protect the freedom of the pornographer to market pornographic materials, we simultaneously reduce the freedom of people to live and raise their children in a pornographic-free community.[3]

Freedom of religion, particularly for the Judeo-Christian majority, is being usurped by nondiscrimination rules that limit even free speech and assembly, as well as health care mandates that defy the consciences of many.[4] In a culture whose supreme values have become diversity and tolerance, both religious and majority voices are often challenged. There are many such challenges to the Christian and to the Christian church.[5] Law professor Robert George explains the critical necessity of preserving religious freedoms: "Religion provides authority structures, and where it flourishes and is healthy, is among the institutions of civil society providing a buffer between the individual and the state."[6]

Ethical and political philosopher J. Budziszewski, in his book on natural moral law, writes that there are some things "we can't not know." "There are some moral truths that we all really know—truths which a normal human being is unable not to know."[7] Reflecting on his own early rejection of these laws, he writes, "Clear vision of the moral law is crushing . . . because the first thing that an honest man sees with this clear vision is a debt, which exceeds anything he can pay. Apart from an assurance that the debt can somehow be forgiven, such honesty is too much for us."[8]

The advantages of living within the laws of optimal human and social flourishing are evident even outside of religious faith or biblical text. These natural laws are self-evident across cultures, ages and religions. Thus, as Budziszewski suggests, in our more reflective moments we all know certain things. We know, for example, that divorce is always traumatic for children and leaves a trail of brokenness and poverty, as does having children outside of marriage; we know children need mothers and fathers. People know it is wrong to kill babies no matter what language is given to describe their early developmental stages and that it's wrong to let children die when we live in excess. We know that in the entire history of humankind, no living being ever came from the union of two men or two women and that male and female bodies are made to be complementary.[9]

That it is difficult to submit our human desires to these truths is also self-evident. Truly, I have broken most every moral law. We are all born with desires we need to suppress; I had many of these and, like everyone, still have some. Former radical lesbian professor of English and women's studies Rosaria Champagne Butterfield, who writes eloquently of her conversion and her critique of simplistic versions of following Christ, writes, "I was working from a historical materialist [secular Marxist or critical theory] worldview. . . . Christians maintained that Jesus Christ was historically and globally true, but his entrance into history violated a core value of my research: no one, according to the tenets of historical materialism, enters history; rather, we all emerge from it. . . . Two incommensurable worldviews clashed together: the reality of my lived experience and truth of the word of God. In continental philosophy, we talk about the difference between the true and the real. Had my life become real, but not true? . . . Do I believe that I'm healed? Yes. My life shows the signs. My life went from black-and-white to color. At first I didn't recognize myself in the [Christian] world. Today, I don't recognize myself in the pictures from my life as a lesbian."[10]

Philosopher John Rawls said tolerance is the only response we can have to diversity and that we have to accept the fact of "overlapping consensus."[11] That is, tolerance has to be a two-way street. This has been more challenging than at first glance it appears; as we add new norms to what we will tolerate, we become simultaneously more intolerant of those who live, vote or even speak of traditional values. Radical tolerance is often a reaction to fear ultimately descending into an uneasy indifference—"whatever" or "all good" we shrug.

Steven Smith elaborates,

One who advocates tolerance ought to be prepared to defend that suspect virtue not only against the familiar modern criticism which holds that tolerance is too insipid or unambitious a goal for a "liberal" society, but also against the opposite and older (but, I think more formidable) objection which insists that tolerance is a political or psychological or even logical impossibility. . . . It is precisely our theistic heritage and commitments that make tolerance an achievable virtue.[12]

Regarding new efforts to restrict religious freedom, free speech and freedom of assembly, Harvard law professor Mary Ann Glendon writes, "At the deepest level, we are witnessing an attack on the institutions of civil society that are essential to limited government and are important buffers between the citizen and the all-powerful state."[13] She suggests that if the trend continues, and it has, "religious believers in secular America will come to resemble *dhimmitude*—the status of non-Muslims in a number of Islamic countries."[14] Pulitzer Prize–winning journalist George Will calls the conundrum we find ourselves in "conformity for diversity's sake."[15]

The editor of *First Things* magazine, R. R. Reno, notes,

> What we are seeing today is a secular liberalism that wants . . . to silence articulate religious voices and disenfranchise religiously motivated voters, and at the same time to narrow the scope of free exercise so that the new secular morality can reign over American society unimpeded.

Particularly hard hit in the university have been Christian student organizations, which offer students a way to stay connected and grow in their faith during their time on campus. Recognition as an official university student organization garners them student activity funds (a portion of the mandatory student fees collected along with tuition), as well as free access to such things as speakers, use of facilities, mail servers, bulletin board posting and official recognition on the campus website. In the eighteen months prior to March 2012, forty-one colleges and universities threatened to revoke (and some did) the status of Christian groups on campus because they require their leaders (not their members) to share the Christian principles of the organization.[17] The Hastings Law School, a part of the University of California system, suspended the Christian Legal Society, which then sued the law school. However, in a chilling turn from religious freedom, the Supreme Court backed Hastings.[18]

While anyone can belong to Christian student organizations, the organizations require that students seeking or holding leadership positions be Christian and be living a Christian lifestyle, which means restraining from drugs, maintaining a good academic record, being able to lead Bible studies and restraining from sexual activity outside of heterosexual marriage. It is the fact that those living an active homosexual lifestyle would be excluded from leadership (not membership) in the Christian organizations that has caused the challenge, even though the policy is applied equally to heterosexual relationships.

Vanderbilt University is one example that has attracted a good deal of media attention. It suspended fourteen Christian student organizations for failing to comply with new rules supposed to conform to Title IX nondiscrimination rules. The following are excerpts from testimony to the Civil Rights Commission by Professor Carol Swain, the faculty adviser for the Christian Legal Society (CLS) at Vanderbilt, as she lays out the events over the past two years.

> In the spring of 2011, the University Administration informed CLS and three other religious groups (Fellowship of Christian Athletes, Graduate Christian Fellowship, and Beta Upsilon Chi, a Christian fraternity) that they would lose university recognition unless they agreed to a new policy stipulating that religious groups could no longer require their leaders to share their beliefs. More specifically, the new policy was interpreted by administrators to mean that Christian groups could no longer expect their leaders to head Bible studies or worship.
>
> After several rounds of having its revisions rejected, CLS joined forces with other Christian ministries who sought to persuade the university to reinstate its longstanding policy of allowing religious groups to have religious leadership requirements. Meetings with University officials, who announced with the introduction of the policy that it was non-negotiable, were to no avail. Our efforts to set up meetings with members of the Board of Trust were thwarted at every turn, as university administrators refused to deliver materials and letters that would have helped Board members understand the issues at stake. Throughout the process, the University repeatedly changed its explanation of the policy and what it was designed to accomplish. After months of framing the issue around its "non-discrimination" policy, the university made a sudden switch and began referring to the new policy as an "all-comers."
>
> In the spring of 2012, CLS and 13 other Christian groups at Vanderbilt applied for organizational status with constitutions that included affirmations of faith. As expected, the university refused to approve the applications of the groups who stated that their faith required them to have leaders

who shared their beliefs. After the University rejected their applications, 14 [now 13] of these groups lost the rights and privileges of registered student organizations. These now unregistered groups are paying a high price for their decision to preserve the integrity of their religious beliefs. On the Vanderbilt campus, unregistered groups can no longer use the University's mail server to announce their meetings. They cannot post notices on bulletin boards, co-sponsor events with other student organizations, or participate in interfaith activities and student fairs.[19]

Swain points out that these are efforts to use nondiscrimination rules to trump Article 1 of the Constitution—freedom of religion, speech and assembly.[20] This forces the university to abdicate its position as the free and open marketplace of ideas, as well as its commitment to diversity.

Today's new strongly sexualized culture on university campuses, complete with irresponsible hookups and fashionable sex weeks, encourages students to have casual sex, explore pornography and experiment with different partners and genders; this culture has had its consequences in a dramatic rise in venereal diseases, abortions and depression.[21] Nathan Harden has written about the paradox of the university's original raison d'être and its support of sex on campuses:

> For every expression of what is high and noble and beautiful and true, there seemed to be another following close behind—of the lowest, basest, ugliest and most cynical ideas the world has to offer. At times, I witnessed attitudes toward and depictions of women that could only be described by one word—evil.[22]

A secular-humanist culture might also try to stem this tide, but not having a permanent moral ethic from which to operate is disadvantageous. Almost all early colleges had explicit Christian values that justified administrators' decisions to restrict harmful student activities; some Christian colleges and universities still maintain these.

It is not only believing Christians and Jews who think there are advantages to the Judeo-Christian ethic. Some of the world's most respected atheists and agnostics agree; for example, the philosophers Jürgen Habermas, David Berlinski and Marcello Pera. Former president of the Italian senate and philosopher of science Pera recently wrote that Europe will doom itself to impotence if it does not call itself Christian.[23] All of them would agree with historian Edward Gibbon's eighteenth-century reflections on the fall of Rome that its prosperity led to its moral decline and ultimately to its fall. Gibbon also observed the way the state used the church: "The various modes of worship, which prevailed in the Roman world, were all considered by the people as equally true, by the philosophers as equally false and by the magistrates as equally useful."[24]

Popular and prolific historian Will Durant, though not religious himself, summed up the recurrent pattern of human history in this passage:

> The Movement of liberation rises to an exuberant worship of reason, and falls to a paralyzing disillusionment with every dogma and every idea. Conduct, deprived of its religious supports, deteriorates into epicurean chaos; and life itself, shorn of consoling faith, becomes a burden alike to conscious poverty and to weary wealth. In the end a society and its religion tend to fall together, like body and soul, in a harmonious death.[25]

Harvard sociologist Robert Putnam reports in his work *American Grace* that citizens who are regular church or synagogue attenders were healthier, happier and more active and generous in their communities (less inclined to bowl alone). Nevertheless, Putnam ultimately attributes this to the impact of social communities established in churches and synagogues and not to the fact that their relationship with a living God grants them an added measure of wisdom, grace and discernment.[26] While they may not be in church, people are inside many secular organizations all their lives from kindergarten to the university, in the workforce, sports, families and social groups. Appealing to the magic of community is a secular way of thinking.

For all their faults, a person who is in communion with God will flourish more than that same person would otherwise. The idea that the advantages shown time and again in research comparing the health and generosity of religious and nonreligious persons are due to some reproducible secular social structures limits our understanding of the critical importance of preserving the intersections of religion and state.

Steven Smith summarizes our unique challenge and opportunity:

> The basic problem is this: because the realms [church and state] are at once independent and yet significantly interrelated, and because both make their valid claims on us, we must somehow find a way to honor both kinds of claims. We must give both Caesar and God their due.[27]

Martin Luther King Jr. declared in his Letter from the Birmingham Jail that "a just law is a man made code that squares with the moral law of God" and "an unjust law is a code that is out of harmony with the moral law."[28] This is why the state needs the church and the church needs the state. Certainly a state must choose a single, unchanging basis for its moral laws; a nation simply can't apply Sharia law in some neighborhoods and Judeo-Christian derivations elsewhere in the nation. The logic of radical toleration and radical individual freedom is simply not logical. While a nation may turn a blind eye to any number of individual choices, it is more problematic when the government privileges these above founding constitutional principles, such as the First Amendment's guarantee of freedom of religion, assembly and speech. Forcing orthodox religious people to agree with decisions that every religion in its orthodox form rejects is dangerous and contradictory to a stable democratic republic.

Freedom in Judeo-Christianity

I still remember the exhilaration of thinking I was living my life in ultimate freedom; I reveled in being called a "free spirit." Gradually the boundaries of what I wanted and what I would do to get it expanded, slowly at first, exponentially as I got older, until I was bored with what I had gotten and then moved on to the next thrill. In the wake of my desires I left any number of serious problems for other people. The paradox was that when I thought I was most free, responsible and reasonable, I was least. I was a slave to my own desires and to the spirits that drove them. Real freedom is something altogether different—it starts on the inside. As martyrs and the persecuted have testified, we can have real freedom inside a prison cell.[29]

In this famous passage, Aleksandr Solzhenitsyn poignantly describes the freedom in breaking with his human rationalizations[30] before his conversion to Orthodox Christianity:

> It was granted to me to carry away from my prison years on my bent back . . . this essential experience: how a human being becomes evil and how good. In the intoxication of youthful successes I had felt myself to be infallible, and I was therefore cruel. . . . In my most evil moments I was convinced that I was doing good, and I was well supplied with systematic arguments. And it was only when I lay there on rotting prison straw that I sensed within myself the first stirrings of good. Gradually it was disclosed to me that the line separating good and evil passes not through states, not between classes, nor between political parties either—but right through every human heart—and through all human hearts. This line shifts, it oscillates with the years. And even in the best of hearts, there remains an unuprooted small corner of evil. . . . It is impossible to expel evil from the world in its entirety, but it is possible to constrict it within each person.[31]

When I began to follow Christ, I had the grace to stop wanting and watching pornography, but that did not stop the sure consequences of having movie scenes enter my mind without intentionally recalling them. All sins, indeed all actions, have spiritual, emotional, intellectual and natural consequences that affect our bodies, souls and spirits. Each time the scenes appeared, I prayed to be forgiven and cleansed: "Lord, you saw that. Please forgive me and cleanse me."[32] After three years I realized that these unwelcome scenes had ceased to torment me; my mind was free of the unwelcome intruders.

In addition to the freedoms that secular humanists and Christians share, individual freedom in Judeo-Christianity is achieved when we see, one glimmer at a time, who we really are. When we take our unrighteousness to God, a spiritual transaction is released that relieves us from the burden. This is followed by a second spiritual transaction whereby one is gradually cleansed from the unrighteous desires that prompted the thought or action in the first place. Are people ever perfect in this world? No, but gradually we can be cleansed more and more, allowing access to an ever widening rationality, less clouded by our own personal desires and error.

I am acutely conscious, as I write about the freedom in Christ, that from where I stood for many years this sounded like some fairy tale or a delusion; it made no sense that freedom was an internal state of human nature available through communion with God in Christ. Though I thought it foolish for forty-one years, my disbelief did not alter the fact that this freedom is and has been available for two thousand years, and it is perhaps the most effectual and progressive of all human realities.

VARIETIES OF SECULAR HUMANISM

*Man is the only animal for whom his own
existence is a problem which he has to solve.
Man's main task in life is to give birth to himself.*

ERICH FROMM, *MAN FOR HIMSELF*

Most theories in the humanities and social sciences draw their foundations broadly from secular humanism. These include social and economic theories, political theories, literary theories and psychological theories. They are themselves widely diverse, but they have in common an exclusive attention to human reason in secular contexts and deny or ignore any religious principles except to critique them.

Romanticism

Self-trust is the first secret of success, the belief that if you are here the authorities of the universe put you here, and for cause, or with some task strictly appointed you in your constitution, and so as long as you work at that you are well and successful.

RALPH WALDO EMERSON, *SOCIETY AND SOLITUDE*

If you have built castles in the air,
    your work need not be lost;
    that is where they should be.
Now put foundations under them.

HENRY DAVID THOREAU, *WALDEN*

Romanticism is an intellectual movement largely associated with the
arts and humanities developed in the eighteenth century in part as a
reaction against the rise of radical empiricism, what we now call scientism. Romanticism secularizes the humanist values of Judeo-Christianity by shifting the transcendental characteristics of God to man and
celebrating the self, imagination and the arts.[1] Romanticists hold great
optimism about the human condition and humankind's ability to transcend the ordinary in life. French philosopher Jean-Jacques Rousseau
was a major figure in the emergence of romanticism in the social sciences and philosophy, as well as being instrumental in the French Revolution. His treatise on the education of Emile recommended that all
young men be educated in nature, away from society, which was held to
be corrupt.[2]

In America, Emerson's and Thoreau's romanticist views were advanced as transcendentalism, and like Rousseau, they emphasized the
primacy of learning from nature, aesthetics, and free and imaginative
expression. Romanticists hold a suspicion of science and objective truth,
and unreserved faith in human nature and the soul. Romanticists advocate self-reliance and the advancement of the soul into higher states
through nature, aesthetics, intuition and imagination. Because of their
acceptance of the transcendent human spirit and their rejection of empiricism (scientism), this form of secular humanism rejects naturalism
and can in some instances even overlap with New Age pantheism.

Judeo-Christianity, while highly supportive of science, also rejects
the exclusivity of empiricism (scientism) as the only way to know. Judeo-
Christianity is also keenly attuned to the issues of the soul and beauty,
often expressed in the arts valued by the romanticists. Early Western
music was almost exclusively Christian, created to worship and glorify
God, and early art depicted biblical stories to the illiterate and literate

alike. At the same time, Judeo-Christian principles suggest a more grounded, less idealized vision of man. In Judeo-Christianity, corruption in social institutions simply reflects the fallen nature of its collective members.

Communism, Socialism, Marxism

The charges against Communism made from a religious, philosophical and ideological standpoint are not deserving of serious examination. Does it require deep intuition to comprehend that . . . man's consciousness changes with every change in the conditions of his material existence, in his social relations and in his social life?

KARL MARX, *THE COMMUNIST MANIFESTO*

Marxism takes a variety of forms today but commonly argues that people's lives are primarily shaped by their material existence (class, labor and economic conditions) and by other forces, such as the media, politics and education. The communist revolution is accomplished when the working class (proletariat) overthrows the upper and middle classes (bourgeoisie). Those who labor at production overthrow those who own and manage production. Marx proposed that the revolution would free the worker in a capitalist system who was alienated (1) from the product he is producing, (2) from meaningful work since the work of the laborer is experienced as torment, (3) from his or her own creative powers and (4) from other human beings.[3]

After the revolution and the material conditions of the people change through government control, it was hypothesized, the ideal communist culture would then emerge since man would have developed a new human nature. Greed would be abolished, and cooperation would become natural and replace the competitive spirit. Though Marx predicted that communism would result in a more just and free society with abundance, Marxist experiments in the last century actually resulted in unprecedented poverty, government oppression, dehumanization, genocide and totalitarianism.[4]

The move toward socialism in the West today is much more subtle than Marxists' overt revolutions of the last century. Nations are moved toward socialism by gradually increasing people's benefits and dependence on government, providing an opportunity for the government to gain more and more control over its citizens, who become increasingly dependent on governmental assistance to survive, thus becoming beholden to its authorities. Today, nearly half of American households have at least one member receiving government benefits due to both the recession and government expansion.[5] Canada, the United Kingdom and Europe have similar percentages. Socialists support progressive taxation, increased government welfare and the subversion of private property. The status quo is to be interrupted by protests, even general anarchy, rather than sudden violent political revolutions. This resulting disorder allows for greater governmental intervention and makes a nation even more vulnerable to excessive government monitoring and intervention, eventually leading to totalitarianism.

Marx believed that the state must eliminate religion because communism can allow no higher allegiance or authority than the government. Judeo-Christianity presents a competing vision of well-being that includes but goes beyond the material. Marx called religion the opiate of the people and predicted religion would become extinct as communism shaped a new moral human being through social evolution and without God. There are aspects of Marxist ideologies that are not foreign to Judeo-Christian principles of justice. The last three popes have all had strong ethics to help the poor but rejected liberation theology, which was essentially Marxist.

Capitalism has also been distorted when, instead of using capital to stimulate human creativity and well-being, banks were selling shaky mortgages to other banks and lawmakers became involved in political scheming. Essentially people were making money on other people's money. I have a colleague who was a student at the Harvard Business School when the faculty invited a group of people to speak to the students about a new strategy called investment banking. He remembers the crowd of fellow students and alumni standing and cheering at the end of the talk, while he sat there thinking to himself, *Well, it isn't illegal, but it sounds immoral.*

Michael Novak defines proper capitalism:

> Capitalism is an economic system, dependent on an appropriate political system and a supportive moral-cultural system, that unites a large variety of social institutions (some new, some old) in the support of human economic creativity. It is the system oriented to the human mind: *caput* (L. "head"), wit, invention, discovery, enterprise. It brings institutional support to the inalienable right to personal economic initiative.[6]

Novak has written on how the recent problems in Wall Street, the banking and mortgage industry and Congress have inhibited the growth of what he has named "democratic capitalism," a force that helped move 500 million out of poverty in two decades.[7]

Critical Theories

Critical, feminist, cultural, multicultural, race and queer theories are contemporary expressions of post-Marxist theory that increasingly dominate the university social sciences and humanities. These theories suggest the rich oppress the poor, the social class of the poor undermines their opportunities, the dominance of men oppresses women, dominant cultures oppress nondominant ones, people of one or more races or tribes oppress others, heterosexuals oppress homosexuals, media oppress societies and wealthy nations oppress poorer ones.

There are aspects of critical theory, like any secular theory, that are true also from a Judeo-Christian view. For example, the kingdom of God is multiracial and multicultural, and Jesus broke through many limits placed on women. In addition, French philosopher Pierre Bourdieu accurately described how social institutions reproduce inequalities—a process he named "social reproduction." For example, students of poor parents are largely educated in such a way as to be prepared only to take on the same jobs as their parents, reproducing their existing social conditions so that the poor stay poor while the wealthy are educated to take positions of power. It is true that public schooling has not broken this cycle of poverty despite having had this goal for the past sixty years.

The No Child Left Behind Act (2001) was the first strategic attempt to disrupt this cycle of underachievement of the poor. It began a movement to evaluate schools, teachers and districts by achievement data disaggregated by race and class to ensure that all of the students were making progress, and there has been progress.[8] Unfortunately, most critical theorists, though committed to increasing equity, worked against the measure because it used conservative measurements of school achievement—standardized tests. This is an example of how ideological commitments can obscure goals: two seemingly progessive agendas collided—teacher unions' ability to control their evaluations, and the need to evaluate teachers based on their students' achievement.[9]

Existentialism and Nihilism

Man cannot will unless he has first understood that he must count on no one but himself; that he is alone, abandoned on earth in the midst of his infinite responsibilities, without help, with no other aim than the one he sets himself, with no other destiny than the one he forges for himself on this earth.

JEAN-PAUL SARTRE, *CHARACTERIZATIONS OF EXISTENTIALISM*

Existential theory proposes that human beings live in a constant state of anxiety. The only way to reduce our anxiety about being in this world is by making conscious choices. These choices in turn make us who we are. Jean-Paul Sartre was famous for saying, "We are our choices." The following excerpt from his work *Nausea* shows the grueling level to which life descends when the navel gazing of existentialism and nihilism becomes habitual:

The Nausea has given me a short breathing spell. But I know it will come back again: it is my normal state. Only today my body is too exhausted to stand it. Invalids also have happy moments of weakness, which take away the consciousness of their illness for a few hours. I am bored, that's all. From time to time I yawn so widely that tears roll down my cheeks. It is a profound boredom, profound, the profound heart of existence, the very matter I am made of.[10]

I sympathize with these kinds of musings because so much of my life was lived in depression. Boredom was my frequent companion and biggest fear. Nihilism is an even more despairing form of existentialism, denying even the possibility that there can be any truth, objective meaning, ultimate purpose, moral values or knowledge. Friedrich Nietzsche wrote, "What then is truth? . . . Truths are illusions about which one has forgotten that is what they are; metaphors which are worn out and without sensuous power. . . . We still do not know where the urge for truth comes from; for as yet we have heard only of the obligation imposed by society that it should exist."[11]

James Sire suggests "every important worldview that has emerged since the turn of the twentieth century has had as its major goal to transcend nihilism."[12] Nihilism in the human soul is parallel to naturalism in the physical world. Our lives, like the materials of nature, are causeless, purposeless and directionless, moved only by random forces and our "reasoned" choices.[13]

Judeo-Christian principles agree that peoples' choices do affect who they become, and what we believe also greatly influences our choices. To know oneself (talents and warts) determines the degree to which one will be able to know and fulfill one's purpose. Anxiety is magnified by separation from God and diminished by intimacy with God. While Judaism and Christianity are very strong on human agency in making choices, this principle is motivated not by a desire to escape anxiety but by a desire to fulfill a destiny—to live a purposeful life. All choices are not equally valid, good or neutral; just choosing is not enough to thrive.

Postmodernism

> *The postmodern condition is an*
> *incredulity toward meta-narratives.*
>
> JEAN-FRANCOIS LYOTARD,
> THE POSTMODERN CONDITION

Postmodern art and architecture are good visual representations of postmodern philosophy and theory. The art and architecture seek to make the world look absurd—to make the familiar appear strange and the strange familiar, to undermine certainty. Postmodern buildings often have areas of inexplicable and unusable space, doors that go nowhere and cannot be entered or exited, and shapes that make the buildings appear to be falling down.

While postmodernism did open a larger space for cultural critique, in its purest form it is the ultimate rejection of any universal story that connects us to one another and to the world (metanarrative). There can be no truth claims, except of course this one. It is characterized by extreme skepticism. Metanarratives on which nations exist and laws are enacted and around which people groups build their lives are merely human constructions used to gain power. There are no universal standards for what is good, true or beautiful (the foundations of Christian education).[14] Literature, art, history, philosophy, economics, architecture and culture are analyzed not for their internal logic or for truth but for contradictions, oppositions and power relations.

Postmodern literary critics profess that the writer is dead—only the current reader's reading of a text is relevant and alive. Various readers can read wildly different things into the text, all equally valid. Analyses offer an infinite contest of meanings: yours versus mine, and the elite and powerful versus the weaker and less powerful.

In postmodernism, language is central to changing moral norms. Sociologist Anne Hendershott explains,

> In major cultural transitions, words often change their meaning as new norms evolve and old cultural constraints loosen. . . . Those involved in the politics of deviance often foster subtle changes in the language as part of a larger campaign to alter perceptions. An effective media campaign—one, for instance that pushes for standards of behavior based on individual desires rather than moral categories—begins the redefinition with a linguistic assault. The man who preys on boys becomes someone seeking only "intergenerational intimacy," and the promiscuous teenager is redefined as simply "sexually adventurous." From a rights-based, pro-choice rhetoric of those promoting assisted suicide, to the medical jargon of those promoting the disease model of addiction, advocates for redefinitions of deviance know that the side that wins the linguistic high ground generally wins the debate. . . . Words like "crazy" and "deeply disturbed" once were connected to suicide. Today they have been replaced with words like "dignity" and "autonomy" while those who oppose . . . are stigmatized as "zealots."[15]

Not all secular humanists believe there is no truth; those whose beliefs are nearer those of the material naturalists would be on the opposite end of the secular-humanist continuum. The highly intellectualized language of postmodernism is sometimes baffling. Atheist Christopher Hitchens said in an interview, "There are people . . . now—sometimes glibly called the postmodernists, who deny that there is such a thing as truth. . . . They only wear people down by boredom and semi-literate prose."[16]

Political Secularisms

Political scientist Elizabeth Hurd writes about the secular assumptions in international relations and its conundrums. She argues that the West must evaluate its "unquestioned acceptance of the secularist division between religion and politics . . . and that secularism needs to be analyzed as a form of political authority in its own right and its consequences evaluated for international relations." She suggests that this division between the religious and secular is not fixed but has been socially constructed, and secularism itself has become a form of productive power. One form of secular politics she defines as Judeo-Christian secularism, which opposes the total abdication of religion from politics.[17]

These varieties of secular theories all share some overlapping intentions with Judeo-Christian thought—stimulating human creativity, increasing justice, examining human existence and purpose, and exploring thoughtful and just ways of relating across international boundaries. While the purposes are similar, the absence of God in the equation limits both the analysis of the problem, as suggested by Hurd, and the generation of effective, just and true solutions.

PRINCIPLES OF SECULAR
AND CHRISTIAN PSYCHOLOGY

The goal towards which the pleasure principle impels us—
of becoming happy—is not attainable: yet we may not—nay, cannot—
give up the efforts to come nearer to realization.

SIGMUND FREUD,

CIVILIZATION AND ITS DISCONTENTS

Most secular psychology is directed at the valiant goals of understanding and overcoming psychological pain or stress and increasing happiness. A trained therapist generally guides clients to greater mental health by using one or more techniques drawn from the various schools of thought.

Psychoanalysis

Psychoanalysis's well-known founder, Sigmund Freud, proposed that certain unconscious drives and defense mechanisms are functions of our psyche or soul. These are often revealed in unconscious fantasies, dreams and free associations. The goal of psychotherapy is to uncover these unconscious desires and mechanisms so that they can be put under the conscious control of the individual's mind and will. Psychotherapy involves a person reliving and consciously renaming past events in order to better direct the person's present and future.

Carl Jung, at first a protégé of Freud, proposed that all human beings had an unconscious dark side. Consciously recognizing and accepting this dark side held keys to releasing the creative force. Though his methods do not conform to biblical principles, Carl Jung, unlike his predecessor, believed in God.[1] He noted that people became neurotic when they believed wrong answers to the meaning of life. He wrote, "The majority of my patients consisted not of believers but of those who had lost their faith."[2]

Freud, on the other hand, believed human beings invented God as a sort of wish fulfillment, a childish reaction to feelings of powerlessness, guilt and anxiety. One might ask why, if one were going to invent a god, would it be a god with rules? Why would human beings around the world invent a similar god or such similar moral and ethical rules?[3]

Behaviorism

Behaviorism is the most pragmatic and naturalistically oriented school of psychology. Behaviorism is a product of the empirical work of B. F. Skinner, Ivan Pavlov, John Watson and Edward Thorndike. Behaviorism recognizes that human behavior is shaped by environmental and social reinforcement. So rather than dealing with hypothesized internal drives and mental states, behaviorists address human problems by controlling the environment in order to reshape human behavior. When challenged about his coercive and reductionist view of man, Skinner maintained that human beings were already being controlled by their environments. Why not systematically control human beings to benefit the whole of society?[4]

Humanistic Psychological Theories

Humanistic psychological theories operate closer to romanticist notions of human nature. Erich Fromm and Carl Rogers were prominent authors of these theories and methods that concentrate on affirming the dignity and value of the human being. Erik Erickson developed a stage theory for identity development whereby people moved from childhood to adulthood—from trust to autonomy, initiative, industry, identity, intimacy, generativity and integrity. Abraham Maslow developed a hierarchy of needs that led one toward self-actualization. Each of these concentrates on man's ability to direct his or her life in a positive direction, a kind of natural evolutionary development of the human being becoming increasingly independent and self-sufficient.

Cognitive Psychology

Cognitive psychology was first developed by Donald Meichenbaum, who adapted behavioral therapy to help clients construct more positive narratives about themselves. His method is called cognitive behavior modification.[5] Here the client is led to understand his or her maladaptive thoughts; to identify errors, such as thinking too negatively or positively or fearing new situations; and to strategically replace these with healthier thoughts and more adaptive behaviors. The client may use relaxation strategies, particular forms of self-talk or imagery in order to replace negative thoughts and behaviors with more productive ones. Albert Ellis developed a similar form called rational emotive therapy; he held that religion was detrimental to psychological health. He taught clients to identify, challenge and replace negative thoughts about themselves.[6] Aaron Beck developed cognitive therapy, which helped clients consciously realize the negative thoughts they held about themselves and replace them.[7] All of these are forms of cognitive psychology.

Positive Psychology

Positive psychology is a newer form of humanistic psychology developed by Martin Seligman and Mihaly Csikszentmihalyi. It encourages the client to define character strengths, build a vision of the good human life and focus on increasing events that lead to wholeness. This focus helps the client to overcome problems by redirecting attention from psychological problems to each client's own vision of living a good human life.[8]

These various strategies are often taught to returning veterans, though some have been critical of its use here as too unrealistic for the problems they face.[9] Secular humanist and naturalist approaches can overemphasize a mindset of illness and disability. Every year more psychological illnesses are added to the list. Psychology and psychiatry increasingly view psychological problems as illnesses that can be treated with drugs. However, there are increasing concerns that these may actually make the client more ill.[10] One particularly disturbing manifestation of secular psychology today is the way in which the media sets our expectations that the women and men who return from war will be afflicted with a host of psychological disorders. Biblically, men were honored and celebrated as heroes upon their return from battle, whatever their other issues happened to be.

Professor of psychology Paul Vitz explains the emphasis on the self in psychology: "The modern self is characterized by such things as freedom and autonomy, by strong will, and by the presumptions that the self is self-created by the will, operating freely in the construction. The self is assumed to be strong, capable, and above all coherent; it is also largely conscious and heavily indebted to reason or at least reasonableness. . . . In recent years the presumed goal or ideal is the self of self-actualization or self-fulfillment." He suggests that most secular psychology encourages a detrimental self-worship.[11]

The Freedom in Divine Forgiveness

To be a Christian means to forgive the inexcusable,
because God has forgiven the inexcusable in you.

C. S. LEWIS, "ESSAY ON FORGIVENESS"

For the most part, research finds that religion is a positive force in people's lives—mentally and physically.[12] Though Christian psychology addresses many of the same psychological issues, it does so using different starting places and principles and also depends on God's ever-present grace. Forgiveness is perhaps the single most significant psychological principle in the Judeo-Christian approach to psychological health. Forgiveness is a two-pronged principle—people receive forgiveness from God for things they do or fail to do, and people forgive others unconditionally for the same.

Psychologists have also explored forgiveness and psychological well-being. But what happens to the Judeo-Christian principles when they are fit into secular language and research? I use the following example because it is particularly insightful and methodologically rigorous. It extends the long line of research that demonstrates generally positive relationships between forgiveness and various aspects of physical and mental health. Neil Krause and Christopher Ellison surveyed and interviewed over thirteen hundred adults, ages sixty-six and older (Christian and non-Christian, African American and white) regarding aspects of forgiveness and well-being (i.e., depression, death anxiety, life satisfaction and religious participation). The authors report their most significant statistical finding ($p < .0001$): "Older people who feel they are forgiven by God are approximately two and a half times more likely to feel that transgressors should be forgiven unconditionally than older people who do not feel they are forgiven by God."[13]

First, note the authors' use of the term *feel* three times, not *know* or *believe,* even though the survey question asked about *beliefs.* To be fair, in the summary they return to the word *belief.* I would contend, however, that this slip of tongue reveals the secular culture's assumption that religious belief is largely about feelings, and not about knowledge. In the conclusion of their study, they end with the following:

> Finally, as noted earlier, official church doctrine advocates forgiving others and seeking forgiveness from God. Yet, we know relatively little about how these theological issues are brought into practice in daily life. Two intriguing leads are provided in the literature. First, a recent study by Wuthnow . . . suggests that small formal groups in the church, such as prayer groups and Bible study groups, may promote the forgiveness of others. Second, research indicates that the general psychosocial climate of the congregation may have an important influence on the thought and behavior of church members. . . . Perhaps specific aspects of the congregational climate, such as the overall level of expressiveness, empathy, and social concern among church members, may contribute to a parishioner's willingness to forgive. Because the general psychosocial climate of the church is likely to affect the way that prayer groups and Bible study groups are run, comparing and contrasting these two institutional influences may provide valuable insight into the factors that encourage people to be more forgiving of others.[14]

This last statement regarding institutional influence is a rather odd conclusion because in the results the authors also report, "The relationship between forgiveness by God and the odds of forgiving right away (p < .0001) is substantially larger than the corresponding effects of any other independent variable in the equation, including church attendance (p < .05) and frequency of prayer (n.s.)."[15]

Second, the claim that though "official church doctrine advocates forgiving others and seeking forgiveness from God, . . . we know relatively little about how these theological issues are brought into practice in daily life" is even more curious.[16] There are roughly two thousand years of literature on how this works, beginning with the New Testament, which claims that the Word of God was incarnated in the person of Jesus Christ, who lived for approximately thirty-three years on earth, experiencing every temptation known to humanity and yet did not sin. Because of his divinity and sinless life, even though his physical body could be murdered, death literally could not hold him. He rose from the dead and was seen and heard by many for forty days. He understands and sympathizes with human weaknesses, having once had a physical body and undergone every temptation. Therefore, when a person asks Christ for forgiveness, the spiritual power demonstrated and won by Christ's sinless life, death and resurrection allows him to cover the sin (having taken them all on the cross). A confessed sin is not only forgiven, but subsequently even the desire that prompted the sin (iniquity) is gradually, and sometimes immediately, removed. This obviously encourages the forgiven to do as Christ taught (forgive immediately without conditions), just as he did when he forgave those who were crucifying him, even though none knew they needed forgiveness nor had asked to be forgiven.

This is a spiritual transaction, not the result of secular institutional influences or psychosocial interactions among human beings. Outside of Christ, no one person and no institutional arrangements can bring this kind of power to the act of repentance and forgiveness. This spiritual reality, like anything that is real, is ultimately likely to be measurable in any number of ways, from psychology to biochemistry, because reality should be effectual and knowable. Indeed, Krause and

Ellison have uncovered evidence for the effectiveness of this Judeo-Christian principle.

However, the study's conclusions do not include the hypothesis that an actual spiritual transaction took place between their "subjects" and a living God that set in motion a relief of their burdens, which were assumed by Christ, prompting them to more easily release others. It may be that the authors even believe or suspect there was a spiritual transaction but also know that their work might not have been published had they concluded this.

In the conclusion, the effectual factors that cause people to forgive others unconditionally are summarized as psychological feelings influenced by particular psychosocial institutional characteristics, not by God's forgiveness as the title and the data imply. The actual spiritual experiences of the participants have been reinterpreted through a secular lens. This is a perfect example of what Dallas Willard calls "the calamity of displacing the central points of Christian knowledge into the domain of mere faith, sentiment, tradition, ritual or power."[17]

Forgiving Others

While I was at Mother Teresa's, I read Christopher Hitchens's very critical book about her, *The Missionary Position*.[18] I was aware she knew about it because in the book she is quoted regarding the book's predecessor, the BBC film *Hell's Angel,* and because it was her sisters who told me about the book. In addition to accusing her of taking money from politically incorrect or corrupt characters, the book portrays Mother Teresa as controlling large sums of money in a little personal egotistical empire.

One morning she was telling a priest and me about some college students who had a fundraiser for the poor and brought her some of the money. She planned to use it for her new work, rescuing prostitutes. Because I had just read Hitchens's book, I said to her, "Mother, there are people who write books about you who say that you do not need any more money." She looked at me quizzically at first, then, in recognition said, "Oh, the book. Yes, I haven't read it, but I know it. Some of the sisters read it. Ask them. It matters not, he is forgiven." I pushed her one step further and told her that when Hitchens learned that she had said she had forgiven him, he was indignant because he said he did not need her forgiveness, nor had he asked her for it. She replied as though I had not understood. "Oh, it is not I who forgives; it is God. God forgives. God has forgiven."

Subsequently, I did speak with some sisters about the book. One of them recounted that when they spoke to Mother about how terrible the book was, she told them, "You know, this is a chance for greater love." Mother always taught that humiliations were simply opportunities God gives us to build humility. The permanent sisters had passed around and read their one used copy of the book left by a volunteer. Once they had all read it, they had agreed to fast and pray for a week, asking God to reveal what they could learn from the book, and then come together at the end of the fast. They told me, with great joy, that God had showed them it was a call for them to become more holy.

The experience of having a critical book published against them had actually helped the Missionaries of Charity. It had given them an opportunity to practice more love and humility, drawn them together in prayer and fasting, and encouraged the development of holiness. This was a spiritual transaction, not an intellectual rationalization or an emotional reaction. Thus the encounter with Hitchens's book did not leave any hooks in them that could deter their work or inhibit their union with God. The missionaries could not afford this kind of unproductive wallowing in anger and unforgiveness. There was no need to; they knew the One who would give them the grace to overcome. They knew that unforgiveness is like drinking poison while hoping the other person dies. Hitchens had been forgiven, plain and simple, and in so doing they were also set free.

According to the Missionaries' Constitution, Hitchens qualified for the Missionaries' service because he was an atheist, one of their categories of the poorest of the poor. Thus it was their job to simply pray for him. Today they are free; he died irate about her. Both the Missionaries' and Hitchens's reactions are manifestations of spiritual transactions— very different ones from very different spirits. Hitchens had no intellectual or spiritual categories from which to analyze their actions, no way of understanding their beliefs or their work; on the other hand, Mother Teresa and the missionaries understood him. No doubt they had already worked on similar kinds of impulses and sins inside themselves.

Two forms of forgiveness are central to psychological health in Judeo-Christianity—one is forgiving others, such as in the example of Mother Teresa with Hitchens. As Krause and Ellison have found, critical to the ability to forgive others is having had the experience of being forgiven by God. I had my own weighty lesson on this as well.

Being Forgiven by God

When I began to follow Christ, I grew deeply remorseful over my two abortions. It was undeniable to me that I chose this solely to make my life more carefree. I am certain problems remain in my body, soul and spirit that directly relate to those decisions. Historian Elizabeth Fox-Genovese wrote about the cultural mindsets that have led to an explosion in abortions worldwide.

> How have the advocates of abortion convinced vast numbers of people . . . that women's prospects for happiness and self-realization depend upon unrestricted access to abortion? The simple answer lies in their success in convincing people that full personhood for women depends upon becoming truly equal to men—which effectively means securing freedom from their bodies and, especially, from children. The more complicated answer arises from the assumptions of our culture as a whole, especially its escalating sexual permissiveness, its loss of spiritual direction, it pathological fear of human mortality and the related cult of youth, its dedication to instant gratification and disdain for sacrifice, and perhaps most portentously, its abandonment of children.[19]

For several years after my conversion to Christianity, I repented over and over for my abortions, unsure whether this most merciful and brilliant God I was just learning to trust could really forgive me for what I now believed was a grievous sin. When I arrived at Mother Teresa's, I was assigned to work with sick and handicapped infants; there are no coincidences in Judeo-Christian understandings. After my return from Calcutta I was at a monastery where we were invited to write on a small index card the names of people we were promising to forgive on one side and the things for which we wanted to be forgiven on the other. We would burn the cards on an altar outdoors during evening prayers.

At the head of my list were my two abortions on the other side of the card was a list of people I was committing to forgive. I put the list in my pocket and began to walk along the river that runs through the monastery's land. All at once I heard a male voice in my spirit clearly say, "Who are *you* not to forgive someone *I* have forgiven?" I stopped, stunned and confused by the question that had appeared in my spirit. Not understanding, I walked further, and the same question came again. I examined my list for missing persons and started forward when the voice recurred yet a third time. Then I stopped, knelt in the grass, looked up at the sky and said aloud, "Lord, I don't know what you are talking about." Into my spirit the Lord spoke one more time, "*I* forgave you the first time you asked me, and I do not want you to ask me again."

Many people had suggested I just needed to confess and forgive myself, but that is not what the Lord was saying to me. He was telling me, "Who do you think *you* are? *You* do not have the authority to forgive yourself. *I* have forgiven you; it is only *I* who can forgive you, and *I* have already done so." I did not need to continue rationalizing that abortion was not all that bad, or was legal, or that many people did it. Nor did I need to remain guilty and try to work off some sort of self-designed penance. I was forgiven and thus free; my staying bound was my choice, and it was limiting my life. My many attempts to forgive myself were never really finished; I always went back and tried again. Things that are not true never completely work.

For a year I searched the Scriptures testing the revelation and discovered there is not a single Judeo-Christian Scripture that suggests we can or should forgive ourselves. Not one person in the Bible does this or is told to do it. Working to forgive myself was an act of pride, a rejection of the free gift of grace already purchased by Christ, who had taken on the sins of the world that only a perfect life could bear.

One of the first times I told this story in public, a young woman came up to me crying and said, "Yes, but I had an abortion after I was a Christian." But David was forgiven for sleeping with Bathsheba and killing her husband Uriah long after he knew God. Most of us unnecessarily carry our sin with us like a permanent companion or karma, some-thing we anesthetize with our human reason. But David simply cried out to God,

> Have mercy on me, O God,
>> according to your steadfast love;
> according to your abundant mercy
>> blot out my transgressions.
> Wash me thoroughly from my iniquity,
>> and cleanse me from my sin! (Psalm 51:1-2)

Hobart Mowrer was the president of the American Psychological As-sociation in 1953. While not religious himself, he was deeply concerned with the state of psychology, whose practitioners increasingly attributed evil actions to illness. He wrote the following, which earned him consid-erable criticism from the psychological community.

> So long as we [psychologists] subscribe to the view that neurosis is a bona fide "illness," without moral implications or dimension, our position will, of necessity, continue to be an awkward one. And it is here I suggest that, as between the concept of sin (however unsatisfactory it may in some ways be) and that of sickness, sin is indeed the lesser of the two evils.[20]

Until I opened my life to Christ, I, like the general secular academic community, absolutely hated the idea of sin; even hearing the word *sin* was like scratching nails on a board, and hearing the name *Jesus* was even more disconcerting. Now I see that the solution to sin—the simple acknowledgment of sin for what it is and seeking God's forgiveness and cleansing—is one of the most brilliant, hopeful and freeing principles of Judeo-Christianity. The Greek word for *sin* means, literally, "to miss the mark." When I miss the mark, I somehow have failed to act in accord with the principles by which I was made to optimally flourish. I have failed to choose the action, thought or emotion that is the most healthy, right and just, not only for me but for others as well.

Without God, I would never have been able to even remotely ap-proach true self-knowledge. I would have simply gotten worse. We see instances all the time of things left unconfessed, unrecognized or ration-alized that simply fester and gradually become magnified. From my previous worldviews, I am painfully aware that it makes no sense that God would come down to earth as a man to offer a way to save the creation he made to know him personally and to bear his image. Even the thought of it seems ludicrous. To this, I can only say, doubt, hate or love it—his love and power are truly that real, effective and unrelenting.

FINDING MORAL TRUTH
IN HUMAN DIALOGUE

But secular humanism goes further, calling on humans to develop within the universe values of their own—as it were, from below. Further, secular humanism maintains that, through a process of value inquiry informed by scientific and reflective thought, men and women can reach rough agreement concerning values, crafting ethical systems that deliver optimal results for human beings in a broad spectrum of circumstances.

TOM FLYNN, "SECULAR HUMANISM DEFINED," COUNCIL FOR SECULAR HUMANISM

One of the most thoughtful and influential philosophic proposals for finding moral truth in human reason is that of German philosopher Jürgen Habermas, an ardent supporter of egalitarianism and constitutional democracies and a "methodological atheist." His theory of "communicative action" encourages wide-ranging participatory dialogue to derive common norms rather than giving power to technocracies to define values (government by experts).[1] Here people come together as equals to search for consensus on matters of common concern.

This reasoned consensus forges a new common secular identity founded on egalitarian constitutional patriotism alone. However, Marcello Pera suggests that constitutional patriotism by itself, with its appeal to loyalty toward universal principles and values, is far too weak or thin an idea . . . to create a strong, specific sense of identity. . . . A bridge is needed, a link between the abstract and the concrete, between the ideal and the real, between the supranational and the national. . . . The link must be something that warms their hearts, stirs their emotions, and produces solidarity.[2]

Habermas's "communicative action" proposal offers a description of "the ideal speech situation"—rules for how reasonable people from various perspectives can deliberate, posit, question, critique and argue central social issues in order to reach a rational consensus.[3] Unlike many of his critical theory counterparts, he suggests that although religious justifications are "pre-political," the religious must also be invited to the table. To participate, the religious will need to translate their contributions into the modern plausibility structure—secularism. Further, when the religious participate, they must accept the authority of secular reason; and in turn secular reason cannot judge the truths of religion. Ultimately, however, the consensus position must be entirely decided on the authority of secular reason. Then, for what purposes are the religious invited?

Indeed, this arrangement has a long history in the academy. While the marginalization of religious voices is obvious, it is by far not the most troubling of the issues here. Rather, the more serious challenge is the limitation set on advancing any truly unique knowledge into the existing secular mindset. The forced translation of religious principles into secular ones continues to perpetuate a dialogue held at the lowest intellectual common denominator.

Steven Smith questions the utility of secular human reasoning alone in building moral criteria and points out the fundamental flaw of consensual ethics:

> The philosophers were committed to using reason, yes, but reason alone does not manufacture moral criteria ex nihilo. . . . The existence or nonexistence of consensus has no obvious relevance to the question of . . . justification. . . . The standard example is pertinent here: if a global consensus through much of the world's history regarded slavery as acceptable, was the consensus correct?[4]

Many other troubling questions surface when considering secular humanism's faith in the development of a universal set of moral and ethical norms from rational human communication and consensus alone. Who chooses and excludes the guests at this new Arthurian roundtable? Indeed, who performs Arthur's mystical function? How are we to negotiate this new set of ethics collectively? How often are moral norms to be renegotiated? Who enforces these decisions upon whom? What exactly will be the rules and the real workings of these rational communications?

In the absence of a set of unchanging God-given moral values, we must constantly renegotiate moral and ethical values and be compelled to live tethered to one of four alternatives: (1) the whims and strength of those in power to resolve the endless moral/cultural wars (technocracy); (2) the changing moral climate of the most influential media and most articulate, perhaps even most seductive, spokespersons; (3) the democratic votes of an electorate; or (4) even the overrule of democratic votes by executive orders, legislatures and court decisions as happens increasingly in Western democracies. No doubt any of these alternatives will provoke a good deal of uncertainty, chaos and contestations created by a constantly shifting moral environment.

In a brilliant essay, the chief rabbi of the British Commonwealth, Jonathan Sacks, explains the situation leading up to the British youth riots.

> In virtually every Western society in the 1960s there was a moral revolution, an abandonment of its entire traditional ethic of self-restraint. All you need, sang the Beatles, is love. The Judeo-Christian moral code was jettisoned. In its place came: whatever works for you. The Ten Commandments were rewritten as the Ten Creative Suggestions. Or as Allan Bloom put it in "The Closing of the American Mind": "I am the Lord Your God: Relax!" You do not have to be a Victorian sentimentalist to realize that something has gone badly wrong since. In Britain today, more than 40% of children are born outside marriage. This has led to new forms of child poverty that serious government spending has failed to cure. In 2007, a UNICEF report found that Britain's children are the unhappiest in the world. The 2011 riots are one result. But there are others.[5]

About all our many controversies, Steven Smith boldly asks us,

"Shouldn't the question be what the truth is, not what we believe?"[6] Here Smith is not writing about human-constructed, consensually determined and changing truths but about objective truths that can be observed as the better choice. This is ultimately the problem of ethics and morals built around renegotiable consensus, public opinion, sheer power and democratic majorities. Without an unchanging moral code that works across time and represents the way the world actually functions best—and the way human beings and the rest of nature most productively flourish—nations, groups and individuals are constantly left adrift in an ever-changing moral environment.

For two thousand years the moral code revealed in Judaism and the life and teachings of Jesus Christ has proved to be most productive and edifying. This code is wide enough to accommodate incredible diversity and bounded enough to keep us free, healthy and safe. His incarnation was and is God's design to manifest the perfect, full and abundant life of Christ and to offer us a model.

Marcello Pera suggests the results of letting this framework go. He proposes that because of radical multiculturalism, postmodernism and relativism, Europe can no longer defend herself against radical Islam and other aggressors; she cannot bring herself to say that one thing is better than another. He elaborates,

> Two divergent theories may be compared on the common ground, . . . and one may be judged better than the other. By better we mean that it has greater empirical content, more heuristic capacity, and so on. . . . Two religious systems may be compared by their cultural consequences, and here too one may be judged better than the other. By "better" we mean that it recognizes and respects more fundamental rights, satisfies more expectation, allows for more efficient, transparent, democratic institution and so on.[7]

Though an atheist, Pera, like Habermas, believes that Europe dooms itself to impotence if it does not return to its Judeo-Christian groundings.[8]

David Bentley Hart articulates both the original logic and the hope of our being able to find moral truth in human dialogue apart from the Judeo-Christian ethic and its results thus far.

Part of the enthralling promise of an age of reason was, at least at first, the prospect of a genuinely rational ethics . . . not limited to the moral precepts of any particular creed, but available to all reasoning minds regardless of culture and—when recognized—immediately compelling to the rational will. Was there ever a more desperate fantasy than this? We live now in the wake of the most monstrously violent century in human history, during which the secular order (on both the political right and the political left), freed from the authority of religion, showed itself willing to kill on an unprecedented scale and with an ease of conscience worse than merely depraved. If ever an age deserved to be thought an age of darkness, it is surely ours.[9]

Marcelo Pera concludes his book with the alternative,

In the end, we must choose. As the history of liberalism and modernity shows, the Christian choice to give oneself to God, or to act . . . as if God existed, has yielded the best results. This choice still has great advantages also in the field of public ethics. If we live as Christians, we will be wiser and more aware of the dangers we face. We will not separate morality from truth. We will not confuse moral autonomy with any free choice. We will not treat individuals, whether the unborn or the dying, as things. We will not allow all desires to be transformed into rights. We will not confine reason within the boundaries of science. Nor will we feel alone in a society of strangers or oppressed by a state that appropriates us because we no longer know how to guide ourselves, . . . our moral norms, and with them our coexistence and our institutions—the very same ones that have passed down and preserved for us the civilization in which we are living, at times troubled and afflicted, at times satisfied and hopeful—would wither and die if they were to cut themselves off from Christianity.[10]

EXORCISING SIN

The fact of sin [is] a fact as practical as potatoes . . .
the only part of Christian theology that can really be proved.

G. K. CHESTERTON, *ORTHODOXY*

In Albert Camus's novel The Plague, *an allegory on the coming of totalitarian terror, one of the protagonists comments acerbically on the naive reactions in a time of crisis of those he calls the "humanists," people who see themselves as living in a reasonable world in which everything is up for negotiation. They believe there is a utilitarian calculus by which to gauge all human purposes and actions. . . . Camus's "humanists" are unwilling to peer into the heart of darkness. They have banished the word evil from their vocabularies. Evil refers to something so unreasonable, after all! Therefore, it cannot really exist.*

JEAN BETHKE ELSHTAIN, INTRODUCTION TO *JUST WAR AGAINST TERROR*

Jean Elshtain aptly identifies the tragedy of secular humanists' utilitarian moral calculus. Human sinfulness in Judeo-Christianity is the single most detested principle by those outside it, and the single most transformative to those on the inside. The Judeo-Christian view of human nature is paradoxically that all people are made in the image of the triune God and that we "all have sinned and fall short of the glory of God" (Romans 3:23). These statements are not contradictory or dialectic; they are both altogether true and fully operative in every human being, and at all times we are each moving in one direction or the other. Having refused to admit the reality of sin and evil most of my life, this was the first lesson I had to learn.

Four months after my hesitant confession to try Christianity, a friend awakened me with a violent physical attack very early one morning. He was suddenly unrecognizable, had uncharacteristic strength and spoke with a different voice. After the incident, he appeared as shocked as I and jumped up saying, "I'm sorry, I don't know what happened. That wasn't me." I believed him.

That evening, when reading a passage that had previously seemed particularly egregious, one where the psalmist once again calls out for God to kill his enemies, I suddenly realized the psalmist was crying out to God about evil, just as David had implored God about his own sin. Like metaphorical scales falling from my eyes, instantly I understood two things—evil does exist, and it operates in and through the world, through other people and through me. The reality of our fallen nature became undeniable.

C. S. Lewis explains the gradual slide I had experienced not having any permanent moral boundaries:

> Good and evil both increase at compound interest. That is why the little decisions you and I make every day are of such infinite importance. The smallest good act today is the capture of a strategic point from which, a few months later, you may be able to go on to victories you never dreamed of. An apparently trivial indulgence in lust or anger today is the loss of a ridge or railway line or bridgehead from which the enemy may launch an attack otherwise impossible.[1]

Secularists interpret sin variously as preposterous, foolish, depressing, oppressive or life limiting, or as a human construction used to limit other people's lives and gain power over them. In our moral free fall, thoughts and deeds that once were considered unthinkable, wrong, illegal or aberrations are simply added to an ever-growing list of viable human choices, often by casting them as attractive and trendy in the media. The primary reason for my not believing (not wanting to believe) in sin as it is defined in Judeo-Christianity was not based on human reason, philosophy, science or utilitarian ethics. It was based on personal desire.

Lifelong atheist Aldous Huxley describes the impulse.

> The liberation we desired was simultaneously liberation from a certain political and economic system and liberation from a certain system of morality. We objected to the morality because it interfered with our sexual freedom; we objected to the political and economic system because it was unjust. The supporters of these systems claimed that in some way they embodied the meaning (the Christian meaning, they insisted) of the world. There was an admirably simple method of confuting these people and at the same time justifying ourselves in our political and erotic revolt: we would deny that the world had any meaning whatsoever.[2]

My problem admittedly was like Huxley's; I thought I was living the good life, and I didn't want to disrupt it. I didn't want to see the truth inside me. Nevertheless, the cold hard facts were laid out before me. Fortunately they came with a toolkit and a carpenter. The truth of God is not constructed and does not grant worldly social or political power or privilege; indeed it is generally the reverse. What it grants is true personal freedom. I long, sometimes ache, to see others experience the same transformative possibilities, especially those people who appear to be locked up in the same things that had my mind and emotions and spirit imprisoned.

In the first letter of John, we read: "If we confess our sins, he is faithful and just to forgive us our sins and to cleanse us from all unrighteousness" (1 John 1:9). I do not believe this sentence on sheer unexamined faith. I believe it because of experience and thorough testing over time; I know it works. I am not the sole agent of my psychological breakthroughs; God is the primary agent of these spiritual transactions, just as he is the primary agent in the creation of the universe. Perhaps I am too much the pragmatist and too little faithful, but I believe God's principles are true because when tested they work. I believe those I cannot test, touch or see—because the many I have tested have proven true and because every time I read the Bible I see new things to test, new insights and understandings about the way things really are. For example, Jesus tells us we can remove the splinter from another's eye when we have removed the plank from our own.

Three years after I had been cleansed of the pornographic scenes, I arrived at the Los Angeles airport very early for an afternoon flight to New York on my way to Buenos Aires. I asked to take an earlier flight, and I was seated next to the window in a plane with nine seats across and very few passengers. A muscular young man dressed in shorts and a tank top with two long black braids was assigned the seat next to me. As I looked around at the many choices of seats behind me, I remembered that Jesus would have sat with the young man. I reluctantly gave up my search. His two cell phones were both ringing. This was 1999; I'm pretty certain I didn't have even one cell phone at the time.

We exchanged the usual, why are you going to New York, and what do you do? It turned out he was on his way to be on the *Ricki Lake Show* to find out whether a woman's newborn son was his; he insisted it most likely wasn't his because "she slept with everyone." He asked if I was a teacher with my book, pen and hair in a bun. I asked him in return what he did, and he first said, "I don't think you want to know." I didn't press the issue; nevertheless, he told me he made adult movies. Without thinking, I revealed to him the struggle I had after having watched pornography and how I had each time confessed and asked God to heal me, until a few years later I realized I no longer had the unwanted visual images.

His demeanor softened, and he said, "Yes, and after you begin to watch them you need more, and it has to be more hardcore." Then he got very serious and a little sad and told me he would like to get out of the business, but he knew he couldn't. I told him if he asked the Lord, he would find the way out before he knew what happened. Then I gave him a little Native American tract I had thought I was carrying to show friends in Argentina.[3] It turned out he was ethnically Native American, African American and French.

He took the tract with him to the bathroom. Then he came back and began showing me pictures of his estranged family. He had decided in the meantime it might not be so bad if this baby was his. After all, he told me, here was his little girl, pictured with his ex-wife, and he had always wanted a son. Soon he fell asleep until dinner. At God's prompting I offered to pray for him after dinner, having no idea what I would say if he said yes. At the suggestion he grabbed both my hands, pulled them to his chest and said desperately—"Please." I don't remember what I prayed, and I don't know what happened afterward. However, one thing I do know is that once God has set us free, he uses us for the next person.[4] The plank in my eye has been removed. God is relentlessly working to bring everyone to real freedom, and it is never too late.

CONTESTING JESUS AS DIVINE

The Secular Humanist tradition is in part a tradition of defiance. . . . Prometheus stands out because he was admired by ancient Greeks as the one who defied Zeus. He stole the fire of the gods and brought it down to earth. For this he was punished. And yet he continued his defiance amid his tortures. This is one source of the humanist challenge to authority. The next time we see a truly heroic Promethean character in mythology it is Lucifer in John Milton's Paradise Lost. But now he is the Devil. He is evil. Whoever would defy God must be wickedness personified. That seems to be a given of traditional religion.

FRED EDWORDS, "WHAT IS HUMANISM,"
AMERICAN HUMANIST ASSOCIATION

"But what will become of men then," I asked him, "without God and immortal life? All things are lawful then, they can do what they like."

"Didn't you know?" [Ivan] said laughing. "A clever man can do what he likes," he said. "A clever man knows his way about." . . .

"Ivan has no God. He has an idea." . . . I said to him, "Then everything is lawful, if it is so?" He frowned.

FYODOR DOSTOEVSKY, *THE BROTHERS KARAMAZOV*

Because humanism emerged from Judeo-Christian roots, secular humanists largely define themselves by their opposition to the Judeo-Christian moral framework. According to the Council for Secular Humanism, "Secular humanists do not rely upon gods or other supernatural forces to solve their problems or provide guidance for their conduct."[1] Political economist Robert Reich even more clearly articulates the animosity to divine authority.

> The great conflict of the twenty-first century may be between the West and terrorism. But terrorism is a tactic, not a belief. The underlying battle will be between modern civilization and anti-modernist fanatics; between those who believe in the primacy of the individual and those who believe that human beings owe blind allegiance to a higher authority; between those who give priority to life in this world and those who believe that human life is no more than preparation for an existence beyond life; between those who believe truth is revealed solely though scripture and religious dogma, and those who rely primarily on science, reason and logic.[2]

Aside from the errors in Reich's analysis that a Christian is simply deluded by dogma; resistant to science, reason and logic; and only preparing for the next life, it seems to me that the very logical philosopher Thomas Nagel's confession rings more honest and less polemical:

> I am talking about something much deeper—namely, the fear of religion itself. I speak from experience, being strongly subject to this fear myself: I want atheism to be true and am made uneasy by the fact that some of the most intelligent and well-informed people I know are religious believers. It isn't just that I don't believe in God and, naturally, hope that I'm right in my belief. It's that I hope there is no God! I don't want there to be a God; I don't want the universe to be like that. My guess is that this cosmic authority problem is not a rare condition and that it is responsible for much of the scientism and reductionism of our time.[3]

Prominent secular scholar Phil Zuckerman has been in the news for beginning a "secular studies" program at Pitzer College. Never mind that it is impossible for a student at his college or any other secular college to get any other kind of degree, even most who get degrees in religion and theology. Zuckerman published an often-quoted book, *Society*

Without God, suggesting one reason to abandon divine authority is that the most prosperous, happy and healthy cultures are secular.[4] Zuckerman asserts in his book that as Denmark and Sweden became more secular they became more prosperous.

The methods and facts related to his observations are important. Zuckerman's data compare statistics from Denmark and Sweden (more secular) to the United States (less secular). First, Denmark is less than twice the size of Massachusetts and has about 20 percent fewer inhabitants. The population of Denmark is less than 10 percent immigrants, 54 percent of whom are European. So one cannot simply compare the culture of Denmark to the United States. A more scientifically accurate investigation of his hypothesis would compare, for example, Denmark to Denmark or Sweden to Sweden as each became more secular.

In 1960, Denmark had 100,000 crimes committed; in 2000 it had five times as many (500,000) with only 13 percent growth in population. In 1960 there were 300,000 people of working age who received full-time government welfare; in 2000 there were three times as many (900,000). From 1970 to 2002, the divorce rate grew from 18 percent to 37 percent. In 1970, 83 percent were married and 47 percent in 2002.[5] These are not signs of improvement or even stasis; these are the same signs of decline experienced everywhere in the West.

Swedish scholars Kjell Lejon and Marcus Agnafors reviewed Zuckerman's book and also pointed out that these two societies are still largely shaped by their Lutheran backgrounds, which encourage many of the virtues that Zuckerman exalts—literacy and the work ethic that lies behind Denmark and Sweden's economic prosperity and values. While only 2 to 3 percent regularly attend church, 80 percent say they belong to the church and 50 percent attend church on occasions such as baptisms and weddings.[6] But Zuckerman's faith is that human beings, freed of God, will create better cultures.

Jesus as Divine

Since the contest of the secular humanist is ultimately between the authority of man and the authority of God, the God/man Jesus stands abruptly in the way of the secular humanist's goal of man being supremely in charge. Jesus can be a great man, famous prophet or good teacher but not what he is, fully divine and fully human. His existence and ethics can be seen as slightly better than ours, but he has to have been one of us. In secular humanism, where man is the measure of all things, there can be no higher authority than man—certainly not a divine man.

In Judeo-Christian knowledge, Christ is both the creator and the measure of all things. He is our yardstick, our redeemer and our only real hope across the ages. He was born as a baby on the earth that was made by him and through him; he experienced every temptation ever known to man, and he overcame them all without giving in. This perfect man/God was then judged guilty by the religious and secular authorities and condemned to die. Dying sinless, he was able to take on the sins of the world, before and after his physical death and resurrection, breaking the barrier between God and man. As humans confess their failings to him, he not only takes away their sin, but his Spirit moves in to begin to cleanse us of the cause of our sin, and we are freed to be ever in communion with God, whom we can now call our Father.

To counter the best of identities given to Jesus by the secular humanists and liberal theologians, C. S. Lewis writes:

> I am trying here to prevent anyone saying the really foolish thing that people often say about Him: "I'm ready to accept Jesus as a great moral teacher, but I don't accept His claim to be God." That is the one thing we must not say. A man who was merely a man and said the sort of things Jesus said would not be a great moral teacher. He would either be a lunatic—on the level with the man who says he is a poached egg—or else he would be the Devil of Hell. You must make your choice. Either this man was, and is, the Son of God, or else a madman or something worse. You can shut Him up for a fool, you can spit at Him and kill Him as a demon; or you can fall at His feet and call Him Lord and God. But let us not come with any patronizing nonsense about His being a great human teacher. He has not left that open to us. He did not intend to.[7]

Part 4

PANTHEISM

*There is a theory which states that if ever anybody
discovers exactly what the Universe is for and why it is here,
it will instantly disappear and be replaced by something even more
bizarre and inexplicable. There is another theory which
states this has already happened.*

DOUGLAS ADAMS,
THE HITCHHIKER'S GUIDE TO THE GALAXY

IMMANENCE—THE SPIRIT WITHIN US

By self alone is evil done, by self alone does one suffer.
By self alone is evil left undone, by self alone does
one obtain Salvation. Salvation and Perdition
depend upon self; no man can save another.

BUDDHA, *DHAMMAPADA*

L ike many in college in the late 1970s, my friends and I were swinging away from Western thought. As a graduate student at the University of Texas, I avidly read the *Whole Earth Catalog,* had friends who left to build communes in the countryside and frequented new "organic" restaurants and shops with their bulletin boards announcing endless opportunities to join all manner of "spiritual" lectures and workshops, all of which were pantheist. Within two weeks of starting graduate school, I was also enrolled in Transcendental Meditation classes. Subsequently, over the years I tried many varieties of pantheism, including Zen, Yoga, feminist theology, Wicca and less rigorous forms of American pantheism and paganism—the New Age, New Earth varieties. Eventually I was bending spoons at friends' houses while more adventurous friends were trying hypnotism. For me it was something of a spiritual hobby; I was surfing the spiritual net to find my bliss.

Shortly after my decision to "try on" Christianity, I remember hearing

a Buddhist monk on campus answering a young student who was also
surfing the spiritual net. The monk told him, "If your religion isn't really
difficult, you don't have one." Clearly there are devout followers of pantheist religious systems, such as Buddhism and Hinduism, but many of
these religions also have been Westernized and have lost their orthodoxy, not unlike the effect of secularism on Christianity in the last
century. The monk's admonition that an authentic religion is difficult
rang true. Even as a new Christian explorer, I knew the real thing would
not be easy.

Pantheists' fundamental faith is that there is a spiritual reality that
is one with observed natural and human reality. In pantheism, this
immanent spirit is in all human and physical nature (pantheism), or
we are one and the same with this eternal immanent spirit or force,
making us also the expression of the divine itself (panentheism). This
singular reality posits that there is only one substance—spirit—from
which all else emerges and exists. The important point in defining the
difference between these views and monotheism is that the divine
spirit is not a personal but an impersonal animating force coexisting
with all things whether it is one and the same with the universe or in
but also outside the universe. Like all worldviews, these metaphysical
presuppositions are also not subject to scientific verification; they con-
stitute the faith of pantheism.[1]

Though this immanent spirit is not always defined in terms of good
or evil, orthodox pantheist religions do maintain that particular attitudes or virtues are to be cultivated and their opposites avoided. The
Dalai Lama suggests the most important virtues are the opposites of the
acts condemned in Buddhism (and would be also in Judeo-Christian
thought): murder; theft; sexual misconduct; covetousness; malice;
speech that is lying, offensive or frivolous; and holding perverted views
such as nihilism and extremism. C. S. Lewis documented the virtues that
many cultural and religious traditions share in the appendix of his book
The Abolition of Man,[2] and some suggest the shared virtues alone are
evidence of there being one universal God who has written his universal
natural laws on our hearts.[3]

Pantheists achieve various degrees of "spiritual enlightenment" by becoming increasingly one with the ultimate spiritual reality (Nirvana in Buddhism) or by actualizing their god-nature or real self (Atman in Hinduism, when the soul becomes united to Brahman, the ultimate reality). Disciplines such as meditation, the study of sacred texts, chants, ceremonies, trances, veneration of deities and other spiritual practices are designed to free us from the ignorance and desire that block our enlightenment. Salvation and enlightenment are solely the responsibility of the individual person. Connecting with the ultimate spiritual reality and becoming enlightened is said to enhance both our human well-being and consciousness and in turn positively affect the world.

The reality of spiritual transactions is one of the primary principles shared by Judeo-Christianity and pantheism. Judeo-Christian thought and the more orthodox expressions of pantheistic and panentheistic worldviews share common beliefs in the existence of a spiritual world. This spiritual reality affects human beings and nature, and human beings coexist and interact with spiritual reality. Both worldviews distinguish between the natural and the spiritual while recognizing their inextricable connections. They each practice spiritual disciplines (prayer, study, fasting) and are committed to practicing particular virtues, such as reverence, compassion and humility. However, there are also significant differences between Judeo-Christian and pantheist worldviews. They do not both lead to the same place. In an interview regarding Christianity and Buddhism, the Dalai Lama explained, "Once a certain degree of realization has been reached, a choice between two paths will become necessary."[4]

In Judeo-Christianity, God is neither immanent (coexistent with human and physical nature) nor mythical or metaphorical (as in the gods and goddesses of early Greco-Roman empires and of Hinduism). God is alive, and both active in and transcendent to the universe as its Creator. So God cohabits with his people and creation, as well as transcends them. Spiritual growth in Christianity is obtained and sustained in a strong relationship with God through Christ, who gives us the grace to live in the world without being completely consumed into it (to be in the world without being of it). This relationship transforms (not transcends) the inner man through the effectual working of the Holy Spirit.

Karma and Consequences

In pantheist worldviews, karma is an impersonal force that embodies the consequences that follow a person's choices (actions and inactions) in this lifetime. The Dalai Lama defines karma as "the intentional acts of sentient beings . . . all of which have impacts upon the psyche of an individual, no matter how minute. . . . The entire process is seen as an endless self-perpetuating dynamic. The chain reaction of interlocking causes and effects operates not only in individuals, but also for groups and societies, not just in this lifetime but across many lifetimes. . . . This karmic causality is seen as a fundamental natural process and not a kind of divine mechanism."[5]

These consequences are believed to follow us into the next life. The Buddha taught, "All that we are is the result of what we have thought. If a man speaks or acts with an evil thought, pain follows him. If a man speaks or acts with a pure thought, happiness follows him, like a shadow that never leaves him." These karmic consequences are irreparable, offering no process for complete redemption in one's lifetime, though one can decide to change their thoughts, feelings and intentions, thus changing their actions. Some pantheists believe through good works these consequences can be diminished.

There was a heartbroken Hindu couple who came for quite some time to volunteer at Mother Teresa's Shishu Bavan while I was there. They were apparently in hopes that their good works would help their son, who had tragically died at college, ascend to a higher reincarnation by working off their son's and their own harmful karma, which they suspected had something to do with the loss of this only child whom they deeply loved.

Christians also believe there are consequences to wrong actions, thoughts and words. However, unlike pantheist religions, Christ opened the way to be forgiven and cleansed in this lifetime for anyone who believes in him and admits their errors. This spiritual transaction transforms one from the inside out and grants more desire and ability to overcome and thrive—to live more abundantly in this life and the next.

Hinduism and Buddhism encourage us to confront our selfish desires and recognize that the "self" is the core of the problem. So we work to diminish this self and become nothing through spiritual disciplines. Christianity also believes that focusing on one's self is problematic, but one faithfully confesses thoughts, feelings, intentions and actions and trusts in the work of Christ to help us overcome our selfishness. As in the example of my abortions, my only task, which was difficult enough for an independent-minded person like myself, was simply to confess, repent—turning my mind around to agree with God about the error—and accept Christ's free offer. Without God's forgiveness through Christ, I would still be making excuses, or trying to pray away my sins, my karma.

Some pantheists believe that all living creatures are equal—we are all sentient beings (any being that can sense and feel); there is no species above another. This position closely parallels that of secular animal rights ethicist Peter Singer. However, pantheists who believe in karma obviously do presume levels of being when they suggest that one's actions in this world determine one's reincarnated life form in the next life.

TO ELIMINATE SUFFERING, JETTISON DESIRE

What is evil? Killing is evil, lying is evil, slandering is evil, abuse is evil, gossip is evil, envy is evil, hatred is evil, to cling to false doctrine is evil; all these things are evil. And what is the root of evil? Desire is the root of evil, illusion is the root of evil.

GAUTAMA SIDDHARTHA, THE FOUNDER OF BUDDHISM

Siddhartha Gautama, the Buddha (enlightened one), was born of Hindu nobility around the sixth century B.C. As a prince, he spent his early life in luxury inside the confines of his father's palace estates. The story is told that Siddhartha ventured out of his protected environs and witnessed the great sufferings of the common people. His life's quest then became to understand suffering and how to eliminate it. The Buddha proposed that the cause of suffering was human desire, which when unmet led to disappointment and sorrow.

His moral teachings developed the Buddhist path of enlightenment to the no-self or Nirvana.[1] In Hinduism the goal is to become absorbed into the Brahman, the ultimate spirit. The attainment of these states (Nirvana or Brahman) is entirely dependent on the individual's relinquishing of all desire through various stages. If we desire nothing, we will not want, strive, compete or struggle to obtain these desires, and we will not suffer for their lack. Various spiritual practices, particularly various forms of meditation, chanting, walking and sitting, are used to clear one's mind and separate one from the earthly desires that block a person's movement toward enlightenment. Escaping desire and thus suffering allows the Hindu soul (Atman) to ascend to Brahman, the ultimate reality, and the Buddhist to move closer to the ultimate state of nonbeing (Nirvana). A secular offshoot of this is often called achieving "mindfulness," a derivation of the pantheist steps to enlightenment that allow the mind to transcend lower states and achieve a state of calm, reflective awareness.

Desire and Suffering—To Rid or Redeem

Delight yourself in the LORD,
and he will give you the desires of your heart.

PSALM 37:4

The single most critical difference between pantheism and Judeo-Christianity is the role of desire and suffering. There is no attempt in Judeo-Christianity to negate the mind or emotions (to reach a state of Nirvana or merge with Brahman). Judeo-Christian principles do not deny that people's wrong desires lead them to suffer and cause others to suffer. We can suffer even in right desires. Rather than seek to overcome all desire and thus not suffer, Christ called people to understand and purify and embrace their desires through an ongoing relationship with God, who reveals our true self, real purposes and desires. Right desire is the essential fuel for one's knowing and accomplishing one's unique purpose in life.

Suffering can come as a result of thwarted desire and is a reality in this fallen world. In Judeo-Christian thought it is unavoidable as well as potentially redemptive; suffering can be a major tool for human growth. I am quite certain that I have made very little progress in my spirit or soul without suffering first. Some of the things that have happened to me, which from a practical point of view have been the most hurtful, have in fact been the most helpful. In retrospect, were I to be given the choice now, I would actually choose to have gone through them. Godly desire and suffering together propel us to realize and fulfill our destinies, our purposes in life.

A person's calling or purpose unfolds little by little throughout life as desires are not abdicated but cleansed. Mother Teresa told me that if God had told her his whole plan for the Missionaries of Charity, she would have been too afraid to help the first person. Her desire and purpose to serve Jesus by serving the poor also brought her much personal grief, a grief that was overcome by her stronger desire to know and honor God and serve in India.

When she was sixteen, Anjezë Gonxhe Bojaxhiu (Mother Teresa) told her mother she wanted to become a nun and serve in India. Her mother went in her bedroom and closed the door. She came out twenty-four hours later, took her daughter's hand and told Gonxhe to put her hand in God's and never look back. At eighteen, Gonxhe left home to serve in India and, because of the Iron Curtain, never again saw her mother or sister.[2]

In Judeo-Christianity, to deny or rid oneself of desire would be to render one impotent to act in the world for good or evil. It is obviously not a trade-off that God was willing to make. The essence then of Judeo-Christian teaching on desire is to seek God to clarify and purify our desires, not to relinquish them. All Judeo-Christian principles aim to produce a fuller and more abundant life (human flourishing), rather than mental and spiritual states such as no-mind or abstract oneness.

Vishal Mangalwadi, Indian scholar and Hindu convert to Christianity, suggests that the principle of giving up desire was detrimental to the development of India and that Judeo-Christian principles are the primary reason why the West excelled.[3] He observes that even the early art of Western Christendom and Eastern mysticism expose the differences. In Christian art the eyes of Jesus and the saints are wide open, alive and looking up. Even if they are being tortured, the saints are always looking up, striving for something better. He claims Eastern mystics' eyes are often depicted as closed or half-opened. He asserts that this reveals the differences between the hope embedded in Judeo-Christian principles and the resignation of the Eastern philosophies.

PANTHEISM'S MANY FACES

Do not believe in anything simply because you have heard it. Do not be-
lieve in anything simply because it is spoken and rumored by many. Do
not believe in anything simply because it is found written in your religious
books. Do not believe in anything merely on the authority of your teachers
and elders. Do not believe in traditions because they have been handed
down for many generations. But after observation and analysis, when
you find that anything agrees with reason and is conducive to the good
and benefit of one and all, then accept it and live up to it.

GAUTAMA SIDDHARTHA, *KALAMA SUTTA*

Like secular humanism, pantheism also has a diverse range of expressions. Pantheism's most orthodox forms include what we typically call
the Eastern religions and philosophies of Buddhism, Hinduism, Taoism
and Confucianism. Realistically, all major religions originated in the
East; Jesus, Moses and Muhammad were not Westerners. The Buddha,
Lao Tzu and Confucius were early founders of pantheist religions. The
current fourteenth Dalai Lama and Mohandas Gandhi are among the
best-known contemporary representatives of these more orthodox
Eastern religions. Below are some insights regarding the most prominent
forms which also share some overlap with Christian principles.[1] Chapter
21 will look at pantheism as it is often expressed in Western culture.

Most pantheist religious and philosophic frameworks emerged during what is called the Axial Age. This is roughly from 800 B.C. to 200 B.C. Between 400 B.C. and the advent of Christ, the Hebrew prophets are silent, thus the gap between the Old and New Testaments (with the exception of the books of the Apocrypha). Sociologists Robert Bellah and Hans Joas suggest that during this age intellectual sophistication and awareness of the transcendent evolved worldwide.[2] During this time we have the emergence of the written canonical texts of the Hebrews (Old Testament); the philosophy of Socrates, Plato and Aristotle; the Analects of Confucius; the Bhagavad Gita; and the life and teachings of Buddha. Indeed, pantheist religions and philosophies emphasize intellectual enlightenment and control of our thoughts, feelings and actions. All the major religions, with the exception of Islam, were established during this time. Judaism was already well established, and Christ appeared at the end of the Axial Age.

According to Hegel, Christ comes on the scene as the "crucial dividing line, the axis of world history."[3] Christ extends the Judaic knowledge of the one God. In Charles Taylor's words, "The enfleshment of God extends outward, through such new links as the Samaritan makes with the Jew, into a network which we call the church."[4] Bellah and Joas write,

> The original Christian insight . . . has much in common with [some] perspective[s] of the Buddhists. . . . [T]he incarnation of God in Jesus pushes us outward, beyond the boundaries of all tribes and nations, beyond all civilizational rules, into direct encounters with other persons based on the unconditional love which God has for us.[5]

Buddhism

Buddhism in its orthodox form is formally practiced in most Asian countries and accounts for approximately 6 percent of the world's religious.[6] However, its influence is considerably larger because its philosophic (versus religious) ideas can be made compatible with the secular philosophic outlook on life that many in the West have accepted; witness the loyalties of actor Richard Gere and Apple founder

Steve Jobs. Many New Age teachers also draw principles from Buddhist thought. The current (fourteenth) Dalai Lama notes on his official website that one of his three goals is "the promotion of basic human values or secular ethics in the interest of human happiness." The other goals are "the fostering of inter-religious harmony and the preservation of Tibet's Buddhist culture, a culture of peace and non-violence."[7]

A Buddhist believes four noble truths—the truth of misery, the truth that it comes from within us because of our desires, the truth that it can be eliminated, and the truth that to eliminate it a particular path must be followed. To rid oneself of desire, one follows the discipline of the eightfold path of having right views, right intentions, right speech, right conduct or actions, right livelihood, right effort, right mindfulness, and right meditation or concentration. Ultimately one enters the state of Nirvana, in which one is no longer subject to rebirths due to karmic flaws, thus completely free from suffering and internal afflictions such as anger, sorrow and pain. This state of complete peace marks the end of one's separate identity; one becomes free of all boundaries, of striving for desires and of suffering and becomes a part of the eternal oneness.[8] In his still-popular 1951 novel, *Siddhartha,* Herman Hesse depicted the struggle of this process:

> He went the way of self-denial by means of pain, through voluntarily suffering and overcoming pain, hunger, thirst, tiredness. He went the way of self-denial by means of meditation, through imagining the mind to be void of all conceptions. These and other ways he learned to go, a thousand times he left his self, for hours and days he remained in the non-self. But though the ways led away from the self, their end nevertheless always led back to the self. Though Siddhartha fled from the self a thousand times, stayed in nothingness, stayed in the animal, in the stone, the return was inevitable, inescapable was the hour, when he found himself back in the sunshine or in the moonlight, in the shade or in the rain, and was once again his self and Siddhartha, and again felt the agony of the cycle which had been forced upon him.[9]

Hinduism

*When we think of failure, failure will be ours. If we remain undecided,
nothing will ever change. All we need to do is want to achieve something
great and then simply to do it. Never think of failure, for what we think
will come about.*

MAHARISHI MAHESH YOGI

Hinduism accounts for 14 percent of world population; most of its adherents live in India, Nepal, Bangladesh and Indonesia. This makes it
the third largest religion. Spiritual disciplines such as various forms of
meditation and chanting, the study of sacred texts, Yoga and the veneration of deities in Hinduism help one ascend and draw closer to becoming one with the ultimate Absolute (Brahman, that which sustains
the universe and causes growth).

Hinduism is the most diverse tradition; it includes the veneration of
innumerable male and female deities, each representing some aspect of
the ultimate spirit—Brahman. The tradition includes moral teachings,
the notion of karma and numerous sacred texts (the primary texts being
the Bhagavad Gita revealed by Krishna and the Vedas, Upanishads and
Puranas) as well as a wide range of practices, such as vegetarianism,
worship of deities often through images, veneration of the cow, chants,
meditations and temple worship. Because of the diversity and complexity
of Hindu beliefs, it is difficult to characterize Hinduism's major tenets.

The concept of Brahman figures prominently as the ultimate non-
material, spiritual reality. Atman is the soul of an individual, which is
the human emanation of Brahman. Hinduism holds that human beings
are one with this ultimate reality—spirit. The Atman becomes Brahman
in four stages—the waking life, the dreaming life, the sleeping life and
the Atman, spirit itself, which is unseen and untouched and exists
beyond all thought. This last state is the end of man's evolution; man is
peace itself, the pure state of supreme consciousness.[10] At death, an individual's soul loses its body but is continuously reincarnated until it is
released by being absorbed into the ultimate spiritual reality of pure
consciousness—Brahman.

Hinduism traditionally holds that there is a hierarchy of hereditary castes, which are spiritual/social divisions among people, with the Brahman being the most elite, indicating their higher state of reincarnation and consciousness. This practice was strongly resisted by Gandhi and many others and is slowly losing force. Sister Nirmala, who now leads Mother Teresa's Missionaries of Charity, was born into the Brahman caste and could have lived a very privileged life. Instead, after knowing Mother Teresa, she chose to become a servant to the poorest of the poor, serving the lowest castes, Dalits, as well as Muslims, and thus forfeiting her life as a member of the elite.

Taoism

I have three treasures. Guard and keep them:

The first is deep love,

The second is frugality,

And the third is not to dare to be ahead of the world.

Because of deep love, one is courageous.

Because of frugality, one is generous.

Because of not daring to be ahead of the world,

one becomes the leader of the world.

LAO-TZU

Taoism is an Eastern religious/philosophic approach to harmony that has had a great impact in China. It is symbolized as the cosmic balance, illustrating the path of life, which focuses on the solidarity of nature and man. The Three Jewels of the Tao are compassion, moderation and humility. The Tao Te Ching is the primary text, which was written by Lao Tzu (c. 600 B.C.) and the Chuang-Tsu written by Chuang Tzu (c. 300 B.C.). The Tao (the way of virtue) is nameless since it has always existed; it is superior to Being, the ultimate source of creation, the way of nature, and is often simply translated "The Way."

The mind of the Taoist must become empty of desire so that the Tao can flow freely through the person. The *tao* is the mysterious power at the heart of the sage. To master *wu-wei* (the flow of the natural order) is to achieve harmony with nature by acting in such a humble way that the actors leave no trace of themselves in the work. When one functions fully inside the natural order, actions are effortless. Religious practices and rituals of Taoism include offering sacrifices of food to deceased ancestors; worshiping deities; fasting; alchemy; astrology; telling the future or fortunes; the application of Feng Shui to the design of buildings to maximize or harmonize the positive energy of the heavens and the earth; meditation; martial arts, such as Kungfu and Tai Chi; the reading and chanting of sacred texts; and the use of spirit mediums or shamans.[11]

Confucianism

> *Speak the truth, do not yield to anger;*
> *give, if thou art asked for little;*
> *by these three steps thou wilt go near the gods.*

> CONFUCIUS

Confucianism (developed by the philosopher Confucius, 551–479 B.C.) is an Eastern philosophy similar to Taoism; the two systems are often practiced together. While Taoism emphasizes the natural order, Confucius emphasizes more the social order—society and humans' responsibility to others. Religious practices center on proper social behaviors, such as the younger person's duty to the elder, politeness, formal manners showing respect and particular rituals. The proper social order is characterized in the Five Bonds—ruler to the ruled, father to son, husband to wife, elder brother to younger, and friend to friend. Self-realization is possible through proper actions; particularly critical are self-knowledge, self-discipline and the performance of appropriate rituals. For example, a person's speech should be simple not artful, as artistic speech demonstrates pride. Rulers are to exemplify virtue, humility and thankfulness. The major content of Confucian education centers on morality, proper speech, respect, government and the arts, respected also in Christianity.[12]

Shintoism

Shintoism ("the way of the gods") is the native spiritual worldview in Japan, with roots also dating back to the Axial Age. Today it is generally a mix of Buddhism, panentheism and even polytheism. In Shintoism everything is filled with the essence of spirits or gods (*kami*), abstract forces that can be good or evil. Because of the belief that this spirit resides in all things, Shintoism is more akin to panentheism where all things are one and the same with gods or spirits. The spiritual disciplines include worshiping ancestors, worshiping in shrines and particular spots in nature, purification rites, priestly blessings of buildings and businesses, prescribed prayers and procedures such as bowing, as well as periodic rituals to appease spirits and purify geographic areas, buildings, homes and individuals.

Summary

Pantheists have varying commitments to the world as real or illusory. The Dalai Lama has a firm commitment to the real world and to science. He says,

> My confidence in venturing into science lies in my basic belief that, as in science so in Buddhism, understanding the nature of reality is pursued by means of critical investigation: if scientific analysis were conclusively to demonstrate certain claims in Buddhism to be false, then we must accept the findings of science and abandon those claims.[13]

The Dalai Lama announced that because of this he no longer believes the Buddhist holy text regarding the movement of sun and moon and their relationship to earth.[14] While he understands Darwinian evolution, he has several concerns about the theory's inability to account for altruism, the origin of sentience and karma, and its "dangerous tendency to turn the visions we construct of ourselves into self-fulfilling prophecies."[15] The Dalai Lama's interest in science is one place where naturalism and pantheism meet. On the other end of pantheism, most orthodox Hindu doctrines claim all reality to be an illusion constructed by the mind, more similar to the Western postmodern secular humanist's position.

The principles of the various pantheist religions morphed when they entered the West; in part, they became less distinct and their practices less demanding. The secular urge and relaxed prosperity of the West made the demanding and distinctive forms less appealing, just as it diluted some Judeo-Christian thought and theology.

WESTERN PANTHEISM—
SPIRITUAL, NOT RELIGIOUS

I still use words like "spiritual" and "mystical." . . .
People have self-transcending experiences. And people have the best
day of their life where . . . they seem at one with nature.

SAM HARRIS, WWW.YOUTUBE.COM/WATCH?V=KFBZBY7MLIW

When a man stops believing in God, he doesn't then
believe in nothing; he believes anything.

G. K. CHESTERTON, *ORTHODOXY*

The category "spiritual but not religious" is the fastest-growing religious category in the West.[1] Researcher Michael King and his colleagues at University College London published their results of interviews with over seven thousand people in England who were religious, nonreligious/nonspiritual, or spiritual but not religious.[2] They found that those who were "spiritual but not religious" were more likely to suffer from depression and other mental health problems; to take psychotropic medication; to use or be dependent on recreational drugs; and to have anxiety, eating and other neurotic disorders than either the religious or nonreligious. The religious were less likely to have used drugs and more likely to have education beyond secondary school than either the nonreligious or the "spiritual but not religious."

From the time I entered graduate school in 1975 to the time of my conversion in 1993, I called myself "spiritual but not religious." What I was actually trying ever so cleverly to communicate is that I was "good" without religion; I didn't need a crutch. Particularly to my Christian acquaintances I was denigrating their beliefs in a God and sin. I needed no savior, no rules and no help from some socially constructed God figure. In fact, I believed I was actually more advanced spiritually than religious people because of my self-reliance and ability to connect the spirit within me to the universal spirit.

I was actively engaged in pursuing my own spiritual awakening, spiritual power and spiritual goodness in any number of what, for lack of a better term, are Westernized pantheist expressions. I was also using drugs and, in retrospect, had many of the mental health issues identified in the study. While in graduate school I had to go off campus for such teachings and practice; today they are well integrated into the daily life of universities.

For example, only a few days after the graduation event in which the faculty objected to the commencement prayer, the entire faculty, staff and students received another email, an invitation from the college's campus Health and Wellness Club.

Summer Greetings:

Congratulations to everyone who graduated this year, and to all of us for the completion of another semester!

The Health and Wellness Club would like to extend an invitation to you and your friends and family to attend a Day of Mindfulness Event taking place on Saturday, May 28th from 9am-3pm. . . . This should be a fun and relaxing day full of activities designed to celebrate ourselves, build community and encourage mindful habits. Please see the attached flyer for additional details and RSVP . . . if you will be able to join us. We hope to see you there!

Wishing you all the best in health and happiness this summer.

There were no protests for the official school-sponsored pantheist opportunity to celebrate ourselves and become "mindful." Most were probably unaware this emanates from a pantheist framework—nevertheless one that does not pose much challenge to the secular humanists' urge to celebrate human achievement and potential.

A few months later, we received an email inviting the whole college community to a lecture to be given by a man who is described on the brochure as being "known for his exceptional shamanistic performances . . . to engage the mystical and transformative power of Shamanic ritual" whereby he reportedly has helped tenants in "a social housing block scheduled for demolition . . . by participat[ing] with him in the recreation of a . . . shaman ritual, so that animal spirits, via the medium of the artist, might offer them guidance for the uncertain times." He is pictured wearing sunglasses, holding a stuffed hawk mounted on a long stick in his outstretched hand.

James Sire outlines some of the basic goals of the Western pantheists. They seek to (1) bring on a New Age via increased consciousness, (2) understand the invisible cosmos through altered states of consciousness, (3) use the cosmic consciousness whereby ordinary categories of time, space and morality disappear, (4) use the cosmic consciousness to overcome the fear of death, and (5) achieve cosmic consciousness via the occult, psychedelics or conceptual relativism.[3] Although I had tried various methods of achieving cosmic consciousness, I never really reached anything close to the expressed goal except while taking various drugs.

These Westernized pantheist expressions and performances place an emphasis on individual human spiritual power, well-being and goodness. Oprah Winfrey, Eckhart Tolle, Deepak Chopra, Rhonda Byrne, Shirley MacLaine, Carlos Castaneda, don Miguel Ruiz, Gary Zukav, Marilyn Ferguson, Andrew Weil, Marianne Williamson and Fritjof Capra have all been popular promoters of various manifestations of pantheism in the West, only a few of which will be described here.

The New Age, New Earth Movement

The New Age, New Earth movement has many manifestations such as Wicca (white witchcraft) and various pagan, neo-pagan and Gaia movements and other secular forms of spirituality such as Buddhists without

Beliefs.[4] Regardless of the prefixes *new* and *neo-,* these beliefs and practices existed in ancient cultures; witness for example the "medium at En-dor" during King Saul's reign.[5] Today the movement's most popular proponent in the United States is Oprah Winfrey, who encourages these movements through the guests on her shows and her book-club choices, such as *Siddhartha* and *Zen and the Art of Motorcycle Maintenance.* Films such as *Seven Years in Tibet, Star Wars, Avatar, Eat Pray Love,* and the *Twilight* movies also represent Westernized pictures of Buddhist, Hindu and other pantheist beliefs.

Rather than the secular humanists' pursuit of the power of human reason and politics or the naturalists' pursuit of power over nature via science and technology, pantheists pursue individual power in the spiritual realm. Today's plethora of spiritual teachers and gurus encourages a reverence for the earth and a focus on individual self-improvement, spiritual power, psychic knowledge and mindfulness. They share with pantheism a belief in the "spiritual" methods of meditation to clear the mind and advance human wisdom, health and transcendence but generally deviate in rigor, tradition and devotion.

In Rhonda Byrne's bestselling book *The Secret,* she summarizes various proponents' conclusions, which are typical of many Western pantheist principles.[6] Some of them include:

- Everything is energy.
- You are a spiritual being.
- The Universe emerges from thought.
- We are creators not only of our own destiny but also of the Universe.
- We are all connected and all One.
- Your power is in your thoughts.
- The only thing you need to do is feel good now.
- Now is the time to enhance your magnificence.
- We are in the midst of a glorious era.
- Let go of limiting thoughts, experience humanity's true magnificence.
- What you do with the Secret is up to you.

- Whatever you choose is right.

- The power is all yours.

The Secret, A Course in Miracles, A New Earth and *The Ultimate Happiness Prescription* all emphasize similar principles to enhance spiritual power, happiness and peacefulness.[7] Unlike orthodox pantheist religions, these expressions generally do not reject desire; they frequently orient desire toward the self—individual wellness, spiritual power and peace. Deepak Chopra's center offers programs on such topics as wellness, Ayurveda medicine, harnessing the power of coincidence, meditation, Yoga and mind/body healing.[8]

Westernized pantheism is fairly compatible within a highly individualistic secular culture, and, in point of fact, it could easily be argued that pantheism is more individualistic than any monotheistic religion. It is not an accident that the Westernized Buddhist advocate Steve Jobs, of the high-tech industry, named his inventions i-everything and his Apple emails "@me.com." In Herman Hesse's classic book, *Siddhartha,* the protagonist says, "It had to be found, the pristine source in one's own self, it had to be possessed! Everything else was searching, was a detour, was getting lost."[9]

Earlier forms of contemporary Western pantheism included the theosophists, who sought to transcend their minds in order to reach a divine revelation of truth. The underpinnings of theosophical ideas go back to the third century A.D. and have included the famous educator and founder of the Waldorf Schools, Rudolph Steiner.[10] Similarly, the Unitarian Universalists[11] encourage open-mindedness toward all religious teachings and earth-centered traditions and are heavily influenced by pantheist philosophies.

Transcendental Meditation

Transcendental Meditation (TM) is the ancient Vedic tradition brought to the West in the twentieth century by Maharishi Mahesh Yogi (1917–2008). These practices focus the mind on breathing, chanting mantras or concentrating on objects in order to assist the person in reaching a state of deep relaxation, which allows the mind to transcend to higher states of consciousness. TM practitioners of the last century have been active in collecting data to support the health and psychological benefits of TM; proponents have been granted government funds to study its effects on various aspects of health.[12]

Native American Religions

Native American religious frameworks also emphasize the role of nature in spirit. Carlos Castaneda popularized these in the publication of his encounters with Don Juan, a Yaqui sorcerer, stories that may have been fictional. His books had a strong influence on several generations of seekers.[13] Don Miguel Ruiz offered a series of books, beginning with *The Four Agreements,* that distill his view of Native American wisdom. His *Fifth Agreement* is a guide to self-mastery.[14] Philip Jenkins has done extensive work on actual Native American spirituality as well as the ways in which their authentic beliefs have been distorted by New Age movements. He writes, "What the recent discoveries [of ancient sites] prove is that early Native peoples were profoundly attuned to the natural world, were close observers of the skies, and recorded their observations as accurately (and beautifully) as they could, none of which involves any claims about supernatural powers."[15]

"Engaged" Buddhism

Vietnamese Buddhist monk Thich Nhat Hanh's "engaged" Buddhism combines Western psychology with Eastern meditation and political liberation to promote world peace.[16] He has built villages in France and elsewhere, actively working to help refugees around the world and others whose lives have been limited by government oppression and war.

A Course in Miracles

The Course in Miracles is a spiritual but not religious course of study designed around messages that were reportedly scribed by Helen Schucman with assistance by William Thetford, both psychologists, now run by Kenneth Wapnick. The scribed messages were from an inner voice, which Schucman identified as Jesus. God is discussed in the texts but in a nonsectarian and nonorthodox manner. The goal is to teach universal love by learning to think spiritually. The course emphasizes forgiveness as the way to make relationships holy and to rid oneself of guilt and fear, which block living the miraculous in life. The ultimate goal is to help the student to develop their inner voice to achieve peace and happiness. The actual Course in Miracles includes texts, workbooks and seminars, as well as a yearlong self-study program. The book has reportedly sold millions of copies and is available in twenty languages. Spiritual teacher and author Marianne Williamson updates and teaches these principles in her work.[17]

Magical Realism

Magical realism is a new genre in literature, which embodies pantheism by combining the mystical with the real. For example, characters may suddenly and inexplicably float in the air or be transported in time. In these narratives the spiritual, the magical and the mystical are mixed into realistic settings. Characters blur the lines between fantasy and reality. Authors of this literature include award winners such as Gabriel García Márquez, Ana Castillo, Octavio Paz and Isabel Allende.

New Scientific Mythologies

"New scientific mythologies" is the designation given by communications scholar James Herrick to a set of contemporary beliefs that extend pantheism into science, producing a new spirituality. These beliefs include the following:

- We will discover benevolent, helpful extraterrestrial beings.[18]

- These beings will help us know the universe better so that we can know ourselves better.

- The extraterrestrials will have an enlightened religion or worldview.

- We can use science to force the evolutionary forces to make us a more enlightened superior race.[19]

- Outer space is where we will achieve our destiny.

- There is hope of limitless progress.

- A new and better humanity (post-humanity) will arise from the combination of technologically directed interventions (genome-assisted).

- With technology human physical and mental life will be greatly extended or even become eternal.[20]

Herrick points out that once science stripped the West of the supernatural, science fiction stepped in to fill the gap.[21] These new scientific spiritualities offer various hopes of human enhancements via advanced genetic, nanotech and robotic technologies designed to produce a more socially evolved human race or to contact a more advanced species in outer space. These differ from most forms of pantheism in that they do not believe the universe is an illusion or that human desire needs to be quelled. They are seeking a higher consciousness via technology and science. Herrick uses popular cultural expressions, such as movies, to demonstrate the principles of the new scientific spiritualities. Advocates of scientific spiritualities ultimately believe we will "save" and "redeem" ourselves through technological advances.

Ray Kurzweil, inventor, scholar and futurist, embodies the scientific side of these hopes in the principles he labels "singularity."[22] Singularity is the coming together of nanotechnology, genetic engineering, robotics and artificial intelligence to enhance human functioning and extend life. Science will usher in a post-human or trans-human world. Kurzweil posits six stages of evolution of the universe: (1) physics and chemistry, (2) biology and DNA, (3) brains, (4) technology, (5) the merger of technology and intelligence when singularity is accomplished and, finally, (6) the control of matter and energy in the universe by human intelligence and technology in order to harness matter and energy and transcend boundaries such as the speed of light.[23] We are in the fourth stage moving into the fifth, according to Kurzweil.

Of the self-proclaimed "four horsemen of the anti-apocalypse," Sam Harris is slightly representative of the new scientific spiritualities, giving an ever so slight nod to pantheism. His early books were direct attacks primarily on Judeo-Christianity. In addition to continuing the theme of religion as dangerous, his later books also suggest that science will define the new moral landscape at last separated from religion because of our increasing knowledge of psychoneurology.[24] Harris's spirituality is more akin to peak experiences than true spiritual ones. His "spiritual" experiences are the result of neurological activity rather than a spiritual world transcendent to the physical material. "Spiritual feelings" produced by neural activity make up his pantheism. For Harris, human neurology holds secrets to our moral life and our happiness. Those moments of most happiness he calls spiritual, self-transcending and mystical. *Spirituality* for Harris is what brain scans and other neuroscience can reveal. Richard Dawkins calls it "sexed-up atheism."[25]

The Spiritual as Good

Eckhart's profound yet simple teachings have already helped countless people throughout the world find inner peace and greater fulfillment in their lives. At the core of the teachings lies the transformation of consciousness, a spiritual awakening that he sees as the next step in human evolution. An essential aspect of this awakening consists in transcending our ego-based state of consciousness. This is a prerequisite not only for personal happiness but also for the ending of violent conflict on our planet.

ECKHART TEACHINGS, WWW.ECKHARTTOLLE.COM/ABOUT/ECKHART

In an organic, holistic restaurant, one of the unofficial high priestesses of a city's New Age movement was holding court with her admirers. She got up to leave just before a friend of mine also prepared to leave. As he walked out, she was just backing out her rather large car and turned too sharply, hitting my friend's car. He walked up to his car and looked at her. She jumped out of her car, miffed he had seen her, and began raving. His very old, well-worn Celica was centered in the space, and though she was the only one driving, somehow it was not her fault. As she went on, he stood calmly, facing her in silence. When she stopped to take a breath, he said with no expression, "This is who you really are." Infuriated, she shrieked even louder. At the next breath, he said again, "This is who you really are." She then got in the car and sped away. As I heard this, I knew this was who I was also.

When I was calling myself "spiritual and not religious," I had little, if any, recognition of evil, particularly of the evil inside me. Good was spiritual, but evil, if it existed, was just poor human choice or nonprogressive ideologies and political stances. I talked in terms of positive and negative energy; it fit with my impersonal life force. I said I believed that all religions led to the same place, but it seemed to me that if there could be a universal religion it would be a sort of Westernized pantheism girding up and enhancing secular progressive politics. This would bring about a new global order and peace (the proverbial Age of Aquarius). I was most at home with the Wicca (white witchcraft) and feminist theology movements as they combined my spiritual yearnings with my radical feminist urge; I used their early works in my classes.[26] As "spiritual" feminists we worshiped nature (Mother Nature). Primarily, I was worshiping myself. I was an atheist regarding a transcendent God, but I believed there was a spirit world. Like many people in the West today, I used the word *spiritual* as a synonym for *good*.

My own experience suggests that this vague mindfulness or no-mindness is more easily believed and pursued in privileged environments. The woman who held court in the restaurant and I both lived comfortably among highly educated middle-class people. She was most likely single like myself. Thus, it is easy to hide our real selves from most people and even from ourselves. Even without Facebook, we could build our own public identities. We were in fact filled with ego, and if we had lost it, really given up desire, we still would have been useless to the larger world. But we thought we were good; after all, we were spiritual.

The question I could not have answered was, spiritual power for what purpose? Many of us practicing these methods were looking for *personal* spiritual power. Bending spoons hardly contributed to helping another person, group or culture. The pantheist focus on individual spiritual enlightenment, self-discovery, self-transcendence and the utopian pursuit of goodness, peace and bliss (happiness) suited me well. I deluded myself that I was actually making progress and that my personal enlightenment was helping make a better world. As contemporary Western pantheist Eckhart Tolle proudly proclaims, "You are here to enable the divine purpose of the universe to unfold. That is how important you are."[27]

Just prior to my investigation of Christianity I got a glimpse of just how good and important I really was. In May 1992, I was granted full tenure, and six months later at age forty-one, I had a dream that revealed the true condition of my soul.

In the dream I am in a long line of people dressed in gray robes and looking very depressed. We are suspended in a dark night sky (with no obvious floor) where everything is some shade of gray. We are single file, not looking at one another, and silent. Except for shuffling slowly forward, we are hardly moving—a bit zombie-like. I am curious to see the length of the line and my place in it, so I break out of line a bit by leaning to my left to see where the line begins, and I see that the line snakes around and disappears. Then I lean to my right and look behind me to see the end. The line appears endless in both directions. As we move forward, I notice that we are about to pass by something on our right. There is light coming from it, and the scene is in color though those of us in the line are not; we remain in the gray. As I approach, I see the Last Supper, similar to Leonardo da Vinci's depiction. However, it is live, and the disciples are eating together, moving around and talking with one another. I notice that Jesus is not at the table with them; he is standing up ahead (also in color), and each of us is passing by him. When I get up to him and look in his eyes, he is looking at me as though he can see through me. I suddenly have a strong awareness of every cell in my body; I realize that my body, while a unified whole, is actually composed of individual cells, and I am aware of both their singularity and wholeness. Immediately I have a second revelation that every cell in my body is filled with filth. At that, I can no longer look at Jesus, and I fall at his feet and begin to weep. In the dream, Jesus bends over and places his hands gently on my shoulders, and I begin to be flooded with a "peace that surpasses understanding."

I woke to find I was actually crying. This dream was unlike any other in that I remembered every detail—sights, emotions, thoughts and colors (a first for me). The dream affected my entire being. It had revealed the true condition of my soul in such a way that I was both horrified and yet strangely hopeful. God, who knew every cell in my body, every thought in my mind, every deed I had ever done, and knew how disgusting it all was, still had great compassion for me. He had touched me with his own peace, a taste of what was possible. This was a spiritual encounter with the living Christ, totally undeserved and uninvited. I had at last encountered a completely knowledgeable, holy and loving God who would reveal, demand and help me become the person I truly desired to be. Even though I could not have named it at the time, my spirit knew it. Gradually I began to emerge out of my confusion to discern the true God from all the spirits I thought I was enjoying.

The most significant distinction between Judeo-Christian and New Age pantheists' understanding of the spiritual world is that spirits and the spiritual are not synonymous with goodness or even neutrality; spiritual expressions and transactions can be evil. The demonic is spiritual. In its most extreme form, evil manifests itself in satanic cults and demonic possession. Some evil disguises itself as good. In the Judeo-Christian worldview, evil is a spiritual force waging a constant war against God by using those God made in his image. The war is not between people, although people are used.

For four years after I became a Christian I occasionally struggled to break free of the many spirits to which I had given myself. Indeed, this included a number of demonic encounters, which manifested as visitations by sheer evil in the middle of the night, intended to frighten or kill me. They were stopped in all cases by calling out for Jesus. Krister Sairsingh, a convert from Hinduism to Christianity whose degrees are from Yale and Harvard, now teaches philosophy and history. In his conversion testimony he tells also of demonic attacks, of being strangled and of subsequent tormenting fears. While I was not formally practicing strict Hinduism, my own experience resonates with the description he gives of the transition from pantheism to Christianity.

> For a while I tried to incorporate Jesus into the pantheon of deities arrayed on the altar of the puja room. Each morning, after I offered incense and changed mantras before the altar, I would then turn to recite the mantras to the picture of Jesus beside that of Gandhi. . . . But I had the uneasy feeling that Jesus did not belong to their company, that he was

without equal, and that he would not wish to be honored in a way that made him one among many, just another avatar among others. . . . He was unique, utterly different. I did not know how to worship and honor him. And yet in the depths of my heart, I desired to adore him.[28]

SPIRITUAL TRANSACTIONS IN PEOPLE, NATURE AND NATIONS

Our human minds, with all their variety, need different approaches to peace and happiness. It is just like varieties of food. Certain people find Christianity more appealing; others prefer Buddhism because it does not advocate a creator—everything depends upon your own actions.

DALAI LAMA, *HOW TO SEE YOURSELF AS YOU REALLY ARE*

In January of 2002, Buddhist monks from the Drepung Loseling Monastery offered and were subsequently invited by the Smithsonian's Freer Gallery to develop an intricate mandala or sand painting to draw forth various spirits of healing and protection for the United States after 9/11. There is hardly a major city, art museum, or even small college or university in North America and Europe where similar ceremonial spiritual acts have not taken place. The purpose is to invite various Buddhist spirits of peace, healing and protection into a geographic area.[1]

The events begin with chanted prayers and sacred horns, drums and other instruments to consecrate the area, to purify it of other spirits and to invoke the divine energies of the deities that will reside in the mandala's "palace." Mantras, chants and prayers garner the deities' blessings and continue throughout the multiday productions of the elaborate, colorful mandalas. The 9/11 mandala in the Smithsonian was seven feet in diameter and took twenty monks working in shifts for two weeks to create. I observed a similar process at the Los Angeles County Museum of Art in the fall of 2003.

There are levels of spiritual meanings in the mandalas, described in a report from the Aspen Chapel, where one of the mandalas was developed in the fall of 2011:

> In general all mandalas have outer, inner and secret meanings. On the outer level they represent the world in its divine form; on the inner level they represent a map by which the ordinary human mind is transformed into enlightened mind; and on the secret level they depict the primordially perfect balance of the subtle energies of the body and the clear light dimension of the mind. The creation of a sand painting is said to effect purification and healing on these three levels.[2]

A final ceremony with incantations, chants, sacred horns and drums is held before the sand in the mandala is swept together, destroying the images (indicating the impermanence of existence), and then dispersed into a body of moving water (ocean, rivers, streams) whereby the spiritual energy and power of the deities that have been called forth are released into a particular geographic area.[3] Small vials of sand are often available to the audience to place where they will draw forth the same spirit.

While most North Americans and Europeans experience the mandala creations as prestigious intercultural or interfaith events, as elite art productions, or as quaint but harmless spiritual productions, the monks know they are releasing particular spiritual powers that have consequences for transforming minds and geographic territories; they are infusing particular geographic territories with the spiritual power of particular deities. Their website describes the spiritual reality:

> The Tibetan mandala is a tool for gaining wisdom and compassion and generally is depicted as a tightly balanced, geometric composition wherein deities reside. The principal deity is housed in the center. The mandala serves as a tool for guiding individuals along the path to enlightenment. Monks meditate upon the mandala, imagining it as a three-dimensional

palace. The deities who reside in the palace embody philosophical views and serve as role models. The mandala's purpose is to help transform ordinary minds into enlightened ones.[4]

There are spirits of peace that can deliver us into a kind of ennui and others that produce individual concentration, and there is a spirit of peace that makes us get up and fight against the oppression that inhibits peace. The peace in Judeo-Christianity produces both gentleness and peace in the natural realm as well as guidelines for just wars, such as the war against the Nazis in the last century.[5] The spirit of Christ's peace and the deities in the mandala are not the same; they are manifestations of different spirits. This is but one example of why Christians and Buddhists know that all religions do not emerge from or end up in the same place and why, as the Dalai Lama puts it, "a choice between two paths will become necessary."[6]

Spiritual Transactions in Judeo-Christianity

Both pantheists and monotheists pray, and both believe that individuals, spiritual atmospheres and geographic areas can change as a result of rituals, meditative practices, and prayer or other spiritual disciplines directed to God (Judeo-Christian) or various deities/spirits (pantheism). Though these spiritual transactions are largely invisible, those gifted and trained in spiritual discernment can recognize their effects. Among the early monks there were three groups—the practical monks, the scholastics and the mystics. The mystics best understood spiritual reality, but it was the scholastics who established the early universities. Mystical writings from the early church fathers still exist and are still studied, revealing more about spiritual phenomena.

The absence of this spiritual knowledge in many Western Christian churches and the concomitant longing to understand the more spiritual or mystical reality clearly defined in the Gospels and the Hebrew Scriptures have led many young people in the West to explore pantheist spiritual frameworks. This longing to recover a deeper understanding of spiritual reality and laws has also led to an increase in charismatic or Pentecostal Christianity[7] and a proliferation of alternative seminaries, Bible colleges and literature.[8] Charismatic and Pentacostal evangelicals now number twice the total of non-charismatic evangelicals worldwide, 26.7 percent to 13.1 percent, and 160 million Catholics are charismatic.[9]

Missiologist Charles Kraft notes that spiritual laws can be grouped under six major headings:

1. There are dispensers of spiritual power.

2. There is a close relationship between spiritual and human realms.

3. There is a major difference between God and other less powerful spirits.

4. Authority and spiritual power flow from allegiances, relationships and obedience.

5. Cultural forms can be spiritually empowered.

6. Territories and organizations are subject to spiritual power.[10]

Often churches in the technologically developing world have a clearer understanding of these spiritual phenomena (good or evil), and it is widely known that these are the same places where miracles most frequently occur.

Throughout biblical accounts, spiritual transactions take place not only between God and man but also between God and nature and God and nations. The Hebrew Testament is replete with examples of God allowing catastrophes to overtake the Israelites because of their rebellion. More than anything else these Scriptures suggest that God simply withdraws his hand of protection from rebellious individuals and nations while continuing to draw, woo, call, wait and long for their return. Deuteronomy 28 captures the consequences of faithfulness and unfaithfulness to God's laws. Though it is unlikely this would be the pantheists' explanation, the Buddhist monks who develop the mandalas in the West know something has gone wrong spiritually.

An example of spiritual transactions across nations is recorded in 2 Kings 3, when Israel is engaged in a war with the Moabites. The Israelites are advancing; the prophet has foretold their victory. The desperate king of Moab puts seventy of his best swordsmen on the front lines; still they cannot break through. Finally, he takes his firstborn son and sacrifices him on the wall as a burnt offering to Moab's pagan deities in exchange for victory. While they are not wholly victorious against Israel, a great wrath comes against the army of Israel that forces them to retreat. This was a spiritual transaction, one that has corollaries even today.

Spiritual transactions in nature abound also in the New Testament. On the day of Christ's crucifixion, the earth quaked, the sky grew dark and the dead were raised and seen walking in the city (Matthew 27:45-56). Paul said that all creation groans and waits to be set free, and that even our spirits groan when we do not know how to pray so that the Holy Spirit prays through us (Romans 8:18-30). Jesus instructed his followers to preach the gospel to all creation (Matthew 28:18-20). As he went about the regions of Israel and Samaria, Jesus regularly cast out demonic spirits from people, both young and old, and even calmed storms (for example, Matthew 4:23-25; 8:23-27, 28-34).

Historian Steven Keillor has proposed that more investigations of the category of divine judgment are warranted in the academy. His own work has investigated divine judgment and US history.[11] While the US media jump to find the most extreme people to defend judgment theories of disasters, there is biblical precedence regarding divine judgment. William Koenig has compiled a list of what would appear to secularists as coincidences between events in Israel and the United States.[12]

Consensus in many orthodox Christian churches, even in North America and Europe, is that the West is under judgment for such things as poor stewardship of resources while those in desperate need suffer, rampant abortions, divorce, child abandonment, pornography, sexual sins, actions against Israel, uncontrolled greed (love of money), governments forcing people to act in ways that deny their consciences, and increased limitations of freedom of religion. God may well have lifted his hand of protection from the West and left us to live with our own consequences without his heavy grace.

Christ taught that many who have eyes actually do not see even the obvious, not because people become physically blind but because they are spiritually blind. Thus even common discernment evades us. For example, given secular knowledge alone, one might wonder how it is that Israel, a nation of only 8,019 square miles (about the size of New Jersey) would be pressured to give up more land to so many much larger nations who are so hostile. We forget sometimes the Israelites were an extremely oppressed small tribe that God chose to love and to use to communicate his existence, his laws, his Son, and through which he demonstrates his power. The extraordinary success of the Jews and the intense hostility toward this small people group makes little sense in the natural, only in the spiritual.[13]

The absence of spiritual knowledge in secular Western culture is tragic, and the forced silence and humiliation of those who know something of the spiritual world (pantheist or monotheist) is detrimental to all knowledge, scholarship and life. Accomplished journalist Nathan Schneider interviewed eminent sociologist of religion Robert Bellah, who said,

> The academic world is one of the few places where prejudice is supposed to be totally banned, and we're politically correct on everything, but it's still a place where you can attack religion out of utter, complete, bottomless ignorance and not be considered to have done anything wrong. It's astounding to me to hear what some people can say with the assumption that everyone would agree with them, based on nothing whatsoever.[14]

If the spiritual exists, as approximately 95 percent of the world's inhabitants believe, then it matters a great deal to our being able to understand all things. It matters that we not only understand various spiritual worldviews but investigate the truth of spiritual reality, because it holds implications for science and all of human life. The spiritual world and its laws operate with or without our knowledge just as surely as do the laws of physics.

CONTESTING THE HOLY SPIRIT

Nevertheless, I tell you the truth: it is to your advantage that I go away, for if I do not go away, the Helper will not come to you. But if I go, I will send him to you. . . . When the Spirit of truth comes, he will guide you into all the truth, for he will not speak on his own authority, but whatever he hears he will speak, and he will declare to you the things that are to come.

Jesus to his disciples, John 16:7, 13

Pantheism and panentheism would deny that the Holy Spirit is above all other spirits in the earth and the universe. In Judeo-Christianity there is a hierarchy of authority in the spiritual world, with the Holy Spirit being all perfect and the most powerful force on earth. In Judeo-Christianity we are all under some spiritual authority. To not choose God does not leave us without spiritual authorities; it leaves us with other ones whether we are conscious of them or not.

The Holy Spirit hovered over the waters and moved in the physical realm at the word of God in creation. He acted in the incarnation of Jesus, the Word of God, when he became flesh, incarnated as fully man and fully God, and continues to move in perfect harmony within the Godhead with Christ and God. He is the Spirit of truth that searches our hearts and convicts us in such a way that we can receive the truth about ourselves. He instructs and counsels with a wisdom that includes and is greater than solely human reasoning.

In Christianity the Holy Spirit was in the beginning an animating force in creation as God spoke his word, and remains both the personal and animating spirit of God's truth and Christ's power on the earth. No other spirit is as pure, true or powerful. The Holy Spirit is the source in man of love, joy, peace, patience, goodness, faithfulness, kindness and self-control. While everyone by virtue of being alive has some access, the Holy Spirit's presence is more effectual and available to those who belong to Christ, whose spirits, through being born again, are more open to the Holy Spirit's anointing and become more sensitive to his leading.

Thomas Aquinas (1225–1274) remains one of the most respected theologians and philosophers. Though he followed closely Aristotle's method of logic laid out in *Nicomachean Ethics,* Aquinas criticized "pagan" philosophers for not being able to access the higher wisdom that only God could provide. In his short life this Dominican priest wrote five volumes of *Summa Theologica,* among many other works. Four months before he died, this highly rational theologian had an undefined experience with God and told his superior he could never write again because compared to God everything he had written was "as straw." He died four months later having never written another word. Aquinas's works are among the most highly valued in Christian theology. And yet one powerful encounter with the Holy Spirit made it all look insignificant. He had a glimpse of the brilliance, power and love of the living God.

WHAT IF JUDEO-CHRISTIANITY IS TRUE?

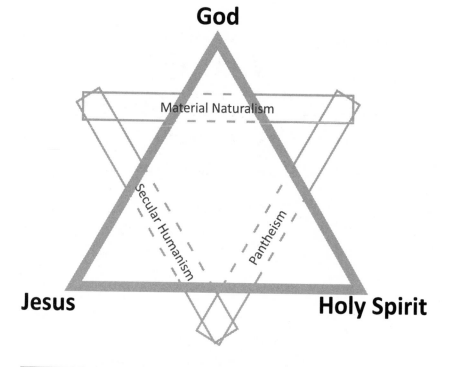

Figure 1. The tri-unity of reason: A wider rationality

A WIDER RATIONALITY

[I]t is fatal to imagine that everybody knows quite well what Christianity is and needs only a little encouragement to practice it. The brutal fact is that in this Christian country not one person in a hundred has the faintest notion what the Church teaches about God or man or society or the person of Jesus Christ. . . . Theologically this country is at present in a state of utter chaos established in the name of religious toleration and rapidly degenerating into flight from reason and the death of hope.

DOROTHY SAYERS, *CREED OR CHAOS?*

Christianity is a statement which, if false,
is of no importance, and, if true, of infinite importance.
The only thing it cannot be is moderately important.

C. S. LEWIS, *GOD IN THE DOCK*

Lesslie Newbigin describes the reality that I have learned over the past twenty years: "The Christian claim is that though the Christian worldview can in no way be reached by any logical step from the axioms of [the other worldviews], nevertheless the Christian worldview does offer a wider rationality that embraces and does not contradict the rationality of [these other worldviews]."[1]

Those who come to Christ have access to a wider capacity for human reason than they had before. For this to be effective we have to jump ship, so to speak, from our old worldviews to a new, higher and larger place. From here we can see how Christian thought is both inclusive and exclusive of our previous mindsets. The Judeo-Christian worldview is exponentially richer, greater and more effective. This does not mean that every Christian is smarter or better than every non-Christian, just that those who come to Christ will begin to experience an increase in human reasoning capacity.

From the Christian worldview the principles of the other worldviews of secular humanism, naturalism, pantheism and even the other mono-theisms can be easily understood. However, from these other worldviews the Christian worldview cannot be fully understood. C. S. Lewis's picture of this is that "man is a tower in which the different floors can hardly be reached from one another but all can be reached from the top floor."[2]

Figure 1 is a rough sketch of the four global worldviews and their intersections, illustrating the reality that Newbigin and Lewis are describing. Outside the triangle lie some of the principles of secular humanism, naturalism and pantheism that are distortions of truth caused by the addition of false principles, such as secular humanism's utopian vision of human reason or naturalism's insistence that everything is material or pantheism's amorphous, impersonal spirit. All these worldviews and their standing philosophies, theories and methods have some overlap with the principles of Christianity, depicted in their intersections with the triangle. According to Judeo-Christian principles, evil cannot create; it can only distort. It is not possible for any worldview to stand if it does not contain some truth (inside the triangle).[3]

Jesus taught that though people could predict the weather from looking at the skies, they lacked spiritual discernment to judge the "signs of the times" (Matthew 16:2-3; Luke 12:56)—the limitation of reasoning solely based on sense experiences (naturalism). Yet those who can discern the "times" also can read the natural weather signs.

Christianity is the one worldview that actually encompasses the true and reasonable principles of all three other worldviews and more. The Trinity holds all things together within truth's boundaries; the Godhead is the ultimate force of spiritual gravity. For example, the truths of naturalism and pantheism are actually reconcilable inside the triangle; they are part of the same totality. In its independent form, scientific naturalism ultimately excludes the possibility of spiritual transactions, which makes spiritual knowledge both unnecessary and inaccessible. Pantheism, in its most extreme forms, proposes that the world is ultimately an illusion, which makes science both unnecessary and impossible. Christ's teachings unify the spiritual, natural and human worlds. Here it is possible to study the interactions of spiritual and natural phenomena. We can study the natural effects of spiritual prayer or God's forgiveness.

Thus, Judeo-Christianity gives us science without naturalism, humanism without relativity, and the spiritual beyond the impersonal and individual. Christianity gives us the grace for spirituality with a larger purpose, sin with redemption and restoration, and the ability to discern good and evil. The Judeo-Christian framework builds spiritual discernment in a world that has both good and evil, and provides the means to fight the evil and expand the good, first in ourselves and then in our culture.

From inside the triangle we are not blind men surveying the elephant, each discerning the universe from our limited worldviews. Inside the triangle the whole picture emerges of the coherent unity of all truth because "in [Christ] all things hold together" (see Colossians 1:15-20). Christian errors, like secular worldviews, also come from too much emphasis on one or the other worldview or concentration on one person of the Trinity to the exclusion of others. Like the secular humanists on the left, error leads some who seek to follow Christ to posit that there is no possibility of eternal consequences for turning away from God.[4] Like the secular humanists on the right, error also leads some Christians to be overly legalistic. The closer we come to Christ, the more balanced we will become.

In many of Paul's letters he instructed Christians to renew their minds so that they would not be deluded by plausible arguments (see Romans 12:2; Colossians 2:4). The false principles of each of these worldviews are expressed variously in the dialogues of this Jewish intellectual. In Galatians 4:9, he calls these "weak and worthless elementary principles of the world," possibly a reference to the prin-

ciples of naturalism that reject all but elementary material phenomena. In another letter, Paul refers to "deceitful spirits and
teachings of demons" (1 Timothy 4:1), most likely a reference to the
spirits of some pantheist and pagan religions such as those that had
seduced the Israelites from time to time. To the Colossians, Paul says,
"see to it that no one takes you captive by philosophy and empty deceit,
according to human tradition" (Colossians 2:8), most likely the errors
of secular humanism. He refers to a number of other principles that
humans have concocted that err against Christ's teachings: "myths
and endless genealogies" and "speculations" (1 Timothy 1:4); "irreverent, silly myths" (1 Timothy 4:7); "craving for controversy" (1
Timothy 6:4); and "irreverent babble and contradictions of what is
falsely called 'knowledge'" (1 Timothy 6:20). Of knowledge alone Paul
cautions that "'knowledge' puffs up" (1 Corinthians 8:1) and that some
are "always learning and never able to arrive at a knowledge of the
truth" (2 Timothy 3:7).

In the second book of Peter (2 Peter 1:5-8), Peter exhorts Christ's
followers to grow: "Make every effort to supplement your faith with
virtue, and virtue with knowledge, and knowledge with self-control,
and self-control with steadfastness, and steadfastness with godliness,
and godliness with brotherly affection, and brotherly affection with
love." The proper order here is for knowledge to be preceded by faith
and virtue. Peter concludes, "If these qualities are yours and are increasing, they keep you from being ineffective or unfruitful in the
knowledge of our Lord Jesus Christ [who is all knowledge]." Right
knowledge, understanding and wisdom are of supreme importance in
Judeo-Christianity. Perhaps the clearest biblical explanation of why
there are limitations on human reason without God is outlined in the
first chapter of Paul's letter to the Romans.

> For the wrath of God is revealed from heaven against all ungodliness and
> unrighteousness of men, who by their unrighteousness suppress the truth.
> For what can be known about God is plain to them, because God has
> shown it to them. For his invisible attributes, namely, his eternal power
> and divine nature, have been clearly perceived, ever since the creation of
> the world, in the things that have been made. So they are without excuse.

For although they knew God, they did not honor him as God or give thanks to him, but they became futile in their thinking, and their foolish hearts were darkened. Claiming to be wise, they became fools, and exchanged the glory of the immortal God for images resembling mortal man and birds and animals and creeping things.

Therefore God gave them up in the lusts of their hearts to impurity, to the dishonoring of their bodies among themselves, because they exchanged the truth about God for a lie and worshiped and served the creature rather than the Creator, who is blessed forever! Amen. (Romans 1:18-25)

I was in fact suppressing the truth because of my unrighteousness, and this passage is the clearest explanation for why I could hardly think myself out of a paper bag. People who come to Christ, particularly later in life, often consciously realize this increased access to a wider rationality and ability to discern. Lesslie Newbigin likens this experience to physicists after Einstein's theory when they had to hold both Newton's and Einstein's laws together in unity because Newton's laws are still true in mechanics and for large objects in slow motion. Newbigin writes,

> Seen from one side there is only a chasm; seen from the other there is a bridge. By analogy, one could suggest that the radical conversion . . . implies a discontinuity that cannot be acknowledged [by the secular world]. . . . Yet it does not imply a surrender to irrationality, since the new understanding of the converted person might make it possible . . . to find a place for the truth that was embodied in the former vision and yet at the same time offer a wider and more inclusive rationality than the older one could. Saul the Pharisee can only see Jesus of Nazareth as a saboteur of the law. Paul the Christian can see the law as the *paidagogos* [tutor] that brought him to Christ; and he can see Christ as the fulfillment of the law.[5]

The Conundrum of Negotiating Global Culture on Secular Reason

This reveals more clearly the dilemma in Jürgen Habermas's and others' proposals to include Christians at the cultural negotiations table while requiring them to present their claims using secular reasoning alone.

Habermas assumes rightly that Christians know and use secular language. Even though it marginalizes believers by limiting their interactions, this is not its most disturbing consequence. Though I am certain Habermas's proposals are sincere and well intended, his restrictions inhibit those inside the Judeo-Christian framework from contributing much-needed knowledge only available in Judeo-Christian thought to those whose minds are limited by secular ideologies. Habermas's ideal speech situation, then, is reduced from the outset to the least common denominator of human reason—secular reasoning.

I am certain from my own experience as well as scriptural principles that it would not have been possible even with the best of translators for me as a secular person to have truly understood the depth of the potentialities and truth that are internal to the Judeo-Christian worldview. As secular people, when we hear these insights we simply translate them into what we already know, which renders them foolish. However, being open to the reality of God makes it possible for people to hear new things and to know in new ways.

With even a tiny opening, God does exponentially more than we can imagine, but without it he will not impose himself on our will. Scriptures suggest that the reason we reject him is because "the god of this world" (2 Corinthians 4:4) has blinded us. Paul, though a religious leader of the Jewish community, had been intellectually and spiritually blinded. After being briefly physically blinded as well, when the "scales fell from his eyes" (Acts 9:18), he became perhaps the greatest apostle, even though he had previously been responsible for the imprisonment and even murder of other apostles and disciples. Related to the dilemma in Habermas's and other similar proposals for Christians to speak only secularly, Paul explains why he refused to bend to similar pressures in the first century.

> We refuse to practice cunning or to tamper with God's word, but by the open statement of the truth we would commend ourselves to everyone's conscience in the sight of God. And even if our gospel is veiled, it is veiled to those who are perishing. In their case the god of this world has blinded the minds of the unbelievers, to keep them from seeing the light of the gospel of the glory of Christ, who is the image of God. (2 Corinthians 4:2-4)

The Wisdom of God Versus Man's Reasoning

*He called himself a sword of slaughter, and told men to buy swords if they
sold their coats for them. That he used even wilder words on the side of
non-resistance greatly increases the violence. We cannot even explain it
by calling such a being insane, for insanity is usually along one consistent
channel. The maniac is generally monomaniac. Here we must remember
the difficult definition of Christianity. . . . Christianity is a superhuman
paradox whereby two opposite passions may blaze beside each other. The
one explanation of the Gospel language that does explain it, is that it is
the survey of one who from some supernatural height beholds some more
startling synthesis.*

G. K. CHESTERTON, *ORTHODOXY*

*Answer not a fool according to his folly,
lest you be like him yourself.
Answer a fool according to his folly,
lest he be wise in his own eyes.*

PROVERBS 26:4-5

When I first began to explore Christianity I had in my mind that it would
be simply about my personal life, mostly my emotions. It might help me
be a better person. Little did I realize it was more rational, all encompassing and intellectually demanding than any secular philosophy, or
scientific, social or psychological theory I had or could ever encounter.

Contemporary social theories emphasize individual rights, but responsibilities loom larger in Christendom, thus pulling together the twin
goals of individual and community flourishing. Free will is an individual
choice granted by God, not a right granted or limited by government
laws. The very concept of rights disconnected from responsibility is incomprehensible in biblical texts. Contemporary man's reasoning today
emphasizes justice, but biblically justice is inextricably linked to righteousness, so much so that it appears impossible for an unrighteous
person or nation to actually be just and vice versa.

I sometimes meet students who were raised in middle- or upper-class evangelical homes who look down on their Christian parents because, in their minds, their parents or churches stressed righteousness over justice. Two things can be said here. Out of their resistance, this generation has a tendency to soften the righteousness requirements and turn instead to justice (mission trips to aid the poor). While all this can be good, one error does not reverse the other. Both justice and righteousness must be fully sought simultaneously. While their parents may not have been going on mission trips, they were very likely tithing faithfully to ministries that supported real missionaries. Mother Teresa could not have done what she did had there not been people making money and sending it to her; that is one reason why she told me God does not call everyone to be poor or live like the poor, even though that was certainly her and the sisters' calling.

The Scriptures present equity as the concept that is most aligned with justice; our contemporary culture uses the word *equality*. Equality is a concept that many scholars have pointed out does not actually exist in nature.[6] G. K. Chesterton once noted, "The Declaration of Independence dogmatically bases all rights on the fact that God created all men equal; and it is right; for if they were not created equal, they were certainly evolved unequal. There is no basis for democracy except in a dogma about the divine origin of man."[7] Like rights, equality appears rarely in biblical principles, except, as Chesterton notes, that God created us all in his image—across cultures, economic conditions, gender, nations and languages. The primary instance of equality in the New Testament is when Jesus "though he was in the form of God, did not count equality with God a thing to be grasped" (see Philippians 2:5-7).

The opposite of love in Judeo-Christian thought is not hate but fear. There is one fear and love that is absolutely perfect and that is the fear and love of God. All other fears lead to oppression, which is the opposite of love. There is a righteous anger, but most anger is personal or political and not necessarily righteous. When Jesus turned over the tables in the temple, it was because the money-changers had turned his Father's house into a marketplace, not because he (or someone else) wasn't getting a fair share of the goods (Matthew 21:12-13). These truths are not contradictory, though at first sight they may appear so. They are not irrational; they are suprarational.

Judeo-Christian thought frequently keeps what appear to be opposites held together, not in a tension as in Hegelian dialectics, which create something new, or in the middle, as in Aristotle's golden mean. Rather, both aspects of the paradox exist side by side in their fullest forms as true, such as the fact that we are fallen beings and are made in the image of God. All these are true, and the dialectic tension between them does not diminish, subsume or reconstitute them but leaves them both fully operable within the principles of Judeo-Christian thought. To get our minds around these opposite passions or supranatural paradoxes we need a relationship with the living God who grants spiritual discernment, which includes, transforms and goes beyond secular human reason, even transforming suffering into spiritual growth.

God's thoughts are higher than our thoughts, and his ways higher than our ways as heaven is higher than the earth (see Isaiah 55:8-9). The two greatest apostles were Peter and Paul. They were very different in temperament. Paul was a highly educated Jew who was also a religious and political leader. Peter was a rough, impulsive Jewish fisherman, more of a common man. But when it came time for God to send someone to the highly intellectual Jews, God chose Peter. And when it was time to send an apostle to the rather barbaric Gentiles, he chose Paul.

In the last days of Christ, he revealed to his disciples that he would soon suffer at the hands of the authorities and be killed and on the third day be raised again. The impetuous disciple Peter rebuked him, saying, "Far be it from you, Lord! This shall never happen to you." Jesus replied, "Get behind me, Satan! You are a hindrance to me. For you are not setting your mind on the things of God, but on the things of man" (Matthew 16:22-23). If we analyze Jesus' remarks from purely secular-humanist reasoning, it seems rather harsh and uncalled for. If we analyze it literally, we may believe that Satan had appeared to him. If we analyze it politically, we wonder why Jesus did not simply leave the area.

Instead, Jesus knew spiritually this was the purpose of his life, the reason he had come to earth. He told them, "For this reason the Father loves me, because I lay down my life that I may take it up again. No one takes it from me, but I lay it down of my own accord. I have authority to lay it down, and I have authority to take it up again. This charge I have received from my Father" (John 10:17-18).

Why then did Jesus say to Peter, "Get behind me, Satan"? Jesus knew Satan was working through Peter's soul; he was not calling Peter Satan, he was calling Satan's reasoning out of Peter's mind. Jesus knew his destiny; he saw what his Father was doing. Peter only saw the death of his friend and the death of the Messiah as evil; thus, at all costs it must be avoided. He could judge the outward circumstances with human reason but could not discern "the times." He did not yet know that time would forever be changed on planet earth. The most earthshattering and restorative event was about to happen, and even the earth and the sun could hardly bear it. This momentary worldly grief was minuscule in comparison to the transformation made possible for all humanity.

Universal Laws

The act of creation always necessitates laws by which the creation will exist and function optimally. God's creation is no different. Laws were not created to limit physical creation or humankind but to allow both to flourish. Christians believe that these universal laws are evident through a number of sources: in the Hebrew and Greek Scriptures, in the life of Christ and through the reasoned study of all that exists. They reveal the created order of the inseparable physical, natural and spiritual worlds. That is why there can be no domains of knowledge that exist separately, such as religion and science.[8]

The physical laws by which the universe operates include laws such as those of gravity, mechanics, thermodynamics, chemistry and electromagnetism, as well as biological laws of genetics, cellular biology, biological chemistry and metabolism. In addition, God provides laws of agriculture, about crop rotation and times of rest for land and prohibitions against hybrids. There are laws by which a family or community best flourishes, including being our neighbors' keeper. In Jesus' parables he made it clear that Jews and Samaritans are neighbors when we are in him, but outside of him worldly cares and histories separate us (see Luke 10:25-37).

The rule of law in government and politics is an attempt to create social order based on the idea that a flourishing society or nation will reflect the same orderliness as the natural world—the orderliness of the mind of God. One spiritual/political law is that the sins of the leader strongly influence the people. This is revealed in many instances in the histories of the righteous and unrighteous kings of Israel.

The laws of human nature govern the optimal operation of our souls. These include a relationship with the living God, self-knowledge, forgiveness through Christ, forgiveness of others and justice. Additionally we have laws of health, laws of family and laws of basic character such as purity, honesty, righteousness, trust and diligence. Many Christians and non-Christians have argued that God's laws are written on our hearts ("natural law" in philosophy, theology and political science), and though we might object, deny or subvert, we do generally know what is right and wrong, normal or abnormal all around the world.[9]

There are also spiritual laws, including laws regarding the movement of spirit and how spiritual laws impact the earth, for example, how sins of people affect the fruitfulness of the land.[10] A violation of laws in one area (spiritual) often results in consequences in another (physical). There are laws of the movement of spirits, such as selfishness or generosity, and laws that govern and restrict the movements of demonic spirits.

When the Philistines stole the ark of the covenant, which contained Aaron's budded rod, a piece of manna and the commandments, they took it to several of their cities. In the first city, they placed it next to the statue of their god Dagon. Dagon fell over on two consecutive nights, breaking this spirit's physical statue in pieces, indicating the power of God over demonic spirits. The ark was moved several times with dire consequences for all the receiving cities (tumors broke out on the people). Once the ark was returned to Israel on the backs of two cows that had never been yoked, the Philistines were safe (1 Samuel 4:1-11; 5:1-12; 6:1-20).

There is no question in my mind that I could not, as a nonbeliever, skeptic or opponent, have ever understood the Christian worldview in its fullness. I could only understand Christianity in a shallow, textbook way. Living in the secular world makes understanding and living the deeper truths of Christianity difficult without strong Christian relationships, personal disciplines and study.

Sometimes the media misrepresentations of Christianity result from a simple lack of understanding (having been deluded themselves). But in other instances members of the cultural elite intentionally ignore and distort the principles of Christendom. For example, inordinate media time has been given to a false prophet who proclaims dates of the apocalypse, despite Jesus' direct exhortation that the date will not be known, or to a pastor of a very small congregation who burned a Qur'an. Media professionals knew full well the outcome of such a report in the Middle East. They were perfectly willing to incite that violence in the Middle East and then zealously film it in order to make it appear that Christianity, rather than the secular media, was the cause of violence. When one understands all the worldviews and the consequences at stake, the real spirits behind these deceptions become clear.

Unlike my constant search for the next "most progressive" framework that invariably ended in boredom, my exploration of Judeo-Christian thought found the riches to be fathomless. Its principles are in some cases more radical than those on the left ("love your enemies, do good to those who hate you," Luke 6:27) and sometimes more conservative than those on the right ("everyone who looks at a woman with lustful intent has already committed adultery with her in his heart," Matthew 5:28). Yet these principles always produce more abundant life and human flourishing.

If Christianity is true, then it is not simply one of many personal options that are equally valid or invalid. If it is true, its precepts will be operative whether or not we believe or agree with them. Spiritual principles, like the principles of physics, are impersonal, though their designer is imminently personal. These laws do not yield to human agreement, and certain consequences follow their rejection. Yet the author of creation is immanently personal, and humans are offered a grace pass. On the front of the pass is printed the name of our benefactor—*Jesus, the Christ.*

THE TRIUNE GOD

I believe in Christianity as I
believe that the sun has risen:
not only because I see it, but
because by it I see everything else.

C. S. LEWIS,
"IS THEOLOGY POETRY?"

True wisdom consists in two things:
knowledge of God and knowledge of self.

JOHN CALVIN,
INSTITUTES OF THE CHRISTIAN RELIGION

Saint Augustine observed, "There are some things which we do not believe unless we understand them, and there are other things which we do not understand unless we believe them."[1] This is true of every worldview because each one begins with faith. Every scientific experiment begins with a hypothesis that is developed from other observations suspected to be true before it is fully confirmed, and that confirmation leads to other beliefs and understandings. The Scriptures are similar, waiting patiently for us to be willing to believe and then to prove them in our lives. I am certain that at first I did not fully believe, but I suddenly had the grace to hold my disbelief and ill-informed opposition to Christianity at bay long enough to swim out in the ocean for a little while until the waves of God's brilliance could wash over me. I gradually became starved for more.

The central earmark of my intellectual life had been boredom. I would find a new theory, love it, work on it, realize it was just a shell of what I was really looking for and discard it for the next one. I had gotten to postmodernism, which seemed too much bother for something that proclaimed it was empty from the outset. There is nothing I can say that will make the entry into this discussion of Christian faith easier for someone who is like I was. It takes only a willingness to consider the possibility that there is another dimension of reality that makes this one more comprehensible and inspiring. On the other side all things do come together because all things coexist and cannot be separate and all the things you or I know make more sense from the standpoint of God's Spirit and revelation through Christ.

By the time I got to the point of putting Christianity on a real trial (as opposed to condemning it first and filling in the evidence in retrospect), I had hardened my heart so much that it is truly a miracle I ever broke through. For a God who wants to be known and who loves everyone does not make himself accessible exclusively to the intellectual or the simple-minded; he has a way for everyone to know him. Indeed, perhaps it is easier for those whose minds have been shaped more by actual experiences with reality than for those of us who are protected by material privilege and education; we can simply sit and read about life and imagine we understand and live this way already. Scriptural principles reveal knowledge is situated in our minds but understanding in our hearts (see, for example, Psalms 49:3; 119:34; Proverbs 2:1-5; 14:33; 15:14). We have to use our entire being to understand.

So here is my far too feeble effort to present a nugget of the unbearable simplicity and brilliant complexity of Judeo-Christianity—the true reality and hope for all times and all peoples.

The Triune God from the Beginning

In the beginning, God created the heavens and the earth. The earth was without form and void, and darkness was over the face of the deep. And the Spirit of God was hovering over the face of the waters.

And God said, "Let there be light," and there was light. . . .

Then God said, "Let us make man in our image, after our likeness. And let them have dominion over the fish of the sea and over the birds of the heavens and over the livestock and over all the earth and over every creeping thing that creeps on the earth."

> *So God created man in his own image,*
> *in the image of God he created him;*
> *male and female he created them.*

GENESIS 1:1-3, 26-27

Each member of the one Godhead (God, the Spirit of God and his spoken Word) is working in perfect harmony with unimaginable intelligence and power, spreading out the heavens, creating light, stars, the sun, the earth, the waters, land, fish, birds and other animals and ultimately creating and communing with human beings. Even in these first few verses of the Bible many things are described that we also know scientifically. For example, the universe had a beginning, and it continues to unfold or expand. And there exist both material elements and living things, including things that are visible and invisible (such as atoms or spirit). Just as one studies the reality of atoms or forces such as gravity not by seeing them but by studying their effects, so people know and study spiritual reality.

The human body, made in the image of God, also mirrors God's tri-unity. Each of us has a physical *body* with a human *soul* (mind, will and emotions) and a *spirit*. In Christianity, each person has a spirit that is distinct from and one with her or his soul. Paul writes a prayer in his first letter to the Thessalonians: "Now may the God of peace himself sanctify you completely, and may your whole spirit and soul and body be kept blameless at the coming of our Lord Jesus Christ" (1 Thessalonians 5:23).[2] Our carnal man is often driven by desires of the body; the natural man is more soulish, operating primarily from our thoughts, emotions and will. Our spirit man in communion with God is increasingly able to judge and discern all things (see 1 Corinthians 2; Romans 8). Ideally our spirit in communion with the Holy Spirit is the command center over our soul and body.

Living the last twenty years of his life in Chinese Communist prisons, Watchman Nee best described the confusion that accompanies our lack of knowledge of the spiritual life of man and our relationship with God.[3] Nee writes,

> As to the matter of soul, I honestly feel most Christians swing from one extreme to the other. We on the one hand usually consider the emotion as soulish; consequently those who are easily moved or excited we normally categorize as soulish. On the other hand we forget that being rational does not at all constitute one as being spiritual. This misjudgment of spiritualizing a rational life must be guarded against equally as much as against that of mistaking a predominantly emotional life for spirituality. . . . One can say [the human spirit] has three main functions. These are conscience, intuition and communion.

Nee suggests we often mistake our souls—emotions, thoughts or will—for our spirits. Mistaking our emotions for our spirits is a common error in contemporary culture, where feelings often become the primary criteria of judgment. Highly educated people tend to mistake their human reason for their spirits. The human spirit is the portal through which the Holy Spirit communes with us in our heart, soul and body, stimulating our reason, conscience, intuition, revelation and spiritual discernment. Spirits other than the Holy Spirit can also influence and even occupy our spirits and souls.[4]

The Faith of Christianity

By the end of the first century, the books we know as the New Testament had been written and were widely circulated. Pieces of the text already had been circulating for years. In the fourth century the Council of Nicaea convened and wrote the Nicene Creed, which has been used ever since.

I believe in one God, the Father Almighty, Maker of heaven and earth, and of all things visible and invisible.

And in one Lord Jesus Christ, the only-begotten Son of God, begotten of the Father before all worlds; God of God, Light of Light, very God of very God; begotten, not made, being of one substance with the Father, by whom all things were made.

Who, for us men and for our salvation, came down from heaven, and was incarnate by the Holy Spirit of the virgin Mary, and was made man; and was crucified also for us under Pontius Pilate; He suffered and was buried; and the third day He rose again, according to the Scriptures; and ascended into heaven, and sits on the right hand of the Father; and He shall come again, with glory, to judge the quick and the dead; whose kingdom shall have no end.

And I believe in the Holy Ghost, the Lord and Giver of Life; who proceeds from the Father and the Son; who with the Father and the Son together is worshipped and glorified; who spoke by the prophets.

And I believe in one holy catholic and apostolic Church. I acknowledge one baptism for the remission of sins; and I look for the resurrection of the dead, and the life of the world to come. Amen.[5]

This statement is the foundational faith of every orthodox Protestant, Catholic and Orthodox Christian believer and has been ever since A.D. 325.[6] Members of many churches formally recite this or the shorter Apostles' Creed every week and sometimes daily. This statement of faith spans all denominations—Catholics, Orthodox and Protestants. In this statement alone, many things are revealed—the relationship between God the Father, the Son and the Holy Spirit; the relationship between God and human beings; the earthly incarnation of God's Word in the form of Jesus, who is fully human and fully God; the universality of the church across denominations, cultures, ages, languages and social classes; the link between justice, judgment and the provision of forgiveness; heaven and earth as made of things visible and invisible; a world that begins, ends and has a new beginning; a kingdom that has no end; and the resurrection of Jesus and eternal life. The apostle Paul well described the outsider's perspective—Christ would be "foolishness to the Greeks" and "a stumbling block to Jews" (see 1 Corinthians 1:20-25).

The Word of God

The canonical books of the Bible were determined by early Christians working together through councils held with extensive prayer. Isaiah described God's inspired and perfect word as written "precept upon precept" and "line upon line" (see Isaiah 28). The believer who reads the Bible faithfully will find that passage after passage is opened up as one pursues understanding. At one reading a passage may enlighten, encourage or even convict in one way; at subsequent times increasingly deeper meanings emerge. All these levels are true and noncontradictory; they are precept upon precept. Maturity and understanding are increased as the Scriptures are continually read, studied and acted upon.

This differs from the postmodern notion that human beings construct the meanings of a text and that these meanings will differ according to a person's culture, language, experience and gender because the text has no inherent meaning. On the contrary, the "word of God is . . . sharper than any two-edged sword, piercing to the division of soul and of spirit, of joints and of marrow, and discerning the thoughts and intentions of the heart" (Hebrews 4:12). It is unlike any other text.

The power of Scripture lies also in the fact that the Scriptures are designed to *read us* as we read them. This is one of the primary paths to self-knowledge. Through the text, God's personal revelation works in us given whatever situation we find ourselves in at the time. The same Scripture speaks to different people at different times in their lives; yet all its revelations are true. Because of the layers and layers of true meanings, our understandings of those levels are always emerging over time. Biblical revelations build on one another.

The biblical writers fully developed every form of literature we know from historic narrative to biography, expository writings, letters, poetry, working manuals of laws and regulations, detailed architectural descriptions, story narratives, prophetic writings, proverbs, songs, and even censuses and genealogies. Its wisdom cuts across all aspects of life—agriculture, psychology, philosophy, sociology, politics, war, history, art, music, health and law. Unlike many pantheist philosophic and religious texts, there are no mythical beings or fictional characters in the biblical text. Of the approximately forty writers of the sixty-six books of the Bible "breathed out by God" (2 Timothy 3:16), all but one is Jewish, Luke being the only known exception. The Hebrew texts were orally transmitted for centuries and then written. The events in the Hebrew and Greek Testaments date from approximately 1500 B.C. through A.D. 100, on either side of the Axial Age.

Christianity's Distinction Among Judaism and Islam

There are similarities in all three monotheisms. Each believes that the uncreated God—a single person in Judaism (Yahweh, G-D) and Islam (Allah)—created the universe, including all that exists on earth. Judaism, Islam and Christianity all recognize Abraham as a central patriarch to whom God revealed himself and who was called to father a special group of people who would know God. Jews and Christians trace their lineage from Abraham's son Isaac, whose mother was Abraham's wife, Sarah. Muslims trace their heritage (including the prophet Muhammad) from Abraham's son Ishmael, whose mother was Hagar, the servant of Abraham's wife, Sarah.

Each of the three also recognizes Moses in their Holy Scriptures as one to whom God spoke. In Judaism and Christianity God reveals himself to Moses as "I AM"—the ultimate being, essence and source of all things who twice gave Moses the tablets containing the Ten Commandments. Islam recognizes that God gave Moses (Musa) tablets but does not specifically refer to the Ten Commandments.

The eternal nature of human existence is a precept of most religious frameworks, including pantheist ones. In Judaism and Islam, one earns a better eternal life by obeying the law and doing good works. To some Reformed Jews, eternal life is defined by the degree to which one's works on earth effectively remain after death, including through children, and not as continuation of an actual eternal life. In both Judaism and Islam, one's access to a better eternal life is dependent upon the works done in one's life on earth. Similarly, Hindus and Buddhists believe rewards, such as reincarnation levels, are dependent on the rightness of one's acts in this life.

In Christianity, salvation by our own righteous works is declared from the outset an impossible task; we simply cannot be that good. Thus, the only way to eternal life is solely through the grace of God because

Jesus fully opened the way to God by taking on our transgressions of the law for those who believe.

Islam proposes that the Bible used by Jews and Christians was corrupted and that the prophet Muhammad set it right six hundred years after Christ. The prophet Muhammad was to have held the newer revelation after Jesus, who Muslims believe was also a prophet named Isa (Jesus). Other prophets since Muhammad, such as Bahaullah, the founder of the Baha'i faith, also have claimed to represent even newer revelations and to correct corruptions in Islam and other faiths. The Baha'i, who are largely pacifists, believe in one God whose character is rendered more clearly across time as human beings evolve. Thus, they believe consecutive prophets will be revealed over time; our revelation of God is said to evolve as humankind evolves. This is similar to a Christian error called process theology, which posits that God changes as he learns from human experience.[7]

Although there are many prophets in the Bible, Jesus is more than a prophet. Rather, Jesus is the Messiah (the anointed one)—"the Alpha and the Omega, the first and the last, the beginning and the end" (Revelation 22:13). He is God's "only Son" (John 3:16), who had been prophesied for over a thousand years. Jesus is the human manifestation of the Word of God (incarnation of God on earth) and both fully God and fully man—the way, the truth and the life.

Jesus—Jews and Gentiles

All the first Christian disciples and apostles were Jews, but soon after Christ's death, resurrection and ascension, many others began to follow Christ, beginning with an Ethiopian eunuch. To magnify the relationship between God and humankind that Jesus had made possible, Christ commanded all his followers to go to all the world and preach the good news (gospel) to all creation. The partial rejection of Christ by the Jews opened the way for Christianity to become universal so that all the world can know him as the Messiah. Paul writes in his letter to the Romans,

> So I ask, did they stumble in order that they might fall? By no means! Rather through their trespass salvation has come to the Gentiles, so as to make Israel jealous. Now if their trespass means riches for the world, and

if their failure means riches for the Gentiles, how much more will their full inclusion mean! . . . For if their rejection means the reconciliation of the world, what will their acceptance mean but life from the dead? . . . And even they, if they do not continue in their unbelief, will be grafted in, for God has the power to graft them in again. (Romans 11:11-12, 15, 23)

The first time the followers of Jesus are called Christians, a multiethnic and multinational group of people is gathered at Antioch. In Acts we read: "For a whole year they met with the church and taught a great many people. And in Antioch the disciples were first called Christians" (Acts 11:26). "Now there were in the church at Antioch prophets and teachers, Barnabas, Simeon who was called Niger, Lucius of Cyrene, Manaen a lifelong friend of Herod the tetrarch, and Saul" (Acts 13:1). Thus began the universal diversity of the body of Christ—a diversity intentionally and purposefully designed by God.

As was predicted, today there is an increase in Jews who are becoming followers of Jesus; these Christians sometimes refer to themselves as Messianic Jews or as fulfilled or completed Jews. It was estimated in 2008 that there were 120 such congregations in Israel with as many as 15,000 members.[8] There are a number of federations of messianic congregations—Association of Messianic Congregations, International Alliance of Messianic Congregations, Union of Messianic Jewish Congregations and Jews for Jesus.[9] Today many Jews who are Christian also attend nonmessianic congregations.[10]

Mortimer Adler, Bob Dylan, Henri Bergson, Edith Stein, Simone Weil and Jay Sekulow are notable messianic converts. Aerospace engineer Andrew Baron wrote after he read the gospel that "God constructed us with souls that can be fed only by His own hand. Believing God cares is not intellectual suicide; believing that He doesn't care is spiritual starvation."[11]

There are also ever-increasing reports out of the Middle East that many Muslims are experiencing dreams in which Christ reveals himself to them.[12] In the last few years there has also been an increase of Christianity in places where it has been less prominent and even signs of renewal in Europe and the Americas.[13] Christ shattered the tradition of spiritual affiliation associated with cultures, people groups, nations, ethnicities, class, race, intelligence and education. Even in Jesus' human genealogy there are multiple ethnicities, and unlike most other biblical genealogies, his includes five women.

Paul summarizes the remarkable global consequences of Christ having opened the kingdom of God to all who desire to enter—"There is neither Jew nor Greek, there is neither slave nor free, there is no male and female, for you are all one in Christ Jesus" (Galatians 3:28; see also Colossians 3:11). God's desire through Jesus was to create a new people by adopting them into the family of his people Israel. He did not replace his chosen people; he added to them.

Peter also describes the reality: "You are a chosen race, a royal priesthood, a holy nation, a people for his own possession, that you may proclaim the excellencies of him who called you out of darkness into his marvelous light. Once you were not a people, but now you are God's people" (1 Peter 2:9-10). From the prophet Hosea, Paul quotes:

> Those who were not my people I will call "my people,"
>   and her who was not beloved I will call "beloved."
> And in the very place where it was said to them, "You are not my people,"
>   there they will be called "sons of the living God." (Romans 9:25-26,
>   quoting from Hosea 2:23; see also 1 Peter 2:10)

Jesus said, "I tell you, many will come from east and west and recline at table with Abraham, Isaac, and Jacob in the kingdom of heaven" (Matthew 8:11). "I am the good shepherd. I know my own and my own know me, just as the Father knows me and I know the Father; and I lay down my life for the sheep. And I have other sheep that are not of this fold. I must bring them also, and they will listen to my voice. So there will be one flock, one shepherd" (John 10:14-16).

In the book of Revelation we see John's prophetic vision of the new earth and heaven:

> After this I looked, and behold, a great multitude that no one could number, from every nation, from all tribes and peoples and languages, standing before the throne and before the Lamb, clothed in white robes, with palm branches in their hands, and crying out with a loud voice, "Salvation belongs to our God who sits on the throne, and to the Lamb!" (Revelation 7:9-10)

As a result, Christianity is the only religion into which no one can be born. It knows no culture and no economic, ethnic, national or linguistic boundaries. Once 80 percent of Christians lived in Europe; today only about 25 percent do.[14] We are not Christian because our parents or our ancestors were. Every person has to choose through her or his own free will. This is why Christ tells us we must be born again. We are reborn when we voluntarily enter into a relationship with Christ. This is God's formula for global unity.

Geography and Monotheisms

Geographic territory holds strong significance in Islam and Judaism. All three monotheisms were birthed in and around Jerusalem. However, Christians have no Jerusalem or Mecca. Jesus proclaimed to the Samaritan woman that with his coming the time had come to worship not on one mountain or another but in spirit and in truth. This same Samaritan woman (a sinner who had had five husbands and was living with another man when she met Jesus) became the world's first evangelist to bring an entire city (of Samaritans, not Jews) to Christ, once again revealing that Jesus came to lead and save all people regardless of their cultural heritage or previous lives (see John 4). He even broke religious rules separating men and women, as in his interaction with the Samaritan woman, as well as in his teaching of women, men and children.

Most Christians, like most Jews and Muslims, do not believe they are called to be pacifists.[15] Jesus did not tell the soldiers to leave the army; he told them to be happy with their pay. He told Pilate that his Father had given Pilate the authority to take his (Jesus') earthly life.[16] Judeo-Christian principles have been significant in the development of the principles of just wars, which form the foundation of most international law. These precepts offer guidelines for deciding (with prayer) whether one should enter a war, for how to behave in combat and for negotiations at the war's end.[17]

Both the Crusades, intended to take back Jerusalem and protect Europe from the takeover of formerly Jewish and Christian lands by radical Islamists, and participation in World War II were decided using just war principles like those first set forth by Augustine in A.D. 300.

Today there are forty-nine Muslim nations[18] surrounding Israel's approximately eight thousand square miles (similar to New Jersey), and they are almost exclusively hostile to the Jewish people. Christians are called to support the Jewish people, who are the true vine of God's people into which all can be grafted or adopted.

Also in Judaism and Christianity, but not in radical Islam, the government is to be informed by the principles of the faith but not be one with it. Jesus recognized the state's authority—"render to Caesar the things that are Caesar's, and to God the things that are God's," he teaches (Luke 20:25). The organizational separation of church and state in the United States was devised to protect both while preserving the support and counsel they gave to one another.

Though not pacifists, Christians are called to be willing to die for others and to give their lives up if necessary to proclaim Christ. The ancient and present tradition of Christian martyrs is a testimony to these principles. A radical fundamentalist Christian may irritate you by explaining the gospel on an airplane, but he won't be blowing up the plane because it is full of nonbelievers.

However, the major difference between Christianity and both Judaism (from which Christianity is founded) and Islam is the difference between a spiritual framework based solely on law (Judaism and Islam) and a spiritual framework based on grace (Christianity). Paul writes, "For by grace you have been saved through faith. And this is not your own doing; it is the gift of God, not a result of works, so that no one may boast" (Ephesians 2:8-9).

By Grace Versus by Law

The Christian does not think God will love us
because we are good, but that God will
make us good because He loves us.

C. S. LEWIS, *MERE CHRISTIANITY*

Grace does not free Christians from the calling to put off the old man and put on the new—to live a holy, just and righteous life. It rather suggests this can only be done in relationship with a personal God who wants to help and has already won our freedom from the law of death (or karma) to pay for our sins. That worry lifted, we press on to fulfill the call on our lives, our life purposes. The grace of God makes it possible to grow ever stronger in living according to the laws of human flourishing laid out in the commandments and Christ's teachings. This grace inspires and supplements our human reason, will and emotions through the Holy Spirit's guiding of our spirits.

Grace is a spiritual transaction, which is necessary because inside each of us is a sinful nature that lures us away from those actions that we should desire and toward those we should not. Grace is the spiritual force of pure love that acts to encourage more wholeness (righteousness, justice, goodness, holiness). As we commune more fully with God, we are made ever more able to fulfill our destinies and to thrive. The grace of God through Jesus makes it more possible to fulfill the law. As Jesus said, "Do not think that I have come to abolish the Law or the Prophets; I have not come to abolish them but to fulfill them" (Matthew 5:17).

JESUS, REDEEMER OF MAN AND THE WORLD

Jesus promised his disciples three things—
that they would be completely fearless,
absurdly happy, and in constant trouble.

G. K. CHESTERTON, *ORTHODOXY*

The Cosmic Christ—Fully God—Son of God

At the most universal level, Jesus is the word of God through which God created the world. He was with God in the beginning, creating alongside God and the Holy Spirit. Everything that exists (visible and invisible) was made by him and for him, and in him all things hold together. He is the beginning and the end of all things (alpha and omega); he is eternal. The universe was both created by and continues to be upheld by the power of his Word, and the fullness of God in heaven and earth dwells in him. He and the Father and the Holy Spirit are one, and they are living and active in the universe and on the earth (see John 1:1-18; 3:16-21; Colossians 1:15-20).

Jesus became flesh (incarnate) and came to earth as the earthly manifestation of God. He is over all spiritual powers (principalities, dominions, rulers and authorities). In Hebrews we are told,

> Long ago, at many times and in many ways, God spoke to our fathers by the prophets, but in these last days he has spoken to us by his Son, whom he appointed the heir of all things, through whom also he created the

world. He is the radiance of the glory of God and the exact imprint of his nature, and he upholds the universe by the word of his power. After making purification for sins, he sat down at the right hand of the Majesty on high, having become as much superior to angels as the name he has inherited is more excellent than theirs. (Hebrews 1:1-4)

Son of Man—Fully Human

Jesus is referred to as both Son of God and Son of Man. His earthly existence began when an angel announced to a very young virgin named Mary God's plan to have her carry and give birth to his Son on earth. Mary and Joseph were engaged when an angel told her, "The Holy Spirit will come upon you, and the power of the Most High will overshadow you; therefore the child to be born will be called holy—the Son of God." And Mary faithfully answered, "Behold, I am the servant of the Lord; let it be to me according to your word" (Luke 1:35, 38).

An angel then told Joseph not to be afraid to take Mary as his wife because the child was of the Lord. His birth in Bethlehem; his childhood in Egypt and Nazareth; his life, death, resurrection and ascension; and his role as the Messiah, the anointed one of God, had been prophesied ever since Moses. In the story of Adam and Eve he is prefigured as the son of Eve who will crush the head of Satan. Even Magi from the East, most likely pantheist priests who were astronomers and astrologists, saw the signs in the heavens that had been prophesied of the birth of this great king. They also obeyed a dream not to inform Herod. Joseph also obeyed four dreams: to marry Mary, take Jesus to Egypt, return to Israel, and finally withdraw to Nazareth in Galilee.

As a child and man, Jesus faced every temptation known to man, including direct taunts by Satan. Because he faced every temptation but did not sin and then voluntarily offered himself up for our transgressions, he was the quintessential and final sacrifice for human sins for all times and all people (the final perfect blood sacrifice—no more unblemished lambs, bulls and goats). The author of Hebrews describes it best:

Since then we have a great high priest who has passed through the heavens, Jesus, the Son of God, let us hold fast our confession. For we do not have a high priest who is unable to sympathize with our weaknesses, but one who in every respect has been tempted as we are, yet without sin. Let us then with confidence draw near to the throne of grace, that we may receive mercy and find grace to help in time of need. (Hebrews 4:14-16)

Jesus Not Just a Great Human Teacher or Prophet

Unlike other religious leaders and teachers, Jesus was not a human being who was troubled by some great question and spent his life trying to answer that question. Buddha, Confucius, Muhammad and others had questions about life and searched their whole lives for the wisdom to answer these questions. They ultimately taught their reasoned answers and then died. But Jesus had no questions; he knew all of our questions and came as the answer.

Jesus did not receive or leave commandments of stone or lead people to a particular geographic place. He came as the personification of the commandments and as God for all peoples and lands. He came to show and teach everyone who wanted to know the way, and, in fact, the first descriptions of Christianity called it simply "the way." Given Jesus' challenges to the Pharisees and the absence of a name for his ministry, it is likely Jesus intended his teaching to simply be seen as the way—like himself—"the way, and the truth, and the life" (John 14:6).

Jesus summarized the Ten Commandments into two when a lawyer questioned him:

"Teacher, which is the great commandment in the Law?" And he said to him, "You shall love the Lord your God with all your heart and with all your soul and with all your mind. This is the great and first commandment. And a second is like it: You shall love your neighbor as yourself. On these two commandments depend all the Law and the Prophets." (Matthew 22:36-40; see Deuteronomy 6:5)

Loving God with all our heart, soul, strength and mind first is the only thing that makes the second commandment truly possible. Secular humanism in all its forms is the worthy goal of achieving the second commandment without the concomitant and necessary first one.

Jesus' Works on Earth

Jesus spent nights in prayer and explained that he did only what he saw his Father doing. He never killed anyone, never led a war, never married or had children, and never had a physical home during his ministry. He obeyed secular authorities but challenged religious leaders; for example, he healed on the sabbath, called God his Father, and taught women, Samaritans and sinners. He lived the Spirit of the Law without legalism and said he had not come to abolish the Law but to fulfill it. He fulfilled all the requirements of the Law by living a perfect life and voluntarily dying a thoroughly unjust death to take on all the sins of the world. Jesus' sacrifice of his life replaced the legalistic requirements that no person, not even Moses, had ever been able to fully live, and at the same time he produced the spiritual power that made it eminently more possible to live them. His perfect life, death and resurrection were the all-sufficient provision for man's redemption for all time. God's love both replaces and fulfills the Law by grace to those who seek, know and follow him; no matter how clumsily we follow, there is always grace.

Jesus spent most of his days teaching his disciples and large numbers of people who followed him. During his three years of public ministry, he healed the sick, blind, deaf and mute; turned water into wine; multiplied food; commanded storms to stop; walked on water; cast out demons; and even raised the dead. Miracles were a normal part of his day, though he did not refer to them as miracles, nor did his disciples.

He never suggested that the spiritual world was something separate from the natural world; there is no principle in Christianity that supports separating natural from supernatural, nor are these words ever used in the Bible. G. K. Chesterton observed, "Believers in miracles accept them (rightly or wrongly) because they have evidence for them. The disbelievers in miracles deny them (rightly or wrongly) because they have a doctrine against them."[1] In fact, Jesus said that after his ascension to the Father and the advent of the Holy Spirit, his followers would do even more than he had done.

Jesus' life embodied the principles and wisdom of the Judeo-Christian worldview. He revealed, for example, that not all disease is caused by sin though some is, and some disease is caused by the demonic. He taught that faith is a central aspect of healing, but even someone else's faith, or an admission that one lacks faith, can substitute for the faith of the repentant. He used different actions for different healings. Sometimes he touched people; sometimes people were healed miles away at his word. In one healing he was aware that power had come out of him when a woman touched him.

None of the extraordinary acts of Jesus were for himself—he never bent spoons, twirled, went into a trance or waged war. He was not being mindful, using his mind to overcome matter, overcoming desire or emptying his mind. He had an all-consuming desire to fulfill his destiny and God's will, which are one and the same. His spiritual acts were for a purpose—to heal, to deliver and set free, to teach, to feed the masses—and all of them brought glory to God, even though they irritated the religious leaders who were not doing the same things. He was revealing a reality beyond and inclusive of human reason.

Jesus and Suffering

One of the most comprehensive prophecies regarding the incarnation, life, death and resurrection of Jesus was written by the prophet Isaiah approximately seven hundred years before Christ's birth. His prophecy is explicit regarding suffering being Jesus' constant companion.

> He was despised and rejected by men;
>   a man of sorrows, and acquainted with grief;
> and as one from whom men hide their faces
>   he was despised, and we esteemed him not.
>
> Surely he has borne our griefs
>   and carried our sorrows;
> yet we esteemed him stricken,
>   smitten by God, and afflicted.
> But he was pierced for our transgressions;
>   he was crushed for our iniquities;
> upon him was the chastisement that brought us peace,
>   and with his wounds we are healed.
> All we like sheep have gone astray;

we have turned—every one—to his own way;
and the L ORD has laid on him
the iniquity of us all.

He was oppressed, and he was afflicted,
yet he opened not his mouth;
like a lamb that is led to the slaughter,
and like a sheep that before its shearers is silent,
so he opened not his mouth. (Isaiah 53:3-7)

It was for our salvation that Christ chose suffering. He did not come to put an end to suffering in this world but prepared the way for anyone to follow him and live in the kingdom of God even while living in this worldly kingdom as well as beyond in the next life. Jesus wept for Lazarus and his sisters, grieved over Jerusalem, wanted to gather them as a hen gathers her chicks, and wept over the death of John the Baptist, his cousin and friend, the one crying in the wilderness. He was in anguish in the garden of Gethsemane knowing of his impending torture and death on the cross and even sensed God's brief absence as he withdrew his presence so that Jesus might take on the sins of the world, by becoming sin for us.

For Christians, growth seems always to involve some suffering; and all people suffer, with Christ or without. Peter tells us we should not suffer as an evildoer but suffer rightly for doing good (1 Peter 4:15-19). C. S. Lewis aptly describes the process of suffering while growing in God:

Imagine yourself as a living house. God comes in to rebuild that house. At first, perhaps, you can understand what He is doing. He is getting the drains right and stopping the leaks in the roof and so on; you knew that those jobs needed doing and so you are not surprised. But presently He starts knocking the house about in a way that hurts abominably and does not seem to make any sense. What on earth is He up to? The explanation is that He is building quite a different house from the one you thought of—throwing out a new wing here, putting on an extra floor there, running up towers, making courtyards. You thought you were being made into a decent little cottage: but He is building a palace. He intends to come and live in it Himself.[2]

To be honest, I have never grown spiritually without suffering. I simply don't have the will to do difficult things that are absolutely necessary even though it is my desire to mature and I know that suffering spurs growth. I must admit I am too much like Mother Teresa's descriptions of Americans; I can be too content to pursue spiritual growth because I don't sense its necessity while living in a good deal of comfort. She said Americans were spiritually the poorest of the poor because we were so rich we didn't think we needed God.

Jesus taught that there is an ultimate justice in the kingdom of God, where the suffering poor are rewarded and those who reject God and are rich in their own eyes are cast out. In Jesus' teachings we see Lazarus, a poor man, who had begged all his life at the gate of the rich man. In their eternal dwellings the principle of ultimate justice is revealed. Lazarus is carried by angels while the rich man burns (Luke 16:19-31). Another man who had many storehouses decided to hoard his goods and sit back to rest. The night he announces his plans his life is taken away, and the goods are divided among others (Luke 12:15-21). Even the problem Christopher Hitchens had with Mother Teresa taking money from the corrupt is explained in Proverbs 13:11, 22, where we are told, "Wealth gained hastily will dwindle," and "the sinner's wealth is laid up for the righteous."

In Christianity, Scriptures about suffering indicate there is a way to make it redemptive. In Romans, Paul writes, "we rejoice in our sufferings, knowing that suffering produces endurance, and endurance produces character, and character produces hope, and hope does not put us to shame, because God's love has been poured into our hearts through the Holy Spirit who has been given to us" (Romans 5:3-5). We are made more perfect through overcoming the temptations of evil and experiencing righteous suffering, which is "experienced by your brotherhood throughout the world" (1 Peter 5:9). Pastor Graham Cooke teaches that every trial of the Christian has hidden within it a potential spiritual upgrade when we meet it with faith, hope and love in Christ.[3]

C. S. Lewis wrote that "God whispers to us in our pleasures, speaks in our consciences, but shouts in our pain. It is his megaphone to rouse a deaf world."[4] Lewis advised, "I didn't go to religion to make me happy. I always knew a bottle of Port would do that. If you want a religion to make you feel really comfortable, I certainly don't recommend Christianity."[5]

Those who seem to have the most trouble desiring God or even considering the fact that there is a God who made the world a certain way—physically, humanly and spiritually—are often those with the most wealth, health, power and fame and those who have a good deal of natural self-discipline and control. The more we have of native talent, economic sufficiency, self-control and confidence, the less we seek him. Sadly, this is the frequent state of the cultural elite, though on the inside there is frequently a good deal of angst and uncertainty.

The prodigal son was much the same. Living in his father's abundance, he took his share of the inheritance and spent it in reckless living. Then he became destitute and decided to go home, repent and offer to become his father's servant. But his father would not allow it. Instead he did what Jesus does for all who ask; he took him in, cleaned him up and threw a party for him (Luke 15:11-32).

Jesus and the Problem of Evil

I freely admit that real Christianity (as distinct from Christianity-and-water) goes much nearer to Dualism than people think. One of the things that surprised me when I first read the New Testament seriously was that it talked so much about a Dark Power in the universe—a mighty evil spirit who was held to be the Power behind death and disease, and sin. The difference is that Christianity thinks this Dark Power was created by God, and was good when he was created, and went wrong. Christianity agrees with Dualism that this universe is at war. But it does not think this is a war between independent powers. It thinks it is a civil war, a rebellion, and that we are living in a part of the universe occupied by the rebel.

C. S. Lewis, *Mere Christianity*

*Men do not differ much about what things
they will call evils; they differ enormously on
what evils they will call excusable.*

G. K. Chesterton, *Orthodoxy*

Jesus' primary assignment was to "destroy the works of the devil" (1 John 3:8) and to do this he had to experience and overcome all his encounters with it. He accomplished this by becoming a man, allowing himself to be tempted in all ways and to be murdered, whereupon he became the perfect sacrifice to cover our sins. He also takes on not only our sins but our illnesses. For example, it is recorded that strength went out of him when the ill woman touched him and was healed (Matthew 9:18-26; Luke 8:40-49). This is the plan executed by the Trinity to overcome evil. His resurrection reveals his divinity and the power of his perfect life, which is indestructible.

His life, death and resurrection broke forever the barrier that existed between God and man because of sin. While we all die an obvious physical death, we all are eternal beings and we will always live, with God or without him. While we are still affected by evil, it has no permanent hold on us, and the divine grace of God through Jesus operating through the Holy Spirit provides ways to diminish its effect now and for eternity.

Some of the basic Judeo-Christian precepts related to the existence and operations of evil that Jesus and the early Hebrews taught include these:

- We are all living in a fallen world (nature and humanity are in a fallen state).

- Evil began when Satan, originally an angel who was created by God for good, wanted to take God's place (the very thing with which he tempted Eve—"you will be like God, knowing good and evil," Genesis 3:5).

- Satan is God's enemy but not equal to God.[6]

- Satan took one-third of the angels with him in his rebellion.[7]

- Unable to affect God, Satan seeks to recruit and infect human beings, whom God loves, by using humankind for his rebellion.

- Humans are made in God's image and are special to God.

- Though designed to be good, humans are given free will, which allows the possibility that human beings will choose to do evil.

- The laws by which all creation was made prevail, both physical laws and human ones, and breaking them incurs consequences: "your sins have kept good from you" (Jeremiah 5:25).

- Nature also groans and is affected by evil in part due to the sins of man.[8]

- We are involved in a spiritual war between good and evil—a war not for or against people but against the spiritual powers that humans choose to serve.

- We are always serving one or the other—good or evil; there is no neutral demilitarized zone.

- There is far more good than evil in the world and far more chance that we will live today rather than die.

- God works so that evil tends to destroy itself—falling into the pit it digs for others.

- Evil is irrational.

- There are authorities (in heaven and on earth), and the moral condition of those authorities influences those under their authority.

- There is an ultimate divine justice in eternity.

French Orthodox philosopher and theologian Jean-Claude Larchet tackles the problem of evil in illness. He begins by noting that in the beginning God pronounced all things good; God cannot be the author of illness. We know that Jesus on many occasions healed the sick: children plagued with the demonic; women plagued with disease; those who were blind, lame and deaf; some already dead; and some suffering because of sin. Larchet notes that our constant hope since the Enlightenment that science will solve our illnesses "bear[s] witness to the positive aspirations that are deeply rooted in human nature: that man might escape death, which he rightly considers as foreign to his true nature."[9]

Larchet acknowledges that most medical practices treat the human person as a "purely biological organism." He argues, "The body does not only express the person; to a certain extent it is the person. The person does not merely have a body, it is a body, even though it infinitely transcends bodily limits. . . . By refusing to consider the spiritual dimension of human persons when we seek to alleviate their physical ailments, we do them immeasurable harm." He sets forth a synthesis of "a Christian theology of illness and suffering, and with it . . . consider[s] various modes of healing" in the Christian context.[10]

Jesus as the Way of Forgiveness and Redemption

> *If men will not understand the meaning of judgment,*
> *they will never come to understand the meaning of grace.*
>
> DOROTHY SAYERS, *CREED OR CHAOS?*

God designed human beings like he designed the physical universe, upon a set of principles by which humans function and thrive. To miss the mark of human flourishing (sin) may not result in sudden death, just as falling a few feet will not likely kill me, but there are consequences nonetheless. As human beings we miss the mark a good deal.

Prior to Christ, Jews made elaborate sacrifices of unblemished animals when repenting. After many centuries of people turning away from God and even from admitting their sins, God sent his Son to be the flawless "Lamb of God, who takes away the sin of the world" (John 1:29). Because he was faultless, he could make propitiation for all humanity's sins for all time. He was the quintessential Passover lamb (male lamb without blemish). Just as God led Moses and the Israelites out of Egypt after the Passover (Exodus 12), so too Jesus leads us out of the wilderness, a process that continues throughout our lifetime. He is the ultimate and eternal scapegoat described in Leviticus, upon whose head the sins of the people were placed before it was sent away into the wilderness. Jesus' death in the place of skulls, his resurrection and appearance for forty days, and his subsequent ascension into heaven opened the way for us not only to commune with God through the Holy Spirit but also to enter his presence sprinkled clean with the perfect blood of Christ. This was the final sprinkling of blood to replace the repetitive sacrifices, which are no longer used even by the Jews.

This mystical event is honored, relived and renewed during Communion or Eucharist, where we partake his flesh in the bread and drink his blood in the wine; he is the priceless spiritual food and drink.[11] We are humbled by recollecting our current sins; seeking forgiveness; and receiving, celebrating and confirming our liberation from sin. This spiritual transaction of confession prompts God's forgiveness as well as his cleansing from the very source of the desire to sin. Every person who believes in Christ can experience this freedom. But it is our choice; God will not force a relationship on us.

There is a beautiful depiction of Jesus as the light of the world in a painting titled *The Light of the World* by William Holman Hunt, a pre-Raphaelite artist, at Keble College, Oxford, and Saint Paul's Cathedral, London.[12] Christ is knocking at a door just before dawn with light emanating from his head and from a lantern he is carrying. He appears to have been there for some time; the door to this soul's house is overgrown with ivy and thorns and is encircled by a bat. There is no handle on the door from the outside; the door has to be opened from within.

I have a young friend—wife and mother of four beautiful children—who sometimes has visions during prayer. She had a vision similar to this painting one day. Someone was at her door knocking, but she could not make herself get up. The knocking continued for what seemed a long time. When it stopped, she finally got up (in the vision). And when she looked out of a window in the door, she saw Jesus sitting on the steps outside the door. He had been there a long time and was surrounded with a number of unopened gifts he had brought her. Many of us who have made a commitment to follow Christ and have drunk deeply from his redemptive hand have trouble receiving all the goodness of God because we always know who we still really are.

Strange as it may seem, the more we know our failings the more he wants to give us. Christianity, unlike any other worldview, accepts the fact of human sinfulness while providing an everlasting solution whereby God and man work together to recover, reclaim and advance. The grace of forgiveness drives us not to more sin but to desire to be more like him and nearer to him.

To follow Christ in a world as secular as the West takes a special diligence and commitment to stay in the Scriptures and find like-minded and deeply committed people in a community who can help one another stay focused and growing. We constantly have to overcome the more shallow lures of the world because we are always moving toward a greater or lesser relationship with God; there is no standing still. Fortunately, as we grow older, the spiritual aspect of our lives becomes stronger, as Paul wrote, "So we do not lose heart. Though our outer self is wasting away, our inner self is being renewed day by day. For this light momentary affliction is preparing for us an eternal weight of glory beyond all comparison" (2 Corinthians 4:16-17). For all of this to happen Jesus had to die, be resurrected and return to heaven alive.

The Resurrected Jesus

> *What do we find God "doing about"*
> *this business of sin and evil? . . .*
> *God did not abolish the fact of evil; He transformed it.*
> *He did not stop the Crucifixion; He rose from the dead.*
>
> DOROTHY SAYERS,
> THE WHIMSICAL CHRISTIAN: 18 ESSAYS

The resurrection of Jesus is the ultimate spiritual transaction that has taken place on the earth. It changed life forever for those who preceded it, lived through it, are living now and will live in the future. Much more than the printing press, atomic bomb, Internet or anything else we can imagine, the life, death and resurrection of Jesus irrevocably changed the world. It was the final earthly act that demonstrated the divinity of Christ. For forty days after Jesus' resurrection, hundreds of people testified to having heard and seen him walking and talking among them. Christ still appears today, though not in physical form but in dreams, visions and revelations.

People do not become irrational when they believe the resurrection and all that is meant by it; they indeed have a wider rationality. The resurrection is not simply about a person who died and then came to life; many such events have been reported, from the Old Testament to contemporary ministries in Africa.[13] However, Jesus went on teaching for forty days, and many eyewitnesses saw and heard him. More important, people still perceive his presence and his working in and through them.

The bodily resurrection of Jesus was not God showing off; it was the fulfillment of God's plan to offer man a way to be transformed and redeemed from the inside out and saved for all eternity. It was possible because of Jesus' perfection and divine incarnation; he could not stay dead. The benefits of this most profound spiritual and natural event of all time immediately became available to all who want it, no matter where in the world they live—even the dead before Christ and those yet to be born are offered this gift.

The Prescription for Global Unity—Jesus as the Head of the Body

Something in the human heart longs for unity around the world. After the flood, people began to construct the Tower of Babel in Babylon (Genesis 11:1-9).[14] Throughout history, human beings have sought ways to unite globally and to solve their most fundamental differences. After World War II, the centers of power, particularly in the West, sought to build a global community through various means, including the founding of the United Nations in 1945. Its purposes include facilitating dialogue and cooperation among nations to promote peace, human rights, international law, and general social and economic progress. Today even airplanes are emblazoned with "one world" proclamations, and the words *global* and *glocal* are so common as to be almost indefinable clichés.

The results of these secular efforts thus far have been less than stellar. For example, we have not had fewer wars since the development of the United Nations; we have had more. We continue to pursue the idea that very diverse human beings can reason together productively. Philosophers, artists, educators and politicians evidence the desire to unite humankind. It is a foundational principle of secular humanism and a goal of pantheist spiritual frameworks.

In Judeo-Christianity this same hope exists alongside a principle for its realization—Christ as the head of all people. There is no need for a continual contest over which group on earth at any particular moment is the most dominant. If Christianity is true, Christ is the head of all humanity. The recognition of this binds very diverse peoples together— different nations, cultures, ages and abilities—in the one Spirit. For this to be possible, Christ had to belong to all the earth, not any single subgroup. Christ's headship sets wide parameters of thought and action and potentialities. This is true globalism. We are like cells in the cosmic body of Christ, each performing our unique functions.

In the first letter to the Corinthian church Paul best outlines the body of Christ in form, purpose and principles. No person can deny that he or she is part of the body or deny anyone else's membership in the body. In the inimitable wisdom of Christ, the weaker is more indispensable, and if one suffers we all suffer. Martin Luther King Jr. summed up these Christian principles in this way, "For some strange reason I can never be what I ought to be until you are what you ought to be. And you can never be what you ought to be until I am what I ought to be. That is the way God's universe is made."[15] (See 1 Corinthians 12.)

This body of Christ is not perfect; there is no utopian premise here. Starting with our sinfulness and the knowledge of our fallen nature precludes the possibility that Christianity can deliver a utopia, and yet Christianity does offer a process whereby people and nations can move toward righteousness, justice and unity. There is a life to come that will be different, not a renewed Garden of Eden but a "new city" filled with every tribe and tongue, not made by man but by God. Until it appears (and we can do nothing to speed it along or know its date), we have all been put here to work with and for others and for the planet. To fulfill our work, we have two options as individuals and nations. We can work alongside God seeking his wisdom, power, strength and grace, or we can limp along with pieces of incomplete and partially distorted worldviews that are vague and powerless shadows of what is actually possible.

Jesus as the Way, the Truth and the Life—The Only Way

And the Lord said: . . .

Behold I will again

do wonderful things with this people,

with wonder upon wonder;

and the wisdom of their wise men shall perish,

and the discernment of their discerning men shall be hidden.

ISAIAH 29:13-14

Possibly the most disturbing fact of the life of Christ to secularists and other religious alike, is Christ's proclamation in John 14.

> Jesus said to him, "I am the way, and the truth, and the life. No one comes to the Father except through me. If you had known me, you would have known my Father also. From now on you do know him and have seen him." (John 14:6-7)

This claim that Jesus is the only way to reach God is offensive to holders of secular, other monotheist and pantheist worldviews. In reality, every avid holder of any worldview believes that her or his way is the right one. But logically only one worldview or none of these can be true. If it is true, as Christians believe, there is no reason to be offended. Oddly enough we are not offended by gravity.

I well remember struggling with this myself. In a profound little booklet, John Bowen points out that the arguments against Christ's claim to be the only way to God generally focus on its sounding arrogant, or its being unfair to those of other faiths, or its being oppressive as a truth claim.[16] In retrospect I sense there were two major issues for me. First, I still had in mind the world's definition of Jesus as just a good man. If that were the case, he would be an arrogant man. But not being just a man and being the very embodiment of truth, he could only have told the truth. Lewis points out, "If you look for truth, you may find comfort in the end; if you look for comfort you will not get either comfort or truth only soft soap and wishful thinking to begin, and in the end, despair."[17] We have nothing in any document about Christ's life that would suggest he ever spoke something that was not true. Indeed, he even knew people's thoughts before they spoke.

Second, we are increasingly driven by our emotions and other people's perceptions of us. To believe that God became man and lived to teach us the way causes all our secular friends or friends of other religions to balk at our belief that Jesus is the only way to God. It rubbed against my egalitarian sensibilities, which had morphed into the idea that therefore all religious frameworks must be equal—equally true to the believer and equally false to everyone else—as though there are no criteria for judging moral and spiritual truths.

Jesus came to tell us and show us the truth. Truth is not changed by our feelings, votes, preferences, beliefs or ideas about God, just as gravity is not.

It is worth repeating C. S. Lewis' wisdom about Jesus:

> I am trying here to prevent anyone saying the really foolish thing that people often say about Him: "I'm ready to accept Jesus as a great moral teacher, but I don't accept His claim to be God." That is the one thing we must not say. A man who was merely a man and said the sort of things Jesus said would not be a great moral teacher. He would either be a lunatic—on the level with the man who says he is a poached egg—or else he would be the Devil of Hell. You must make your choice. Either this man was, and is, the Son of God: or else a madman or something worse. You can shut Him up for a fool, you can spit at Him and kill Him as a demon; or you can fall at His feet and call Him Lord and God. But let us not come with any patronizing nonsense about His being a great human teacher. He has not left that open to us. He did not intend to.[18]

Jesus for the Atheist—The True Last Temptation of Christ

Jesus had to experience every temptation known to man in order to redeem us from every form of transgression. Because he came through every temptation without sin, he and only he could open the way for us to God, who is holy. In a brilliant passage in his book *Orthodoxy*, G. K. Chesterton describes the last temptation of Christ—one moment during his torturous crucifixion when he was tempted with the transgression of atheism.

> That a good man may have his back to the wall is no more than we knew already, but that God could have His back to the wall is a boast for all insurgents forever. Christianity is the only religion on earth that has felt that omnipotence made God incomplete. Christianity alone felt that God, to be wholly God, must have been a rebel as well as a king. Alone of all creeds, Christianity has added courage to the virtues of the Creator. For the only courage worth calling courage must necessarily mean that the soul passes a breaking point—and does not break. In this indeed I approach a matter more dark and awful than it is easy to discuss; and I apologize in advance if any of my phrases fall wrong or seem irreverent touching a matter which

the greatest saints and thinkers have justly feared to approach. But in the terrific tale of the Passion there is a distinct emotional suggestion that the author of all things (in some unthinkable way) went not only through agony, but through doubt. It is written, "Thou shalt not tempt the Lord thy God." No; but the Lord thy God may tempt Himself; and it seems as if this was what happened in Gethsemane. In a garden Satan tempted man: and in a garden God tempted God. He passed in some superhuman manner through our human horror of pessimism. When the world shook and the sun was wiped out of heaven, it was not at the crucifixion, but at the cry from the cross: the cry which confessed that God was forsaken of God. And now let the revolutionists choose a creed from all the creeds and a god from all the gods of the world, carefully weighing all the gods of inevitable recurrence and of unalterable power. They will not find another god who has himself been in revolt. Nay (the matter grows too difficult for human speech), but let the atheists themselves choose a god. They will find only one divinity who ever uttered their isolation; only one religion in which God seemed for an instant to be an atheist.[19]

In his very last words from the cross, Jesus takes the victory over this final temptation so that he might also forgive and transform the repentant atheist. Luke recounts the moment: "Then Jesus, calling out with a loud voice, said, 'Father, into your hands I commit my spirit!' And having said this he breathed his last" (Luke 23:46).

Because of the unfailing love and patience of God, Dallas Willard tells us the atheist prayer always works—"Dear God, if there is a God, save my soul, if I have a soul."[20] My own prayer was even more feeble, "If you are real, please come and get me." God is not slow to come in when we crack the door.

> Ask, and it will be given to you; seek, and you will find; knock, and it will be opened to you. For everyone who asks receives, and the one who seeks finds, and to the one who knocks it will be opened. Or which one of you, if his son asks him for bread, will give him a stone? Or if he asks for a fish, will give him a serpent? If you then, who are evil, know how to give good gifts to your children, how much more will your Father who is in heaven give good things to those who ask him! (Matthew 7:7-11)

If Christianity is true, then it is only Jesus who stands between heaven and earth eternally glorifying his Father, inviting us in, granting us entry, redeeming his people and sending his Spirit. There is no need for man to design complicated abstract principles to guide human nature. The way has already been revealed in the flesh, in the concrete manifestation of God on the earth who became the expressway to union with God—the God/man Jesus, the anointed one, the Messiah, the Redeemer of humanity and the world.

SIGNPOSTS OF REALITY

[W]hen so many brands of . . . "fancy souls" and theories of life are offered you, there is no sense in not looking pretty carefully to see what you are going in for. . . . It isn't a case of "Here is the Christian religion, the one authoritative and respectable rule of life. Take it or leave it." It's "Here's a muddling kind of affair called Life, and here are nineteen or twenty different explanations of it, all supported by people whose opinions are not to be sneezed at. Among them is the Christian religion in which you happen to have been brought up. Your friend so-and-so has been brought up in quite a different way of thinking; is a perfectly splendid person and thoroughly happy. What are you going to do about it?"—I'm worrying it out quietly, and whatever I get hold of will be valuable, because I've got it for myself.

DOROTHY SAYERS, *LETTERS OF DOROTHY L. SAYERS: 1899–1936*

A man was meant to be doubtful about himself, but undoubting about the truth; this has been exactly reversed. Nowadays the part of a man that a man does assert is exactly the part he ought not to assert—himself. The part he doubts is exactly the part he ought not to doubt—the Divine Reason.

G. K. CHESTERTON, *ORTHODOXY*

It is not enough to find one or two pieces of evidence for the truth of Christianity. Alone it is insufficient to know that the universe had a beginning, as though that settles it because it makes the first verse of Genesis 1 true. Although it is also a sign, it's still not enough that Christianity is the world's largest religion, as though truth can be determined by some democratic vote. Jesus did not ask the disciples to vote on whether they should go to Samaria the day he met the woman at the well; the disciples simply followed. It's not even enough for me to tell you, and for others to verify, that once I had a dream of Jesus who showed me who I really was and afterward my life was radically transformed. No, it is not enough for even three or four signs to convince most of us, but an avalanche of evidence is another thing. There are endless signposts of the truth of Christianity and only a few will be recounted here.

Signposts in the Heavens and on Earth

The fact that the universe had a beginning and is incredibly fine-tuned to support our life on earth is evidence of a Creator that stands behind his creation with a mind that is so mathematically precise that it has motivated and inspired the minds of the world's greatest scientists and most brilliant mathematicians and philosophers since the beginning of time. God's imagination evident in the radical diversity of plants, animals, celestial objects and human beings both animates our human reason and stimulates our imaginations. The fact that we are made in God's image makes us able to perceive and study all these things from the 248 muscles in the head of the caterpillar (humans have only about 700 muscles in our entire bodies) to the over 100 billion galaxies in the visible universe.[1] The psalmist declares our inborn human desire to understand God and all of his creation, "Great are the works of the LORD, studied by all who delight in them" (Psalm 111:2). This includes the study of the visible and invisible (atoms, energy, spirit): "By faith we understand that the universe was created by the word of God, so that what is seen was not made out of things that are visible" (Hebrews 11:3).

To Galileo Galilei, Francis Bacon, Isaac Newton, Blaise Pascal, Johannes Kepler and Francis Collins, as well as the thousands of scientists who have known God for millennia, every new discovery about the universe, the earth or human beings is a new insight into the mind of God. Nobel Prize–winning physicist Arthur Holly Compton wrote, "The scientist who recognizes God knows only the God of Newton. To him the God imagined by Laplace and Comte is wholly inadequate. He feels that God is in nature, that the orderly ways in which nature works are themselves the manifestations of God's will and purpose. Its laws are his orderly way of thinking."[2] They reflect his created order.

The hypothesis that there is a brilliant God who created the universe and stands outside of it while acting inside it is the most rational and explanatory of all hypotheses. No other hypothesis has ever been developed that can account for the fact that there is something rather than nothing, that the universe does exist and continues to expand, that our minds are able to study and know about the universe and ourselves, and that our observations can be reliable because the universe, earth and human nature are rule-governed.

The alternative hypotheses of random material emerging from nothing and spontaneously creating the universe or aliens seeding life on earth from elsewhere in the universe are simply irrational. Unlike hypotheses derived from scientific and philosophic methods, these hypotheses are not formed out of what is known. Nothing we have ever known has come from nothing. Nothing ever created itself, and no ordered, intricate design has ever emerged without a designing intelligence. God as Creator is simply the single most reasonable hypothesis.

Signposts in the History of the Nations

History reveals that the closer the foundations of a nation are to Judeo-Christian principles the more it flourishes in all ways—health, education, economics, safety, families, communities and international relations. This evidence begins with the rise of Europe and later North America, all founded directly on principles drawn from the Bible. In these countries slavery was first abolished, women have the most freedom, and children and families have the most protection. Laws protect even convicted prisoners.

Christians (Deist or orthodox) founded Western nations and directly applied Judeo-Christian principles, which they understood as the best description of both public and private truth.[3] Presidents over the centuries have called for days of prayer and even days of fasting for the nation.[4] Though gradually becoming more secular, these nations still enjoy more freedom, prosperity, productivity, diversity and generosity to the poor than do nations founded on other religious or secular principles. In his book *A Free People's Suicide,* Os Guinness writes of the loss of vigor in the West, "The way forward is to return to the source that gave rise to [it] in the first place."[5]

Recent evidence reveals that whenever Christianity begins to rise in a culture so does the health, education and prosperity of the nation. See, for example, South Korea, Singapore and now China.[6] This principle works also in reverse: over the last centuries as Europe has continued to back away from Judeo-Christianity all indicators of the health of the society have begun to plummet.[7] As Billy Graham said, "The farther we get from God, the more the world spirals out of control."[8]

One-third of the world professes Judeo-Christianity; its adherents are in every nation on earth. With the increase in international travel and the Internet, communities of Christians around the world are increasingly connected. At the funeral of Pope John Paul II it was estimated that over four million people from every nation gathered in Rome peacefully. It is believed to have been the largest global Christian event ever in the history of the world. Outside of the United Nations it was also the largest gathering of state officials in the world. Judeo-Christianity is the only worldview that offers a vision for globalization with a common moral code that intersects with other religions around the world.

Though no one can be born a Christian, everyone can choose. Under Christ's unique headship, diverse people and groups of people have unique gifts and talents, all of which are necessary to build the kingdom of God on earth as it is in heaven. In Scripture we find particular nations and families mentioned as having special talents (for example, herders, musicians and metalworkers in Genesis 4:20-22 and woodcutters in 1 Kings 5:6).

Signposts of Women, the Poor, the Alien and the Child

A woman's heart should be so close to God
that a man should have to chase Him to find her.

C. S. LEWIS

There is no act, no sermon, no parable in the whole Gospel that borrows
its pungency from female perversity; nobody could possibly guess
from the words and deeds of Jesus that there was
anything "funny" about woman's nature.

DOROTHY L. SAYERS, *ARE WOMEN HUMAN?*

Had I raised my head above my feminist and Marxist texts, I might have noticed that it was not Christianity that had most oppressed women and the poor. One of the most frequent criticisms of Jesus was that he always associated with the poorest and least respectable citizens and that he ministered to shady women, Samaritans as well as Jews. His example has been the driving force behind missions work inside and outside the West and set the example for what has now become foreign aid. In biblical times, immigrants in Israel were to be given the same privileges as the citizens, though they had to submit to the laws of the land; they could not bring in their other gods.

Women are given high value in Judeo-Christianity, and Western cultures built on its principles have led in promoting women's freedom and continue to do so. Even though it would have been extremely difficult during the times of Old and New Testaments for both husbands and wives to work outside the home, even in the Hebrew Scriptures before Christ God called women to lead wars (Deborah), save nations (Esther and Deborah), kill enemies (Jael), prophesy to kings (Huldah), bear and raise up prophets (Hannah and Samson's mother), build up the wall (daughters of Shallum), save Israel (Rahab) and be a head of state (the Queen of Sheba). The woman in Proverbs 31:10-31, a much-dreaded text by radical feminists, owned both a vineyard and a garment business. We are told her arms are strong, and she gives to the needy. Not only her husband praises her but the whole town praises her—not because of her beauty but because of her strength, faith, dignity, wisdom and kindness. She is the quintessential feminist—working woman, business owner, wife and mother.

Jesus had extraordinary, pure relationships with many women: Mary Magdalene, the adulterous woman, Mary and Martha, the Samaritan woman, his mother Mary and the woman who anointed him with her tears. The longest dialogue Jesus has with any person in the Bible is with the Samaritan woman (a woman, a Samaritan and a sinner). In the Gospels she appears to be the only person he tells directly that he is the Messiah, and the first to evangelize an entire city. Women remained at the cross, helped to lead and fund the early church, supported Jesus and his disciples, and were among the first martyrs.[9]

Regarding Paul's teachings on women, we have to look at their entirety to judge them. While women are called to respect their husbands, their husbands are commanded to love their wives even as they love their own bodies, being willing to die for their wives. Once married, a man and a woman become one flesh. Their children are blessings to them and to the community and nation. The family forms the foundation of the culture and mirrors in some ways the Trinity. Neither husbands nor wives have authority over their own bodies, but their spouses do. They are to give each other their conjugal rights unless they agree for a short time to devote themselves to prayer (1 Corinthians 7:1-5). Paul forbade women from teaching men in the synagogue, but Paul was clearly less restrictive than his contemporaries.

Quite a few prominent women in the university have shared their conversions to Christianity.[10] Historian Elizabeth Genovese and columnist Lorraine Murray have both written challenges to their earlier radical feminist faiths.[11] In 1996 Genovese published a study that foresaw the changing attitudes of large numbers of women regarding the feminist movement. The secular culture's denigration of women is now so remarkably strong that one can hardly imagine criticizing Christian views of women. Women are frequently the objects of the most obscene music and films, young girls are frequently sold into prostitution, and females are more frequently aborted. This cannot happen in a culture that believes every woman and her body are sacred and intended either to be celibate or the wife of one man and where laws protect her and her children's lives.

The man is the head of the woman, and Christ is the head of the husband, who is commanded to obey Christ and be willing to die for his wife as Christ did for the church. C. S. Lewis suggests that the only reason there needs to be a head is that on the rare occasions when they disagree, there needs to be a tie breaker, but at all other times there should be great effort to agree on any course of action because they are one. Why the man? Lewis says because the woman is the "special trustee" of the family's interest and the father is its "foreign policy" adviser.[12] At times God told any number of men to obey their wives and even revealed things to women first (Samson's mother; Mary, mother of Jesus; Sarah regarding Hagar).

The husband's charge is equal if not heavier than God's charge to women. The culture falls apart when either or both abdicate their responsibilities to one another and to their children and set their eyes first outside the family and only secondarily inside. This began happening with the advent of no-fault divorce, which has left a culture in which many young people no longer live with their biological parents—a generation of fatherless children. The personal, social and economic costs of this have been unimaginable.[13]

A truly Christian marriage is a brilliant thing to see. Though not perfect, a couple's faithfulness to one another and to their children builds incredible strength of character. While divorce rates of those who say they are Christian are frequently reported to mirror that of the general public, except for Roman Catholics, closer analyses have revealed that among those who are actually active in church, the rates are far lower.[14] Studies suggest children's health and school and later life achievement are better when children live with their biological parents who are religious.[15] Judeo-Christian principles support both spouses being active in the home and outside in different ways. The principles of exclusive and permanent relationships are a far cry from images in movies and other media.

Signposts of the Times

The universal historic markers of time—B.C. (before Christ) and A.D.

(anno domini, the year of our Lord)—are evidence of Christ's preeminence and the fact that his incarnation, death and resurrection changed human history forever. These dates continue to mark human history regardless of secular attempts to rename them without reference to Christ. Nevertheless, Christ's time-shattering appearance is recognized, gratefully or grudgingly, and we are still living in "the year of our Lord"— it was, in fact, not an error.

It is not only Christianity that suggests there will be an end to the earth as we know it. Scientists also predict the end of the earth when the sun burns out, or we are destroyed by asteroids, or other hypotheses. Matthew records Jesus' teachings on the end of this world and the kingdom to come, of which no one will know the day and hour, not even the angels. Jesus did not even know the dates when he was questioned by his disciples (Matthew 24:36). The only thing one can say is that it is closer today than when this book was written, and we will be nearer tomorrow than today.

Jesus described the situation prior to the end. He said in the beginning there will be wars, rumors of wars, famines and earthquakes, and kingdom will rise against kingdom and nation against nation. Next his followers will be hated and some put to death for his name. False prophets will arise and claim to be Jesus in order to lead people astray with signs and wonders. The gospel will be preached to all nations, and there will be a dramatic increase in lawlessness, causing people's love to grow cold. After this, the "abomination of desolation" stands in the holy place, and then comes the final tribulation when the sun will be darkened and the moon not give its light; stars will fall, and the powers of heaven will be shaken. At last, the gospel will have been preached to all nations and then the sign of the Son of Man will appear in the heavens (Matthew 24).

The end times are also described in the book of Revelation as well as in the book of Daniel; all three are similar. The name of the seventh and last church in the book of Revelation is Laodicea. The Laodicean church's problem was that it had become lukewarm toward God and thus ineffective. Jesus told them: "For you say, I am rich, I have prospered, and I need nothing, not realizing that you are wretched, pitiable, poor, blind, and naked" (Revelation 3:17).

Signposts in the Arts

> *A man can no more diminish God's glory by*
> *refusing to worship Him than a lunatic can put out*
> *the sun by scribbling the word "darkness"*
> *on the walls of his cell.*

C. S. Lewis, *The Problem of Pain*

The art, music, drama and literature of the West were birthed from the loins of Christianity. Early Christian art and music set the highest standards of beauty. From the extraordinary Pietà and ceiling of Sistine Chapel by Michelangelo and paintings of Rembrandt and Caravaggio to the brilliant, inspiring music of Bach and Handel's *Messiah,* there remain no secular matches. Their purpose was to teach and inspire all people to greatness, goodness, truth and beauty. Now novelty and trendiness have replaced grander artistic vision. Witness the *4'33"* (four minutes and 33 seconds of silence), a composition by John Cage that requires the audience to listen to the sounds in the environment, and Marcel Duchamp's urinal placed in museums.[16] How have the intellectual elite been this deluded? When placed next to the products of earlier artists and musicians, they signal better than anything the breakdown of the culture from one that once sought the beautiful, tender, melodic, inspiring and meaningful to one that offers vain, simple, disturbing expressions of anxiety, dullness and farce.

In his book *The Cathedral and the Cube,* George Weigel compares the architecture and the ethos of the Cathedral of Notre Dame to the new Parisian Grande Arche or the Cube. He suggests that the Cube, a stark, gigantic glass cube, mirrors the bankruptcy of the new secular Europe— a prophetic picture of the secularist's project. Though it boasts that it can hold the cathedral inside of it, it cannot hold the intellectual, social and moral richness of the Judeo-Christian worldview. Weigel suggests it is a striking metaphor for the loss of civilization plaguing the West.[12] Yet within the cathedral all the real treasures of secular and pantheist culture find their place; everything that is true in them is true in Christianity and more. It is the Cube that was built by the wisdom of the cathedral with its impressive stones, carved wood, ironwork and stained-glass windows that tell the story of God, man and history that fostered the engineering of both the cathedral and the Cube. In the cathedral lies the uncompromising reality of both the pain and triumph of God—bound together with man by crucifixion, resurrection and ascension and the way to freedom and purpose in this life and the next.

Signposts in Education

The center of all early education in the West was Christendom. Monasteries spawned universities and town centers. These universities, though now largely secularized, served as the model for universities all over the world. The concept of unity in diversity (embedded in the word *university*) holds that there is an ultimate unity undergirding and connecting knowledge across the diverse academic disciplines, a unity evident, perfect and effectual in the Trinity.

Inventors of the Gutenberg press directed their first efforts toward printing the Bible, which was the preeminent text to be studied by all. Missionaries have given many ethnic groups their written languages. Plays and paintings of the biblical stories also became educational texts. The plays of Shakespeare and subsequent Western literature can hardly be understood without biblical knowledge. Early schoolbooks used Proverbs for spelling and Bible stories to teach children to read.

Public schooling in America historically emerged out of church schools. When public schools took over the function, education in the church began to be called "Sunday school."[18] Roman Catholic schools and other Christian schools and home schools, especially Classical Christian schools, continue to use the biblical text as the backbone of their instruction.[19] These students generally do better than their public school peers on all measures.[20] Religious participation is positively linked to higher school achievement.[21]

Signposts of Scriptural Truth

Most of us believe that Alexander the Great lived and performed the exploits we have learned in school; however, the first history we have about Alexander appeared four hundred years after his death.[22] The

New Testament about the life and teachings of Jesus and his first apostles is considered one of the most well documented and reliable texts in early history. By A.D. 95 (about sixty years after Christ's death and resurrection) the New Testament as we know it was complete, and many copies of the various books and letters were repeatedly copied, quoted and widely circulated in various languages. Long before the actual New Testament, identical verses of the text had been found scattered in the writings of many of the early followers of Christ.

After an extensive analysis, Norman Geisler and Peter Bocchino state,

> An honest comparison of the three observations: (1) the number of manuscripts, (2) the time span between the original and earliest copy, and (3) the accuracy of the New Testament, all bear witness that the New Testament is the most historically accurate and reliable document from all of antiquity. If one cannot trust the New Testament at this point, then one must reject all of ancient history, which rests on much weaker evidence.[23]

The historical facts in the Old and New Testaments continue to be verified by archeological digs and other documents, including secular histories. The most recent finds include a coin pointing to the life of Samson, evidence of the rule of David as king, burial boxes with a drawing of a man being eaten by a fish (Jonah) and another with the inscription "James brother of Jesus." The youngest and much loved disciple John ends his Gospel with this statement: "Now there are also many other things that Jesus did. Were every one of them to be written, I suppose that the world itself could not contain the books that would be written" (John 21:25).

Signposts in Human Diversity

God created human diversity, and he must have had a reason, one that offered hope and unity in its massive diversity. Christianity encourages the full development of every individual person to fulfill each unique calling to the larger community and to the world. Among Christian leadership alone, we can witness enormous diversity. Picture the carefully reasoned John Polkinghorne, Oxford scientist, theologian and university chancellor, beside the extroverted and flamboyant T. D. Jakes; the quiet, humble servant Mother Teresa next to Uganda's fiery prophetic minister, John Mulinde; the Chinese dissident and ex-prisoner Brother Yun next to the brilliant emeritus Pope Benedict XVI; and the humble and strong Argentinian Pope Francis next to the charismatic evangelist Carlos Annacondia. These are as different from one another as people can possibly be in culture, language, social background and personality, and yet they all belong to the body of Christ in the world, and they all would agree on basic fundamental truths about reality. They are fully themselves, fully expressions of their own cultures and fully Christ's. It is the headship of Christ that binds them together and gives them very unique callings in the body of Christ on earth.

Signposts of the Global Zeitgeist

Films reveal the undergirding ethos of a culture. All around the world films repeat the story of Christianity in varied forms. In these stories and films there is a spirit world, which is both good and evil; people have choices to join either good or evil; and ultimately a savior ensures that good prevails over evil. My favorite film of this genre became a sort of cult film in 1984—*The Adventures of Buckaroo Banzai Across the 8th Dimension*. Buckaroo is a physicist, brain surgeon, rock musician and leader of a small band of like-minded souls who invent a racecar (a converted pickup with a jet engine) that breaks the sound barrier while traveling through matter (a mountain in west Texas). Not stopping with this accomplishment, they move on to discover, take on and defeat a band of evil aliens from the eighth dimension who have come to take over the earth (Planet 10) and who are under contract with NASA.

While clearly a bit of a spoof on the salvation motif, *Buckaroo Banzai*, like *Superman, Batman, Star Wars, Star Trek, Harry Potter, The Lord of the Rings, Narnia, Avatar* and thousands of other films all around the world, illustrates how the ultimate truth story is endlessly reinvented.[24] It is the story written deeply on our hearts of a Savior's triumph of good over evil—the story lived by Christ two thousand years ago and still alive and well.[25]

Signposts of the Battle over Truth

While our films depict the battle between good and evil generally as a battle between two distinct groups, in the Judeo-Christian framework it is not nearly so simple. There is good and evil inside each of us, and the degree to which we connect with God's grace to diminish evil and expand good is the degree to which we overcome the battles that rage inside us. The battle on the outside is also not against people but against spirits like the battle inside us. Paul writes, "For though we walk in the flesh, we are not waging war according to the flesh. For the weapons of our warfare are not of the flesh but have divine power to destroy strongholds. We destroy arguments and every lofty opinion raised against the knowledge of God, and take every thought captive to obey Christ" (2 Corinthians 10:3-5).

Whenever evil prospers, so does irrationality, sometimes disguised as human reason in the form of rationalization. Evil comes against truth at every turn. In C. S. Lewis's brilliant book *The Screwtape Letters,* a senior devil instructs a younger one. For example, the devil advises his apprentice on how to capitalize on human flaws:

> Man has been accustomed, ever since he was a boy, to having a dozen of incompatible philosophies dancing about together in his head. He doesn't think of doctrines as primarily "true" or "false," but as academic or practical, outworn or contemporary, conventional or ruthless. Jargon, not argument, is your best ally in keeping him from the Church. Don't waste your time trying to make him think that materialism is true! Make him think it is strong or stark or courageous—that it is the philosophy of the future. That's the sort of thing he cares about.[26]

Lewis's ability to capture the movements of evil inside our reasoning is unsurpassed and shockingly real; even the most hardened people can recognize their souls in this work. Lewis was also quick to note in the introduction that evil would like nothing more than for us either to disbelieve its existence or overestimate its power.

The reality that evil fights good and that the battle is often over the mind is another sign of the truth of Christianity. Small battles often mask larger spiritual battles and truths. For example, why would there be such an irrational contest over crosses in public and historical places and prayers in schools unless they were perceived as having power? If people do not believe that there is a God, why does anyone care about the display of crosses? We do not believe in Disney characters, but no one objects to their images in public places. The reality is that Christianity is true and prayer is effectual; thus the fight is fierce.

Signposts of the Transformation of the Human Person

> *Amazing grace, how sweet the sound*
> *that saved a wretch like me.*
>
> JOHN NEWTON,
> "AMAZING GRACE"

> *The Christian ideal has not been tried and found wanting;*
> *it has been found difficult and left untried.*
>
> G. K. CHESTERTON,
> *WHAT'S WRONG WITH THE WORLD*

Even these universal and cultural signposts of the truth of Christianity are not the most convincing evidence. Rather the quintessential proof lies in the transformation of every individual human being who experiences the life-changing effects of knowing and following Christ. There is no other completely accurate, safe and effective way to know oneself and to grow ever stronger in character and destiny. There have been perhaps billions of lives transformed over time.[27] Some are sitting in our homes, workplaces and neighborhoods. These stories involve some measure of what we call supernatural, like the alcoholic who is transformed and never wants another drink, the prisoner who becomes a national leader or the Amish parents who forgive the unforgiveable.[28]

Even small moments in people's lives proclaim the power and truth of Christianity. One often-repeated story is of Corrie ten Boom, a woman who lived through the Holocaust but whose sister, Betsie, and father died in Nazi camps. The family had been arrested and imprisoned because they were hiding Jews. She wrote about a time after the war when she was teaching on forgiveness and a man came up to her afterward whom she recognized as one of their captors, a man who had made her and Betsie pass by him naked. He thrust his hand out to thank her for the message; her arm literally froze. He told her he had become a Christian; still she was unable to forgive. She writes:

> Betsie had died in that place—could he erase her slow terrible death simply for the asking?
>
> It could not have been many seconds that he stood there—hand held out—but to me it seemed hours as I wrestled with the most difficult thing I had ever had to do.
>
> For I had to do it—I knew that. The message that God forgives has a prior condition: that we forgive those who have injured us. "If you do not forgive men their trespasses," Jesus says, "neither will your Father in heaven forgive your trespasses."
>
> I knew it not only as a commandment of God, but as a daily experience. Since the end of the war I had had a home in Holland for victims of Nazi brutality. Those who were able to forgive their former enemies were able also to return to the outside world and rebuild their lives, no matter what the physical scars. Those who nursed their bitterness remained invalids. It was as simple and as horrible as that.
>
> And still I stood there with the coldness clutching my heart. But forgiveness is not an emotion—I knew that too. Forgiveness is an act of the will, and the will can function regardless of the temperature of the heart. ". . . Help!" I prayed silently. "I can lift my hand. I can do that much. You supply the feeling."
>
> And so woodenly, mechanically, I thrust my hand into the one stretched out to me. And as I did, an incredible thing took place. The current started in my shoulder, raced down my arm, sprang into our joined hands. And then this healing warmth seemed to flood my whole being, bringing tears to my eyes.
>
> "I forgive you, brother!" I cried. "With all my heart!"
>
> For a long moment we grasped each other's hands, the former guard and the former prisoner. I had never known God's love so intensely, as I did then.[29]

I have had the sheer joy in the last two years of getting to know a dozen women in a yearlong program at a Christian women's refuge built for them by Christians in the community. The women have been in and out of prison, have had to relinquish their children, are on probation and have been through scores of secular treatment programs. The chaos and pain many of them have experienced are difficult for most of us to even imagine. And here they are—they have given their lives to Jesus, and he is delivering them from addictions, answering their prayers and sending people to supply basic physical and spiritual needs. The women participate in two Bible studies a day. Now they want three. They want to form a praise and worship group to sing in nursing homes "because the old people there are so lonely." They are beautiful, and the power of God is palpable when you are around them. He is bringing order out of chaos and hope out of despair.

Twenty years ago I would have said, well, of course, they need a crutch; let them have their delusions. But twenty years ago I was not much different from these women. I was better placed in the culture and in the economic system so when I did what they did, it was avant-garde, not illegal; I wasn't arrested.

In the spring of 2013 I spoke with some graduate students. A young Latina graduate student who was getting a degree in social work came up to me crying. She asked how could she help her desperate clients, who were all young people on juvenile probation, to know Christ when it was expressly prohibited. She had even been warned about doing so. She said, "I know it would help them; I feel so terrible not helping them." I was at a loss for what to suggest; her question still haunts me.

In 2011, Byron Johnson, a social scientist at Baylor, published a book documenting research on the effectiveness of faith-based programs in reducing crime and recidivism. His empirical evidence makes up over twenty pages of references. He writes, "In an age of political correctness, perhaps the last acceptable prejudice is the one leveled against the involvement of highly religious people and their faith-based approaches to social problems—problems the government cannot fix without them."[30]

I want to close with this observation: though we think of ourselves in the West as brilliantly reasonable and guided by empirical evidence, we are, in fact, neither. We are ideological; we are led by our prejudices—secular ones. We are living in a secular political age where politics has displaced knowledge as the impetus for action. That is why to bring Christ to a prisoner or parolee is made very difficult, if not impossible, regardless of sound research data that would suggest the value of doing so. So how will our culture answer this sobbing young social worker's plea, how are we going to allow her to help her clients to have the same kind of life transformation that she and I and billions of others have experienced?

In his biography of Saint Francis of Assisi, G. K. Chesterton writes, "To this great mystic his religion was not a thing like a theory but a thing like a love affair."[31] If Christianity is true, it is most certainly a love affair—one also filled with all manner of delights, including science, mathematics, literature, art, music, politics, law, business, family, friends, natural exploits, and tastes, sights, sounds, as well as the way to fulfull the longing for understanding, purpose, love and holiness.

Yes, if Christianity is true, it is clearly not a theory. It is a love affair with life and its author. It is reality.

> *You will seek me and find me, when you seek me*
> *with all your heart.*
>
> JEREMIAH 29:13

ACKNOWLEDGMENTS

I am deeply indebted to Dallas Willard, who was a model of impeccable scholarship and incredible faithfulness, relentlessly pursuing the truth and challenging the exclusivity of secularism. If ever there were a professor who looked like Jesus, it was Dallas. While grieving over his passing, we can rejoice over his life and all the gifts he left for us. May we never forget his admonition to re-infuse the knowledge that is in Christ back into the world.

I am also tremendously grateful to James Sire, Art Battson, Johnelle Donnell, Carol Swain, Molly Sutherland and Jim Motter—friends who generously read all or parts of the manuscript and gave invaluable feedback.

Once again I am deeply indebted to my editor, Al Hsu, who over the years has been a strong source of encouragement and wisdom. The fabulously accomplished people at InterVarsity Press, as well as Dan Cho and the wise and passionate team at the Veritas Forum, made the book a much better one.

I have for many years been enriched by the camaraderie of colleagues and students at Claremont, who have taught me invaluable lessons and who keep me growing. I owe special thanks to Lorelei Coddington, who helped structure the references.

My sisters are always a blessing. I owe a special debt of gratitude to Anne for letting me write at her house twice a year for who knows how many years now, to Sue and Warren for endless tea parties, and to Jane and her family for constant encouragement.

Last, but certainly not least, I am extraordinarily grateful for the remarkably generous diligence and love of friends who have prayed for me over the years. They know who they are and I know to whom they belong.

May the Lord do for each of you as he did for Moses:
Thus the Lord used to speak to Moses face to face, as a man speaks to his friend.

EXODUS 33:11

NOTES

Chapter 1: Truth and Consequences

[1] *Secular, secularism* means not connected with religious or spiritual matters, the worldly rather than the spiritual, the worldly as opposed to the church; http://oxforddictionaries.com/definition/english/secular.

[2] Charles Taylor, *A Secular Age* (Cambridge, MA: Harvard University Press, 2007).

[3] *Hegemony* is the dominance, mastery and rule of one group over another; the subordinate group(s) are convinced, coerced or simply submit to this control even when it is not in their best interest.

[4] At Yale in 1934, philosopher John Dewey called religious views "pre-scientific" in his lectures on developing a common secular faith (see his *A Common Faith* [Hartford, CT: Yale University Press, 1991]). Jürgen Habermas calls religious justifications "pre-political" as he seeks to establish procedures for negotiating common norms based on human reason, though he does recommend the presence of religious persons in his "ideal speech" actions (see his *The Theory of Communicative Action*, vol. 1, *Reason and the Rationalization of Society*, trans. Thomas McCarthy [Boston: Beacon Press, 1984]).

[5] Heather Horn, "Where Does Religion Come From?" interview with Robert Bellah, *The Atlantic*, August 17, 2011, www.theatlantic.com/entertainment/archive/2011/08/where-does-religion-come-from/243723. Bellah is talking about evolution as broadly conceived; his book is an outline of the historical evolution of religious thought in the world across the ages. See Robert Bellah, *Religion in Human Evolution* (Cambridge, MA: Harvard University Press, 2011).

[6] David Bentley Hart, *Atheist Delusions: The Christian Revolution and Its Fashionable Enemies* (New Haven, CT: Yale University Press, 2009), p. 106.

[7] *Material naturalism* is a worldview that posits that everything that exists is ultimately reducible to its material form and processes that govern the material—such as atoms, electrons, biochemicals, and their natural processes such as electromagnetism. This includes consciousness, mind and religious beliefs, all of which are proposed simply to be the result of natural physical material. There can be no metaphysical explanations and no supernatural phenomena. This view is generally called *materialism* in philosophy and *naturalism* in science.

[8]*Secular humanism* is "liberalism, with regard in particular to the belief that religion should not be taught or practised within a publicly funded education system [or in any public domain]." *Oxford Dictionaries,* http://oxforddictionaries .com/definition/english/secular%2Bhumanism?q=secular+humanism.

[9]Guenter Risse, *Mending Bodies, Saving Souls: A History of Hospitals* (New York: Oxford University Press, 1999); and Gary Ferngren, *Medicine and Health Care in Early Christianity* (Baltimore: Johns Hopkins University Press, 2009).

[10]Samuel Huntington, *The Clash of Civilizations and the Remaking of World Order* (New York: Simon & Schuster, 2011), p. 209.

[11]William Cavanaugh, "Does Religion Cause Violence? Behind the Common Question Lies a Morass of Unclear Thinking," *Harvard Divinity Bulletin* 35 (spring/summer 2007), emphasis original, www.hds.harvard.edu/news-events/harvard-divinity-bulletin/articles/does-religion-cause-violence. See also idem, *The Myth of Religious Violence: Secular Ideology and the Roots of Modern Conflict* (New York: Oxford University Press, 2009); and video interview: "The Myth of Religious Violence," accessed May 24, 2013, http ://vimeo.com/21894360. See also Meic Pearse, *The Gods of War* (Downers Grove, IL: InterVarsity Press, 2007).

[12]I am not suggesting that radical Islam does not severely oppress Christians in the regions they control. I am simply noting that radical Islamists' disdain for the West is largely about its godlessness.

[13]Melanie Phillips, *The World Turned Upside Down* (New York: Encounter Books, 2010), p. 406.

[14]Whether those seeking democracy will succeed remains to be seen; but we have to keep in mind that the original values of the West, regardless of rhetoric, are still strongly valued around the world, though often denigrated in contemporary Western thought.

[15]Jürgen Habermas, *Time of Transitions* (Malden, MA: Polity Press, 2006), pp. 150-51. See also www.youtube.com/watch?v=SjfBqMlr4rk, where Habermas defends the statement to his mocking philosophic colleagues where he points out that while he remains a methodological atheist, the statement is an accurate reflection of his sentiments.

[16]James W. Sire, *The Universe Next Door: A Basic Worldview Catalog,* 5th ed. (Downers Grove, IL: InterVarsity Press, 2009), front page.

[17]See, for example, the critiques of Neil Postman, *The End of Education* (New York: Vintage, 1996); Alan Bloom, *The Closing of the American Mind* (New York: Simon & Schuster, 1987); Mortimer Adler and Charles Van Doren, *How to Read a Book* (New York: Simon & Schuster, 1972); and Thomas Sowell, *Inside American Education* (New York: Free Press, 1992).

[18]The phrase "ideas have consequences" comes from a book title in which author Richard Weaver argued against relativism and consumerism and for tradi-

tional values of the southern United States (*Ideas Have Consequences* [Chicago: University of Chicago, 1948]).

[19]Dallas Willard, *Knowing Christ Today* (New York: HarperOne, 2009), p. 138.

Chapter 2: Confessions of a Professor

[1]See Psalms 101:3 and 119:37.

[2]For Marx, see Paul Vitz, *Faith of the Fatherless: The Psychology of Atheism* (Dallas: Spence, 1999), pp. 124-25. For Ayers, see Alfred Regenry, "They're All in This Together," *American Spectator,* September 2011, http://spectator.org /archives/2011/09/02/theyre-all-in-this-together.

[3]"Pope Francis Warns Church Could Become 'Compassionate NGO,'" BBC, March 14, 2013, www.bbc.co.uk/news/world-europe-21793224.

[4]See Matthew 25:35-40.

[5]Brian Kolodiejchuk, *Mother Teresa: Come Be My Light* (New York: Doubleday, 2007).

[6]Mary Poplin, *Finding Calcutta* (Downers Grove, IL: InterVarsity Press, 2008).

[7]Lesslie Newbigin, *Foolishness to the Greeks: The Gospel and Western Culture* (Grand Rapids: Eerdmans, 1986), p. 64.

[8]C. S. Lewis, *Mere Christianity* (San Francisco: HarperSanFrancisco, 2001), p. 28.

Chapter 3: Worldviews as Operating Systems of the Mind

[1]Jean Piaget described the realization of being in a state of disequilibrium prior to new learning. Once in this state, we apply the cognitive tools of reflection, assimilation, accommodation and equilibration in order to construct new meanings (learn).

[2]James Sire, *The Universe Next Door: A Basic Worldview Catalog,* 5th ed. (Downers Grove, IL: InterVarsity Press, 2009), p. 20.

[3]James W. Sire, *Naming the Elephant* (Downers Grove, IL: InterVarsity Press, 2004); idem, *Universe Next Door;* Chuck Colson and Nancy Pearcey, *How Now Shall We Live?* (Carol Stream, IL: Tyndale, 1999); Nancy Pearcey, *Total Truth* (Wheaton, IL: Crossway, 2004); idem, *Saving Leonardo* (Nashville: B & H Books, 2010); Francis Schaeffer, *How Should We Then Live?* (Wheaton, IL: Crossway, 1983); Glenn S. Sunshine, *Why You Think the Way You Do: The Story of Western Worldviews from Rome to Home* (Grand Rapids: Zondervan, 2009); Steve Wilkens and Mark L. Sanford, *Hidden Worldviews: Eight Cultural Stories That Shape Our Lives* (Downers Grove, IL: InterVarsity Press, 2009); Ronald H. Nash, *Worldviews in Conflict: Choosing Christianity in a World of Ideas* (Grand Rapids: Zondervan, 1992); David K. Naugle, *Worldview: The History of the Concept* (Grand Rapids: Eerdmans, 2002); J. P. Moreland and William Lane Craig, *Philosophical Foundations for a Christian Worldview* (Downers Grove, IL: InterVarsity Press, 2003); Francis J. Beckwith and Gregory Koukl, *Relativism, Feet Firmly Planted in Mid-Air* (Grand Rapids:

Baker Books, 2005); Mark A. Tabb and John M. Yeats, *Worldviews: Think for Yourself About How We See God* (Colorado Springs, CO: NavPress, 2006); Richard DeWitt, *Worldviews: An Introduction to the History and Philosophy of Science*, 2nd ed. (Malden, MA: Wiley-Blackwell, 2010); Ninian Smart, *Worldviews: Crosscultural Explorations of Human Beliefs*, 3rd ed. (Upper Saddle River, NJ: Prentice Hall, 2000); Ergun Caner, *When Worldviews Collide* (Nashville: LifeWay, 2005); Andrew Hoffecker, *Building a Christian Worldview* (Phillipsburg, NJ: P & R, 1986); and David Burnett, *Clash of Worldviews* (London: Monarch Books, 2002).

[4]Hans Joas, "A Conversation with Robert Bellah," *Hedgehog Review* 14, no. 2 (2012): 72, http://iasc-culture.org/THR/THR_article_2012_Summer_ Interview_Bellah.php.

Chapter 4: Tracing History up to Now

[1]See for example Robert N. Bellah, *Religion in Human Evolution* (Cambridge, MA: Belknap, 2011).

[2]I use throughout the text the traditional classification of eras as marked by the life of Christ as we have done for two thousand years. I do so because I believe this was no error, that, in fact, Christ's appearance, life, death and resurrection marked a cosmic change in time on the earth and in human potentiality.

[3]Antony Flew, *Dictionary of Philosophy* (New York: St. Martin's Press, 1984), p. 330.

[4]See 1 Samuel, 2 Samuel, 1 Chronicles (Saul); 2 Kings, 2 Chronicles (Hezekiah); Daniel (Nebuchadnezzar), Psalm 13 (David) and also Romans 1.

[5]Gary Habermas and Michael Licona, *The Case for the Resurrection of Jesus* (Grand Rapids: Kregel, 2004).

[6]Acts 17:21.

[7]See Acts 17:16-34.

[8]See also Jaroslav Pelikan, *What Has Athens to Do with Jerusalem? Timaeus and Genesis in Counterpoint* (Ann Arbor: University of Michigan Press, 1997).

[9]*The Stanford Encyclopedia of Philosophy*, ed. Edward N. Zalta, winter 2010 ed., s.v., "Stoicism," by Dirk Baltzly, http://plato.stanford.edu/archives /win2010/entries/stoicism.

[10]Flew, *Dictionary of Philosophy*, pp. 339, 108.

[11]Philip Jenkins notes that, though we think of Europe as the first site of Christendom, the earliest Christian communities were actually in the Middle East, Asia and Africa and even extended into China. See Philip Jenkins, *The Lost History of Christianity: The Thousand-Year Golden Age of the Church in the Middle East, Africa, and Asia—and How It Died* (New York: HarperOne, 2008).

[12]Jonathan Hill, *What Has Christianity Ever Done for Us? How It Shaped the Modern World* (Downers Grove, IL: InterVarsity Press, 2005); Jonathan Hill, *The History of Christian Thought* (Downers Grove, IL: InterVarsity Press,

2007); Rodney Stark, *For the Glory of God: How Monotheism Led to Reformations, Science, Witch-hunts, and the End of Slavery* (Princeton, NJ: Princeton University Press, 2003); idem, *The Rise of Christianity: A Sociologist Reconsiders History* (Princeton, NJ: Princeton University Press, 1996); idem, *Cities of God: Christianizing the Urban Empire* (San Francisco: HarperSanFrancisco, 2006); idem, *The Victory of Reason: How Christianity Led to Freedom, Capitalism, and Western Success* (New York: Random House, 2005); and Thomas E. Woods Jr., *How the Catholic Church Built Western Civilization* (Washington, DC: Regnery, 2005).

[13]Alasdair MacIntyre, *God, Philosophy, Universities: A Selective History of the Catholic Philosophic Tradition* (Landham, MD: Rowman & Littlefield, 2009), chap. 8; Woods, *How the Catholic Church Built Western Civilization*, chap. 4; Stark, *For the Glory of God;* Vishal Mangalwadi, *The Book That Made Your World* (Nashville: Thomas Nelson, 2011), chap. 12; and Guenter Risse, *Mending Bodies, Saving Souls* (New York: Oxford University Press, 1999).

[14]George Marsden, *The Soul of the American University: From Protestant Establishment to Established Nonbelief* (New York: Oxford University Press, 1994); see also James T. Burtchaell, *The Dying of the Light: The Disengagement of Colleges and Universities from Their Christian Churches* (Grand Rapids: Eerdmans, 1998).

[15]Lesslie Newbigin, *Foolishness to the Greeks: The Gospel and Western Culture* (Grand Rapids: Eerdmans, 1986), chap. 3.

[16]For example, university mottoes or inscriptions, often written in Latin, Greek or Hebrew, include "the truth shall set you free" (California Institute of Technology, Johns Hopkins University, St. Augustine's University, University of Texas at Austin), "in thy light shall we see light" (Columbia University), "truth for Christ and the church" (Harvard University), "under God's power she flourishes" (Princeton University), "light and truth" (Yale University), "let there be light" (University of California, Berkeley), "the Lord is my light" (University of Oxford), "in God our trust" (George Washington University), "a voice crying out in the wilderness" (Dartmouth College), "laws without morals are useless" (University of Pennsylvania) and "in God we hope" (Brown University). See also Burtchaell, *Dying of the Light.*

[17]Marsden, *Soul of the American University,* pp. 5-6, emphasis added. See also Brad Gregory, *The Unintended Reformation: How a Religious Revolution Secularized Society* (Cambridge, MA: Harvard University Press, 2012).

[18]*Secularization*—"a process of decline in the social influence of religion." *Social Science Dictionary,* accessed May 24, 2013, http://sociology.socialsciencedictionary.com/Sociology-Dictionary/SECULARIZATION.

[19]See, for example, "Pope Benedict XVI Warns Against 'Aggressive Secularism' in Britain," *Telegraph,* September 16, 2010, www.telegraph.co.uk/news/religion/the-pope/8006272/Pope-Benedict-XVI-warns-against-aggressive-secularism-

in-Britain.html; Amy Ellis Nutt, "From Election to Resignation: Highlights of Benedict XVI's Term," *Star/Ledger*, February 12, 2013, www.nj.com/news /index.ssf/2013/02/timeline_for_pope_benedict_xvi.html; and Andres Cala, "In Spain, Pope Benedict XVI Lambasts 'Aggressive Secularism,'" *Christian Science Monitor*, November 7, 2010, www.csmonitor.com/World/Europe/ 2010/1107/In-Spain-Pope-Benedict-XVI-lambasts-aggressive-secularism.

[20]John Henry Newman, *The Idea of a University* (Notre Dame, IN: University of Notre Dame Press, 1982), pp. 31, 33, 39, 75. Newman's lectures in this volume date from 1854-1858.

[21]MacIntyre, *God, Philosophy, Universities*, pp. 146-47.

[22]Julie Reuben, *The Making of the Modern University: Intellectual Transformation and the Marginalization of Morality* (Chicago: University of Chicago Press, 1986), p. 269.

[23]Lesslie Newbigin, *Foolishness to the Greeks: The Gospel in Western Culture* (Grand Rapids: Eerdmans, 1986), pp. 41, 45.

[24]Scott Hahn and Benjamin Wiker, *Politicizing the Bible: The Roots of Historical Criticism and the Secularization of Scripture 1300–1700* (Chestnut Ridge, NY: Crossroad, 2012). See also Ari Goldman, *The Search for God at Harvard* (New York: Random House, 1991)

[25]Eta Linnemann, *Historical Criticism of the Bible: Methodology or Ideology* (Grand Rapids: Kregel, 2001).

[26]Dallas Willard, *Knowing Christ Today: Why We Can Trust Spiritual Knowledge* (New York: HarperOne, 2009), pp. 123-24. Dallas Willard completed two unpublished books prior to his passing: *Gentleness: Apologetics in the Manner of Jesus*, to be published by HarperCollins, and *The Disappearance of Moral Knowledge*, also to be published posthumously. For more information see the interview with Bill Heatley, available at http://blog.epsociety.org/2013/06 /on-dallas-willards-work-interview-with.html?utm_source=feedburner&utm _medium=feed&utm_campaign=Feed%3A+EpsBlog+%28EPS+Blog%29. Also see this excellent treatise on secularism in international relations and politics: Elizabeth Shakman Hurd, *The Politics of Secularism in International Relations* (Princeton, NJ: Princeton University Press, 2008).

[27]Sigmund Koch, *Psychology in Human Context* (Chicago: University of Chicago Press, 1999).

[28]Peter Berger, ed., *The Desecularization of the World: Resurgent Religion and World Politics* (Grand Rapids: Eerdmans, 1999); and John Micklethwait and Adrian Woolridge, *God Is Back* (New York: Penguin, 2010).

[29]Philip Jenkins, *The Next Christendom: The Coming of Global Christianity* (Oxford: Oxford University Press, 2002); idem, *God's Continent: Christianity, Islam, and Europe's Religious Crisis* (Oxford: Oxford University Press, 2007); and Jürgen Habermas, "A 'Post-secular' Society—What Does That Mean?" *Reset Dialogues on Civilizations*, September 16, 2008, www.resetdoc.org/story/00000000926.

[30]Jenkins, *God's Continent.*

[31]Assessing Christianity in the West eludes clear analysis because the largest increases of membership are in loosely affiliated nondenominational churches where many members no longer recognize denominational differences.

[32]J. Habermas, "A 'Post-secular' Society."

[33]Pew Forum on Religion & Public Life, "U.S. Religious Landscape Survey: Religious Affiliation; Diverse and Dynamic," February 2010, http://religions .pewforum.org/pdf/report-religious-landscape-study-full.pdf. See summary at http://religions.pewforum.org/reports.

[34]Neil Gross and Solon Simmons, "How Religious Are America's College and University Professors?" working paper, October 5, 2006, www.epi.soe.vt.edu /perspectives/policy_news/pdf/religions.pdf; Elaine H. Ecklund, "Religion and Spirituality Among University Scientists," *Social Science Research Council,* February 5, 2007, http://religion.ssrc.org/reforum/Ecklund.pdf.

[35]Alexander Astin, Helen Astin and Jennifer Lindholm, *Cultivating the Spirit: How College Can Enhance Students' Inner Lives* (San Francisco: Jossey-Bass, 2011); Alyssa Rockenbach and Matthew Mayhew, *Spirituality in College Students' Lives* (New York: Routledge, 2012).

[36]The full text of the prayer: Almighty God, we give thanks for the presence of our alumni, parents, and friends to share in this great day of celebration, the graduation of Claremont Graduate University's class of 2011. We ask that you be with each and every graduate as they receive their recognition for their great achievement and as they prepare to assume their various roles as leaders and nation builders. May this new cadre of scholars and leaders always remember their enriched knowledge and keep their commitment to social justice. And may they continue to add to this great legacy of excellence that has been established by their predecessors, as they take their places in society. We ask you, God, to never let us forget the bond that we have established during our time at CGU. Amen.

[37]These emails within the university community occurred during the week following graduation on Saturday, May 14, 2011.

[38]Hunter Baker, *The End of Secularism* (Wheaton, IL: Crossway, 2009); George M. Marsden, *The Outrageous Idea of Christian Scholarship* (New York: Oxford University Press, 1997); Steven D. Smith, *The Disenchantment of Secular Discourse* (Cambridge, MA: Harvard University Press, 2010); John Sommerville, *The Decline of the Secular University* (New York: Oxford University Press, 2006); Charles Taylor, *A Secular Age* (Cambridge, MA: Harvard University Press, 2007); Carol Swain, *Be the People* (Nashville: Thomas Nelson, 2011); William F. Buckley, *God and Man at Yale: The Superstitions of Academic Freedom* (Chicago: Regnery, 1951); Charles Malik, *A Christian Critique of the University* (Downers Grove, IL: InterVarsity Press, 1987); and Stephen Carter, *The Culture of Disbelief* (New York: Random House, 1993).

[39]Heewon Chang and Drick Boyd, *Spirituality and Higher Education* (Walnut Creek, CA: Left Coast Press, 2011); Michael Waggoner, *Sacred and Secular Tensions in Higher Education* (New York: Routledge, 2011); and Rob Warner, *Secularization and Its Discontents* (London: Continuum, 2010).

[40]Jürgen Habermas, *Time of Transitions* (Malden, MA: Polity Press, 2006); David Berlinski, *The Devil's Delusion* (New York: Basic Books, 2009); Marcello Pera, *Why We Should Call Ourselves Christian: The Religious Roots of Free Societies,* trans. L. B. Lappin (New York: Encounter Books, 2011); and William Connolly, *Why I Am Not a Secularist* (Minneapolis: University of Minnesota Press, 1999).

[41]Steven Smith, *Disenchantment of Secular Discourse,* pp. 23, 225.

[42]Joseph Ratzinger and Marcello Pera, *Without Roots: The West, Relativism, Christianity, Islam* (New York: Basic Books, 2006); Ratzinger and Pera, *Christianity and the Crisis of Cultures* (New York: Basic Books, 2007); Pera, *Why We Should Call Ourselves Christian: The Religious Roots of Free Societies* (New York: Encounter Books, 2011); Jürgen Habermas and Joseph Ratzinger, *Dialectics of Secularization,* English ed. (San Francisco: Ignatius Press, 2006).

[43]Seymour Martin Lipset and Gabriel Salman Lenz, "Corruption, Culture and Markets," in *Culture Matters: How Values Shape Human Progress,* ed. Lawrence Harrison and Samuel Huntington (New York: Basic Books, 2000), pp. 112-24; and Lawrence Harrison, "Promoting Progressive Cultural Change," in *Culture Matters,* ed. Harrison and Huntington, pp. 296-307.

[44]Niall Ferguson, *Civilization: The West and the Rest* (New York: Penguin Books, 2011), pp. 276-77.

[45]See Alister and Joanna McGrath, *The Dawkins Delusion* (Downers Grove, IL: InterVarsity Press, 2010); John Lennox, *Gunning for God: Why the Atheists Are Missing Their Target* (Oxford: Lion House, 2011); Michael Novak, *No One Sees God* (New York: Doubleday, 2008); Hahn and Wiker, *Answering the New Atheism: Dismantling Dawkins' Case Against God* (Steubenville, OH: Emmaus Road, 2008); Antony Flew, *There Is a God: How the World's Most Notorious Atheist Changed His Mind* (New York: HarperCollins, 2007); David Berlinski, *The Devil's Delusion* (New York: Basic Books, 2009).

[46]Willard, "What Is Skepticism Good For?" February 12, 2013, Claremont Consortium, audio, 82:02, Veritas Forum, www.veritas.org/Talks.aspx#!/v/1314.

Chapter 5: Everything Is a Thing

[1]Alvin Plantinga, "Why Darwinist Materialism Is Wrong," review of *Mind and Cosmos: Why the Materialist Neo-Darwinian Conception of Nature Is Almost Certainly False,"* by Thomas Nagel, *New Republic,* November 16, 2012, www.newrepublic.com/article/books-and-arts/magazine/110189/why-darwinist-materialism-wrong.

[2]I will use Nagel's terminology to indicate both naturalism in science and materialism in philosophy. The following definitions are taken from Antony Flew, *A Dictionary of Philosophy,* 2nd ed. (New York: St. Martin's Press, 1984), pp. 240, 222. Naturalism is "the belief that all that is studied by the non-human and human sciences is all there is, and the denial of the need for any explanation going beyond or outside of the universe." Materialism is "the belief that whatever exists is either matter, or entirely dependent on matter for its existence."

[3]Thomas Nagel, *Mind and Cosmos: Why the Materialist Neo-Darwinian Conception of Nature Is Almost Certainly False* (New York: Oxford University Press, 2012), pp. 14-15.

[4]Thomas Burnett, "What Is Scientism?" *The BioLogos Forum: Science and Faith in Dialogue* (blog), June 11, 2012, http://biologos.org/blog/what-is-scientism.

[5]Phillip Johnson, *The Right Questions: Truth, Meaning & Public Debate* (Downers Grove, IL: InterVarsity Press, 2002).

[6]Nagel, *Mind and Cosmos;* Richard Swinburne, *Is There a God?* rev. ed. (New York: Oxford University Press, 2010); Swinburne, *Mind, Brain, and Free Will* (Oxford: Oxford University Press, 2013); Alvin Plantinga, *Where the Conflict Really Lies: Science, Religion, and Naturalism* (New York: Oxford University Press, 2011); and Jerry A. Fodor and Massimo Piattelli-Palmarini, *What Darwin Got Wrong* (New York: Farrar, Straus & Giroux, 2010).

[7]There are several specifically Christian philosophical societies, for example, The Society of Christian Philosophers (www.societyofchristianphilosophers .com), American Catholic Philosophical Association (www.acpaweb.org) and Evangelical Philosophical Society (www.epsociety.org).

[8]Plantinga, *Where the Conflict Really Lies,* p. 350; see also chap. 10. Also see Plantinga, "The Dawkins Confusion: Naturalism *ad absurdum,*" *Books and Culture,* March/April 2007.

[9]Elaine H. Ecklund, "*Science vs. Religion* Discovers What Scientists Really Think About Religion," *Washington Post,* May 30, 2010; idem, *Science vs. Religion: What Scientists Really Think* (New York: Oxford University Press, 2010); Nancy Frankenberry, *The Faith of Scientists: In Their Own Words* (Princeton, NJ: Princeton University Press, 2008).

[10]See for example The American Scientific Affiliation: A Network of Christians in Sciences, www.asa3.org.

[11]Neil Gross and Solon Simmons, "The Religiosity of American College and University Professors," *Sociology of Religion* 70 (2009): 101–29; working paper published online as "How Religious Are America's College and University Professors?" October 5, 2006, http://musicology.typepad.com/dialm/files/religions.pdf.

[12]Gross and Simmons, "Religiosity of American College and University Professors."

[13]John Lennox, "Stephen Hawking and God," *RZIM,* September 28, 2010, www .rzim.eu/stephen-hawking-and-god, based on idem, "As a Scientist I Am Certain Stephen Hawking Is Wrong: You Can't Explain the Universe Without

God," *MailOnline,* September 3, 2010, www.dailymail.co.uk/debate
/article-1308599/Stephen-Hawking-wrong-You-explain-universe-God.html.
For a full review of the issues of naturalism and Christianity, see John Lennox,
Gunning for God: Why the Atheists Are Missing Their Target (Oxford: Lion
House, 2011).

[14]Epistemological beliefs are those that a person's worldview would count as
valid; naturalists' only methodology is the scientific method.

[15]"A Conversation with Daniel Dennett," interview by Harvey Blume, *Atlantic
online,* December 9, 1998, www.theatlantic.com/past/docs/unbound/digicult
/dennett.htm. See also Daniel C. Dennett, *Consciousness Explained* (Boston:
Little, Brown, 1991); and idem, *Breaking the Spell: Religion as a Natural Phenomenon* (New York: Viking, 2006).

[16]Jerry Fodor, *The Mind Doesn't Work That Way: The Scope and Limits of
Computational Psychology* (Cambridge, MA: MIT Press, 2000).

[17]Plantinga, "Dawkins Confusion."

[18]Plantinga, *Where the Conflict Really Lies,* pp. 313-14.

[19]Swinburne, *Mind, Brain, and Free Will.*

[20]Bertrand Russell, *Mysticism and Logic and Other Essays,* published 1918,
republished in *Bertrand Russell Bundle* (New York: Taylor and Francis, 2009),
p. 39.

[21]The latest book by Stephen Hawking and Leonard Mlodinow, *The Grand
Design* (New York: Bantam, 2010), hypothesized multiple eternal universes
(M-verse). This hypothesis is supposed to support the proposition that our own
universe and our place in it are the result of a fluke that was bound to happen
given so many universes, thus galaxies, stars, planets, etc. Hawking also hypothesized that these universes may be eternal. Prior to *Grand Design,*
Hawking used the actual data from red shift (the evidence that the universe is
still expanding as seen telescopically in a red shift of objects as they move
further away) to indicate the universe had a beginning. In *A Brief History of
Time: From the Big Bang to Black Holes* (New York: Bantam Books, 1988), he
had mentioned the possibility of new discoveries helping us to know the mind
of God, giving reviewers fodder for the God hypothesis, unlike his more recent
book where he argues against God. See for example the differences in the *New
York Times* reviews: Marcia Bartusiak, "What Place for a Creator?" review of
Brief History of Time, by Stephen Hawking, *New York Times,* April 3, 1988,
www.nytimes.com/books/98/12/06/specials/hawking-time.html; and Dwight
Garner, "Many Kinds of Universes, and None Require God," review of *The
Grand Design* by Stephen Hawking, *New York Times,* September 7, 2010,
www.nytimes.com/2010/09/08/books/08book.html.

[22]Jonathan D. Moreno, "The Role of Brain Research in National Defense,"
Chronicle of Higher Education, November 10, 2006, p. B6; see also idem, *Mind
Wars: Brain Research and National Defense* (New York: Dana Press, 2006).

[23]Paul Zak, *The Moral Molecule: The Source of Love and Prosperity* (New York: Penguin, 2012), esp. pp. 39-46.

[24]Ray Kurzweil, *The Singularity Is Near: When Humans Transcend Biology* (New York: Penguin, 2005), esp. chap. 3.

[25]Chuck Colson, "Turning Humans into Martians: Space Travel and Genetics," *BreakPoint*, November 8, 2010, www.breakpoint.org/bpcommentaries /entry/13/15733. See also Tim Cavanaugh, "Human Martians: The People Who Settle the Red Planet May Not Look Like Us," *Reason* 43 (2012), http://reason .com/archives/2012/01/27/human-martians, and Center for Genetics and Society at www.geneticsandsociety.org/index.php. For continual updates on bioethics, see http://tennesseecbc.org.

[26]John Lennox, "John Lennox—The 'Religion vs Science' Myth," *YouTube* video, 9:26, uploaded on May 21, 2010, www.youtube.com/watch?v=bxxFhoKn5Tk; idem, *God's Undertaker: Has Science Buried God?* (Oxford: Lion Hudson, 2009); Ian Hutchinson, *Monopolizing Knowledge* (Belmont, MA: Fias Publishing, 2011).

[27]Proverbs 25:2.

[28]Ecklund, *Science vs. Religion*, p. 155.

[29]Michael King, L. Marston, S. McManus, T. Brugha, H. Meltzer and P. Bebbington, "Religion, Spirituality and Mental Health: Results from a National Study of English Households," *The British Journal of Psychiatry* 202, no. 1 (2013): 68-73. Summaries retrieved from www.guardian.co.uk/comment isfree/belief/2013/jan/09/spiritual-but-not-religious-dangerous-mix and www.psychologytoday.com/blog/unique-everybody-else/201301/troubled-souls-spirituality-mental-health-hazard.

[30]Thomas Woods, *How the Catholic Church Built Western Civilization* (Washington, DC: Regnery, 2005); Rodney Stark, *For the Glory of God: How Monotheism Led to Reformations, Science, Witch-hunts, and the End of Slavery* (Princeton, NJ: Princeton University Press, 2003).

[31]"The Pontifical Academy of Sciences is international in scope, multi-national in composition, and non-sectarian in its choice of members. The work of the Academy comprises six major areas: Fundamental science; Science and technology of global problems; Science for the problems of the developing world; Scientific policy; Bioethics; Epistemology." From the official website, accessed May 24, 2013: www.vatican.va/roman_curia/pontifical_academies/acdscien/.

[32]Frankenberry, *The Faith of Scientists*, p. 6.

[33]See also The American Scientific Affiliation: A Network of Christians in the Sciences, which began in 1941. Visit the website at: http://network.asa3.org/.

[34]Nancy Pearcey, *Total Truth: Liberating Christianity from Its Cultural Captivity* (Wheaton, IL: Crossway Books, 2004), p. 54.

[35]See, for example, Sam Harris, *Free Will* (New York: Free Press, 2012).

[36]Paul Zak, *The Moral Molecule: The Source of Love and Prosperity* (New

York: Dutton, 2013); Dean H. Hamer, *The God Gene: How Faith Is Hard-wired into Our Genes* (New York: Doubleday, 2004). See also discussion by David Barash, "A God Gene?" *Chronicle Higher Education*, June 3, 2012. Also see Mario Beauregard and Denyse O'Leary, *The Spiritual Brain* (New York: HarperOne, 2007); and Andrew Newberg, Eugene D'Aquili and Vince Rause, *Why God Won't Go Away: Brain Science and the Biology of Belief* (New York: Ballantine, 2001).

[37]Tom Bartlett, "Dusting Off God," *The Chronicle of Higher Education*, August 13, 2012. http://chronicle.com/article/Does-Religion-Really-Poison/133457/. Bartlett reviews books by David Sloan Wilson, a professor of biology and anthropology at Binghamton University who argues that religion does not poison everything (a phrase used as a subtitle to Christopher Hitchens's *God Is Not Great*). David Sloan Wilson, *Darwin's Cathedral* (University of Chicago, 2002), and *The Neighborhood Project* (New York: Little Brown, 2011). For an alternate view see Stewart Goetz and Charles Taliaferro, *A Brief History of the Soul* (Chichester, UK: Wiley-Blackwell, 2011).

[38]E. O. Wilson, *The Social Conquest of Earth* (New York: Liveright, 2012), pp. 8, 288.

[39]See Bartlett, "Dusting Off God"; David Sloan Wilson, *Darwin's Cathedral: Evolution, Religion, and the Nature of Society* (Chicago: University of Chicago Press, 2002); and idem *The Neighborhood Project* (New York: Little Brown, 2011).

[40]Alvin Plantinga, a philosopher of science, has the most thorough philosophic explanation of where there is and is not a conflict. See Plantinga, *Where the Conflict Really Lies: Science, Religion, and Naturalism* (New York: Oxford University Press, 2011). Michael Ruse, also a philosopher of science, writes from a non-Christian perspective. See Ruse, *Science and Spirituality: Making Room for Faith in the Age of Science* (New York: Cambridge University Press, 2011).

[41]Plantinga, *Where the Conflict Lies,* p. 265.

[42]Ibid., chap. 9.

[43]Nagel, "A Philosopher Defends Religion," review of *Where the Conflict Really Lies: Science, Religion, and Naturalism,* by Alvin Plantinga, *New York Review of Books,* September 27, 2012.

Chapter 6: Science as the Only Truth

[1]Francis Bacon, *Francis Bacon: The Major Works,* ed. Brian Vickers, (New York: Oxford University Press, 2008); idem, *Francis Bacon: Selected Philosophic Works,* ed. Rose-Mary Sargent (Indianapolis: Hackett, 1999); and "The Translation of Certain Psalms into English Verse," in *The Works of Francis Bacon,* vol. 2 (London, 1826), pp. 535-44. Available online at http://books.google.com/books?vid=OCLC06792219&id=nu4N-M8-laoC&pg=PA533&lpg=PA535&dq=bacon+Psalms&as_brr=1#v=onepage&q=bacon%20Psalms&f=false.

[2]Francis Bacon, *The New Organon*, ed. Lisa Jardine and Michael Silverthorne (Cambridge: Cambridge University Press, 2000), p. 13 in the section titled "Preface to the Great Renewal."

[3]Alvin Plantinga, *Where the Conflict Really Lies: Science, Religion, and Naturalism* (New York: Oxford University Press, 2011).

[4]Charles Kraft, *Defeating Dark Angels: Breaking Demonic Oppression in the Believer's Life* (Ventura, CA: Regal Books, 1992), p. 70.

[5]Sigmund Koch, "The Nature and Limits of Psychological Knowledge: Lessons of a Century Qua 'Science,'" *American Psychologist* 36 (1981): 257-69; and Sigmund Koch, David Finkelman and Frank Kessel, *Psychology in Human Contexts: Essays in Dissidence and Reconstruction* (Chicago: University of Chicago Press, 1999).

[6]Stephen Jay Gould, "Nonoverlapping Magisteria," *Natural History* 106 (1997): 16-22.

Chapter 7: The Purposeless Universe Emerged from Nothing

[1]Lawrence M. Krauss, *A Universe from Nothing: Why There Is Something Rather Than Nothing* (New York: Free Press, 2012). See also David Albert, review of *A Universe from Nothing*, by Lawrence M. Krauss, *New York Times*, March 23, 2012, www.nytimes.com/2012/03/25/books/review/a-universe -from-nothing-by-lawrence-m-krauss.html.

[2]Stephen M. Hawking and Leonard Mlodinow, *The Grand Design* (New York: Random House, 2010).

[3]Donald Garner, "Many Kinds of Universes, and None Require God," review of *The Grand Design*, by Stephen Hawking and Leonard Mlodinow, *New York Times*, September 7, 2010, www.nytimes.com/2010/09/08/books/08book.html.

[4]John Lennox, *God and Stephen Hawking: Whose Design Is It Anyway?* (Oxford: Lion Hudson, 2011), pp. 30-31.

[5]Lennox, "Stephen Hawking and God," *RZIM*, September 28, 2010, www.rzim .eu/stephen-hawking-and-god.

[6]Fred Hoyle, "The Universe: Past and Present Reflections," *Engineering & Science*, November 1981, p. 12; http://calteches.library.caltech.edu/3312/1/ Hoyle.pdf.

[7]Alister McGrath, *Surprised by Meaning: Science, Faith and How We Make Sense of Things* (Louisville, KY: Westminister John Knox Press, 2011). See particularly chapter 8.

[8]Guillermo Gonzalez and Jay Richards, *The Privileged Planet: How Our Place in the Cosmos Is Designed for Discovery* (Washington, DC: Regnery, 2004). See also a five-part lecture by Guillermo Gonzalez, "Our Privileged Planet," University of California, Davis, 2007, *YouTube* video, accessed May 24, 2013, www.youtube.com/watch?v=inUlXooWHbw&feature=PlayList&p=67684557 408B24B6&playnext_from=PL&index=0&playnext=1; Paul Davies, *Cosmic*

Jackpot: Why Our Universe Is Just Right for Life (Boston: Houghton Mifflin, 2007); and various articles at Reasons.org.

[9]Scott Hahn and Benjamin Wiker, *Answering the New Atheism: Dismantling Dawkins' Case Against God* (Steubenville, OH: Emmaus Road, 2008), p. 55.

[10]Antony Flew, *There Is a God: How the World's Most Notorious Atheist Changed His Mind* (New York: HarperCollins, 2007), pp. 88-89.

[11]Antony Flew and Gary Habermas, "My Pilgrimage from Atheism to Theism: A Discussion Between Antony Flew and Gary Habermas," *Philosophia Christi* 6 (2005): 198, transcript at www.biola.edu/antonyflew/flew-interview.pdf.

[12]Thomas Nagel, *Mind and Cosmos: Why the Materialist Neo-Darwinian Conception of Nature Is Almost Certainly False* (New York: Oxford University Press, 2012).

[13]Interview with Jerry Fodor: Thomas Rogers, "'What Darwin Got Wrong': Taking Down the Father of Evolution," *Salon,* February 22, 2010, www.salon.com/2010/02/23/what_darwin_got_wrong_jerry_fodor/.

[14]Stephen Jay Gould, "Abscheulich! (Atrocious!): Haeckel's Distortions Did Not Help Darwin," *Natural History* 109, no. 2 (2000): 42-49; idem, *The Mismeasure of Man* (New York: Norton, 1981); and idem, *Wonderful Life: The Burgess Shale and the Nature of History* (New York: Norton, 1989). See also Gould's essays, "Darwinian Fundamentalism," *New York Review of Books,* June 12, 1997; "Evolution: The Pleasures of Pluralism," *New York Review of Books,* June 26, 1997; and a critique by Lawrence Selden, "Abscheulich!—Atrocious!—Stephen Jay Gould on Haeckel's Fraudulent Drawings in Modern Textbooks," *Darwinian Fundamentalism* (blog), June 19, 2007, http://darwinian fundamentalism.blogspot.com/2007/06abscheulich-atrocious-stephen -jay-gould.html.

[15]David Berlinski, *The Devil's Delusion: Atheism and Its Scientific Pretensions* (New York: Crown Forum, 2008); William A. Dembski, *Intelligent Design: The Bridge Between Science & Theology* (Downers Grove, IL: InterVarsity Press, 1999); William A. Dembski and Sean McDowell, *Understanding Intelligent Design: Everything You Need to Know in Plain Language* (Eugene, OR: Harvest House, 2008), p. 58; and Jonathan Wells, *Icons of Evolution* (Washington, DC: Eagle, 2002). Also see Wells at "Is the 'Science' of Richard Dawkins Science Fiction?" Center for Science and Culture, April 21, 2008, www.dis covery.org/a/4809; and Philip E. Johnson, *Darwin on Trial,* 3rd ed. (Downers Grove, IL: InterVarsity Press, 2010). Also see Johnson's *Reason in the Balance: The Case Against Naturalism in Science, Law & Education* (Downers Grove, IL: InterVarsity Press, 1995); *The Right Questions: Truth, Meaning & Public Debate* (Downers Grove, IL: InterVarsity Press, 2002); and *The Wedge of Truth: Splitting the Foundations of Naturalism* (Downers Grove, IL: InterVarsity Press, 2000).

[16]Nagel, *Mind and Cosmos,* p. 5.

[17]Higher taxon-level disparity refers to the fact that major morphological differences appear before minor variations (lower taxon-level diversity), contradicting Darwinian theory, which predicts a bottom-to-top pattern (minor variations should accumulate and precede major changes). In Darwinian theory, species diversity should precede the disparity that differentiates the major body plans. In natural history, however, disparity precedes diversity. See Stephen Meyer's *Darwin's Doubt* (New York: HarperCollins, 2013). Also see essay by Art Battson at www.veritas-ucsb.org/library/battson/stasis/3.html.

[18]Definitions: *mutation*—an unintended change in a gene, rarely beneficial to an organism; *natural selection*—the primary mechanism theorized as the method by which an organism adapts to its environment by selectively reproducing changes in its genotype, for example, reproducing a mutation that would be beneficial; and *gene exchange*—the initially random fluctuation in genetic expression in small populations that results over time in *genetic drift*.

[19]See, for example, definitions at the *BioLogos* blog, accessed May 24, 2013, http://biologos.org/questions/what-is-evolution.

[20] Daniel Dennett, *Darwin's Dangerous Idea* (New York: Touchstone, 1995), p. 310; and idem, *Breaking the Spell* (New York: Penguin, 2006).

[21]"Daniel Dennett: Darwinian Natural Selection," WGBH Educational Foundation and Clear Blue Sky Productions, 2001 (transcript of interview), www.pbs.org/wgbh/evolution/library/08/1/text_pop/l_081_05.html.

[22]Dennett considers himself one of "the four-horsemen of the anti-apocalypse"; all are radical atheists interested in dispelling belief in religion and God. They include Daniel Dennett (American philosopher of science and cognitive scientist), Richard Dawkins (English evolutionary biologist), Christopher Hitchens (the late English-turned-American journalist and secular humanist) and Sam Harris (American neuroscientist and author). Except for Hitchens, they are material naturalists; Hitchens was primarily a secular humanist.

[23]John Lennox, *God's Undertaker: Has Science Buried God?* (Oxford: Lion Hudson, 2009), pp. 45-48; and idem, *Gunning for God: Why the Atheists Are Missing Their Target* (Oxford: Lion House, 2011).

[24]Thomas Nagel, "The Fear of Religion," review of *The God Delusion,* by Richard Dawkins, *New Republic*, October 23, 2006, www.tnr.com/article/the-fear-religion; see also idem, *Mind and Cosmos*.

[25]See *BioLogos Forum* blog at http://biologos.org/.

[26]Hahn and Wiker, *Answering the New Atheism*, p. 50.

[27]Francis Collins, *The Language of God: A Scientist Presents Evidence for Belief* (New York: Free Press, 2006), pp. 228-29. See also John Polkinghorne, *Belief in God in an Age of Science* (New Haven, CT: Yale University Press, 1998); idem, *The Way the World Is: The Christian Perspective of a Scientist* (London: SPCK, 1992); idem, *Exploring Reality: The Intertwining of Science and Religion* (New Haven, CT: Yale University Press, 2005); Karl Giberson and

Francis Collins, *The Language of Science and Faith* (Downers Grove, IL: InterVarsity Press, 2011); Francis Collins, *The Language of Life: DNA and the Revolution in Personalized Medicine* (New York: Harper, 2010); Darrel Falk, *Coming to Peace with Science: Bridging the Worlds Between Faith and Biology* (Downers Grove, IL: InterVarsity Press, 2004); Ard Louis biography and links to essays at *BioLogos Forum: Science and Faith in Dialogue* (blog), accessed May 24, 2013, http://biologos.org/blog/author/louis-ard; Karl Giberson, *Saving Darwin: How to Be a Christian and Believe in Evolution* (New York: HarperCollins, 2009); and Kenneth Miller, *Finding Darwin's God: A Scientist's Search for Common Ground Between God and Evolution* (New York: Harper Perennial, 1999).

[28]See also Elie Hofer, "Toward an Understanding of Intelligent Design Theory: An Assessment of Francis Collins' Critique of Intelligent Design," MA thesis, Trinity Western University, Victoria, BC, July 2010.

[29]See the "About" page of the BioLogos Foundation website, accessed May 24, 2013, http://biologos.org/about.

[30]See an account of the disagreements between theistic-evolution and intelligent-design advocates at the BioLogos Foundation website, http://biologos .org and at the website for the Center for Science & Culture, www.discovery. org/a/3749. See also Francis Collins, *Language of God* and *Language of Life*; Stephen Meyer, *Signature in the Cell: DNA and the Evidence for Intelligent Design* (New York: HarperCollins, 2009); idem, *Darwin's Doubt* (New York: HarperOne, 2013); William Dembski, *The Design Revolution* (Downers Grove, IL: InterVarsity Press, 2004); and Michael Behe, *Darwin's Black Box: The Biochemical Challenge to Evolution* (New York: Free Press, 2006).

[31]Jerry Fodor and Massimo Piattelli-Palmarini, *What Darwin Got Wrong* (New York: Farrar, Straus and Giroux, 2011), p. xv.

[32]Nagel, *Mind and Cosmos*, pp. 5-6.

[33]Michael D. Lemonick, "Found in South Africa: Key Link in Human Evolution?" *Time,* April 8, 2010, www.time.com/time/health/article/0,8599,1978726,00 .html. In this article on the latest "*Homo*-like" skeleton, *Time* interviews paleontologist Tim White, who explains the arguments.

[34]Dembski and McDowell, *Understanding Intelligent Design*; see chap. 4.

[35]Meyer, *Darwin's Doubt*.

[36]Gould, *Wonderful Life,* p. 57.

[37]Jonathan Wells, *The Politically Incorrect Guide to Darwinism and Intelligent Design* (Washington, DC: Regnery, 2006), p. 32.

[38]Michael Denton, *Evolution: A Theory in Crisis* (Chevy Chase, MD: Adler & Adler, 1986); and idem, *Nature's Destiny: How the Laws of Biology Reveal Purpose in the Universe* (New York: Free Press, 1998).

[39]Jonathan Wells, *Icons of Evolution* (Washington, DC: Regnery), chap. 9; Denton, *Evolution*. See also the following for examples: "No Beneficial Muta-

tions—Not by Chance—Evolution: Theory in Crisis," TheWordisalive, accessed May 24, 2013, www.metacafe.com/watch/4036816/no_beneficial_mutations _not_by_chance_evolution_theory_in_crisis/; and Brian Thomas, "More Mutations Mean More Diseases, Less Evolution," ICR: Institute for Creation Research, August 3, 2012, www.icr.org/article/6933/.

⁴⁰Dembski and McDowell, *Understanding Intelligent Design*; see chap. 3.

⁴¹See Elizabeth Pennisi, "ENCODE Project Writes Eulogy for Junk DNA," *Science* 337, no. 6099 (September 2, 2012): 1159-61; Gina Kolata, "Bits of Mystery DNA, Far from 'Junk,' Play Crucial Role," *New York Times,* September 5, 2012, www .nytimes.com/2012/09/06/science/far-from-junk-dna-dark-matter-proves-crucial-to-health.html?pagewanted=all; Jonathan Wells, *The Myth of Junk DNA* (Seattle: Discovery Institute, 2011); idem, *Icons of Evolution: Science or Myth?* (Washington, DC: Regnery, 2001); Encode Project Consortium, "An Integrated Encyclopedia of DNA Elements in the Human Genome," *Nature,* September 6, 2012, pp. 57-74, www.nature.com/nature/journal/v489/n7414/pdf/ nature11247.pdf.

⁴²Stefan Lovgren, "Chimps, Humans 96 Percent the Same, Gene Study Finds," *National Geographic News,* August 31, 2005, http://news.nationalgeographic .com/news/2005/08/0831_050831_chimp_genes.html.

⁴³Ernie Brannon, personal communication, Moscow, Idaho, October 16, 2010.

⁴⁴Johnson, *Darwin on Trial, Reason in the Balance, The Wedge of Truth* and *The Right Questions.*

⁴⁵Behe, *Darwin's Black Box*; Behe, *The Edge of Evolution* (New York: Free Press, 2008); Meyer, *Signature in the Cell;* idem, *Darwin's Doubt;* Dembski, *Design Revolution;* Dembski and McDowell, *Understanding Intelligent Design;* William Dembski and Jonathan Witt, *Intelligent Design Uncensored* (Downers Grove, IL: InterVarsity Press, 2010); Wells, *Myth of Junk DNA*; idem, *Icons of Evolution;* idem, *Politically Incorrect Guide to Darwinism and Intelligent Design;* Denton, *Evolution;* idem, *Nature's Destiny: How the Laws of Biology Reveal Purpose in the Universe* (New York: Free Press, 1998); Henry F. Schaefer III, *Science and Christianity: Conflict or Coherence?* (Watkinsville, GA: Apollos Trust, 2003); James Gills and Tom Woodward, *Darwinism Under the Microscope* (Lake Mary, FL: Charisma House, 2002); and Ann Gauger, Douglas Axe and Casey Luskin, *Science and Human Origins* (Seattle: Discovery Institute, 2012).

⁴⁶Edward Lee Pitts, "Design Flaw?" *World,* February 26, 2011, www.worldmag .com/articles/17648; see also various reports at the website for the Discovery Institute, www.discovery.org/.

⁴⁷Peter Schmidt, "Ball State U Bars Teaching Intelligent Design as Science," *The Chronicle of Higher Education,* August 1, 2013.

⁴⁸*Expelled: No Intelligence Allowed,* directed by Nathan Frankowski and hosted by Ben Stein (Premise Media Holdings, 2008). For critiques, see Joseph P.

Schloss, "The Expelled Controversy: Overcoming or Raising Walls of Division?" *Counterbalance*, 2008, www.counterbalance.org/expelled/index-frame.html; and Terry Gray, "Jeffrey Schloss Review of Expelled," Expelled: ASA Responds (blog), May 8, 2008, http://www2.asa3.org/groups/expelled/blog/.

[49]Dembski and McDowell, *Understanding Intelligent Design*, pp. 138-43; Behe, *Darwin's Black Box*.

[50]See events and news for the Discovery Institute at www.discovery.org.

[51]See definitions and discussion online at the Discovery Institute—Center for Science and Culture, www.intelligentdesign.org/whatisid.php.

[52]See the statement online at A Scientific Dissent from Darwinism, accessed May 24, 2013, www.dissentfromdarwin.org.

[53]See Ben Wattenberg, "Intelligent Design vs. Evolution," interview of Michael Ruse and Stephen Meyer, on *Think Tank,* aired October 12, 2006, on PBS, transcript at www.pbs.org/thinktank/transcript1244.html.

[54]Berlinski, *The Devil's Delusion: Atheism and Its Scientific Pretensions* (New York: Basic Books, 2009). See also Robert Crowther, "An Interview with Devil's Delusion Author David Berlinski," *Evolution News and Views,* September 23, 2009, www.evolutionnews.org/2009/09/an_interview_with_devils_delus025681.html.

[55]John Lennox, *Seven Days That Divide the World* (Grand Rapids: Zondervan, 2011), chap. 3.

[56]Gerald Schroeder, "The Age of the Universe" (blog), accessed May 24, 2013, www.geraldschroeder.com/AgeUniverse.aspx.

[57]Gerald L. Schroeder is an immigrant from Israel who served on the United States Atomic Energy Commission. His PhD in nuclear physics and earth and planetary sciences is from Massachusetts Institute of Technology. Schroeder's books include *Genesis and the Big Bang: The Discovery of Harmony Between Modern Science and the Bible* (New York: Bantam Books, 1990), *The Science of God* (New York: Free Press, 1997), *The Hidden Face of God* (New York: Free Press, 2002) and *God According to God* (New York: HarperOne, 2010). See Schroeder's biography at www.geraldschroeder.com/About.aspx.

[58]Antony Flew, *There Is a God: How the World's Most Notorious Atheist Changed His Mind* (New York: HarperCollins, 2007).

[59]See the Reasons to Believe website at www.reasons.org/.

[60]See the mission statement at Reasons to Believe, accessed May 24, 2013, www.reasons.org/about/our-mission.

[61]See the following books by Hugh Ross: *The Fingerprint of God: Recent Scientific Discoveries Reveal the Unmistakable Identity of the Creator,* rev. ed. (New Kensington, PA: Whitaker House, 2000); *The Creator and the Cosmos: How the Latest Scientific Discoveries of the Century Reveal God,* 3rd ed. (Colorado Springs, CO: NavPress, 2001); *Beyond the Cosmos: What Recent Dis-*

coveries in Astrophysics Reveal About the Glory and Love of God, 3rd ed.
(Orlando: Signalman, 2010); *A Matter of Days: Resolving a Creation Contro-
versy* (Colorado Springs, CO: NavPress, 2004); *Creation as Science: A Testable
Model Approach to End the Creation/Evolution Wars* (Colorado Springs, CO:
NavPress, 2006); *Why the Universe Is the Way It Is* (Grand Rapids: Baker
Books, 2008); *More Than a Theory: Revealing a Testable Model for Creation,*
repr. ed. (Grand Rapids: Baker Books, 2012); *Hidden Treasures in the Book of
Job: How the Oldest Book in the Bible Answers Today's Scientific Questions*
(Grand Rapids: Baker Books, 2011); with Fazale Rana, Patti Townley-Cover
and Jonathan Price, *What Darwin Didn't Know* (Pasadena, CA: Reasons to
Believe, 2009); with Fazale Rana, *Who Was Adam? A Creation Model Approach to the Origin of Man* (Colorado Springs, CO: NavPress, 2005); and
with Kathy Ross and Jonathan Price, *Genesis One: A Scientific Perspective,*
4th ed. (Glendora, CA: Reasons to Believe, 2006).

[62]See *Seven Days That Divide the World,* by John Lennox (who is neither a
young-earth nor an old-earth creationist). For a discussion of old-earth creationism, see Gerald Schroeder, *Genesis and the Big Bang;* and idem, "The Age
of the Universe," accessed May 24, 2013, www.geraldschroeder.com/AgeUni
verse.aspx. For new-earth creationism, see Henry Morris, *The Beginning of
the World* (Green Forest, AR: Green Leaf Press, 1977).

[63]Henry Morris, *The Biblical Basis for Modern Science* (Grand Rapids: Basic
Books, 1984) idem, *The Revelation Record* (Nashville: Tyndale House, 1993);
idem with Arnold Ehlert, *The Genesis Record* (Grand Rapids: Basic Books,
2009); Ken Ham, ed., *Demolishing Supposed Bible Contradictions* (Green
Forest, AR: Master Books); idem, *The Lie of Evolution* (Green Forest, AR:
Master Books, 2012); idem, *The New Answers Book* (Green Forest, AR: Master
Books, 2007).

[64]See statement at "Explore ICR," Institute for Creation Research, accessed May
24, 2013, www.icr.org/explore.

[65]Lennox, "Stephen Hawking and God."

[66]George M. Church, Yuan Gao and Sriram Kosuri, "Next-Generation Digital
Information Storage in DNA," *Science Express,* August 16, 2012, p. 1628. Published online, August 16, 2012, www.sciencemag.org/content/early/2012
/08/15/science.1226355?explicitversion=tru.

[67]John Polkinghorne, *Belief in God in an Age of Science;* idem, Science and
Theology (Minneapolis: Fortress, 1998); idem with Nicholas Beale, *Questions
of Truth* (Louisville, KY: Westminster John Knox, 2009).

[68]Michael Ruse, "How Evolution Became a Religion," *National Post,* May 13,
2000. This preceded Ruse's books on the subject: *Science and Spirituality:
Making Room for Faith in the Age of Secularism* (New York: Cambridge University Press, 2010) and *Darwinism and Its Discontents* (New York: Cambridge University Press, 2006). See also Ruse, "Is Evolution a Secular Re-

ligion?" *Science* 299 (2003): 1523-24, www.sciencemag.org/content
/299/5612/1523.full; and idem, "Dawkins et al Bring Us into Disrepute,"
Guardian, November 2, 2009, www.guardian.co.uk/commentisfree/belief
/2009/nov/02/atheism-dawkins-ruse.
[69]Richard Swinburne, *Is There a God?* rev. ed. (New York: Oxford University
Press, 2010), p. 2. Also see his extensive website with a large collection of short
video interviews, accessed May 24, 2013: www.closertotruth.com/participant
/Richard-Swinburne/103. Swinburne, a member of the Russian Orthodox
church has also written the following: "The Justification of Theism," Ortho
doxyToday.org: Commentary on Social and Moral Issues of the Day, accessed
May 24, 2013, www.orthodoxytoday.org/articles/SwinburneTheism.php.

Chapter 8: No Miracles Allowed

[1]Todd Burpo, *Heaven Is for Real* (Nashville: Thomas Nelson, 2010). See Lynn
Garrett, "*Heaven Is for Real* Juggernaut Keeps on Rolling," review of *Heaven
Is for Real,* by Todd Burpo, *Publishers Weekly,* March 28, 2012, www.publishers
weekly.com/pw/by-topic/industry-news/religion/article/51238-heaven-is-
for-real-juggernaut-keeps-on-rolling.html.
[2]Akiane's paintings can be seen at this website: http://akiane.com/home. See
also Akiane Kramarik, with Foreli Kramarik, *Akiane: Her Life, Her Art, Her
Poetry* (Nashville: Thomas Nelson, 2006).
[3]Craig Keener, *Miracles: The Credibility of the New Testament Accounts,* vol.
1 (Grand Rapids: Baker Academic, 2011), p. 425.
[4]Candy Gunther Brown, *Testing Prayer: Science and Healing* (Cambridge, MA:
Harvard University Press, 2012); idem, ed., *Global Pentecostal and Charismatic Healing* (Oxford: Oxford University Press, 2011); and Tim Stafford,
"Miracles in Mozambique: How Mama Heidi Reaches the Abandoned," *Christianity Today* 56 (May 2012), p. 18, www.christianitytoday.com/ct/2012/may
/miracles-in-mozambique.html.
[5]Relationships of religion and health are reviewed in the following books:
Harold G. Koenig and Harvey Jay Cohen, eds., *The Link Between Religion and
Health: Psychoneuroimmunology and the Faith Factor* (New York: Oxford
University Press, 2002); and Harold G. Koenig, Michael E. McCullough and
David B. Larson, *Handbook of Religion and Health* (New York: Oxford Uni-
versity Press, 2001).
[6]T. M. Luhrmann, *When God Talks Back: Understanding the American
Evangelical Relationship with God* (New York: Knopf, 2012); Tim Stafford,
Miracles: A Journalist Looks at Modern Day Miracles (Bethany House,
2012); and idem, "Miracles in Mozambique." See also Candy Gunther Brown,
Stephen C. Mory, Rebecca Williams and Michael J. McClymond, "Study of
the Therapeutic Effects of Proximal Intercessory Prayer on Auditory and
Visual Impairments in Rural Mozambique," *Southern Medical Journal* 103,

no. 9 (September 2010): 864-69.

[7]Barbara Bradley Hagerty, *Fingerprints of God: What Science Is Learning About the Brain and Spiritual Experience* (New York: Penguin Books, 2009), p. 283.

[8]Keener, *Miracles*, vol. 1, p. 213.

[9]For those interested, see Heidi Baker, *Always Enough: God's Miraculous Provision Among the Poorest Children on Earth* (Grand Rapids: Baker Books, 2003); *Transformations I and II Films,* produced by Sentinel Group and hosted by George Otis Jr. (1999, 2001); *Finger of God,* produced by Darren Wilson and Wanderlust Productions (2006); *Furious Love,* produced by Wanderlust Productions (2007); and C. Peter Wagner and Pablo Deiros, *The Rising Revival: Firsthand Accounts of the Incredible Argentine Revival* (Ventura, CA: Regal, 1998). See Juan Zucarelli's article on prison ministry in Argentina, "God's Kingdom in Olmos Prison," chap. 10 in Wagner and Deiros, *Rising Revival;* and Ed Silvoso, *Marketplace Miracles: Extraordinary Stories of Marketplace Turnarounds Transforming Businesses, Schools, and Communities* (Ventura, CA: Regal, 2008).

[10]For example, Matthew 9:22; Mark 5:34; Luke 8:48.

[11]Charles Kraft, *Christianity with Power: Your Worldview and Your Experience of the Supernatural* (Ann Arbor, MI: Vine Books, 1989), pp. 4-5.

[12]Michael Ruse, *Science and Spirituality* (Cambridge: Cambridge University Press), p. 205.

[13]Alvin Plantinga, *Where the Conflict Really Lies: Science, Religion, and Naturalism* (New York: Oxford University Press, 2011), pp. 130, 118.

[14]Lesslie Newbigin, *Foolishness to the Greeks: The Gospel and Western Culture* (Grand Rapids: Eerdmans, 1986), p. 45.

[15]Ibid., p. 45.

[16]C. S. Lewis, *Miracles* (New York: Collier, 1978), pp. 60-61.

[17]G. K. Chesterton, *Orthodoxy* (Nashville: Thomas Nelson, 2000), pp. 279-80.

[18]British novelist C. P. Snow wrote about the intellectual split between those in the sciences and those in the humanities who each saw the other as illiterate in the opposing fields. His essays regarding these two worlds were published in several places in Britain and the United States in the 1950s. See C. P. Snow, *The Two Cultures and the Scientific Revolution* (Cambridge: Cambridge University Press, 1960).

[19]Ruse, *Science and Spirituality: Making Room for Faith in the Age of Science* (New York: Cambridge University Press, 2010), p. 206.

[20]Newbigin, *Foolishness to the Greeks,* p. 62, emphasis added. See also Gary Habermas and Michael Licona, *The Case for the Resurrection of Jesus* (Grand Rapids: Kregel, 2004); N. T. Wright, *The Resurrection of the Son of God* (Minneapolis: Fortress, 2003); Michael Licona, *The Resurrection of Jesus* (Downers Grove, IL: InterVarsity Press, 2010).

Chapter 9: The Ethics of Things upon Things

[1]Romans 3:1-2: "Then what advantage has the Jew? Or what is the value of circumcision? Much in every way. To begin with, the Jews were entrusted with the oracles of God." Elsewhere Paul calls the Jews "children of the promise" (see Romans 9:8). Throughout the Hebrew Scriptures they are "the people of God."

[2]Richard Weikart, *From Darwin to Hitler: Evolutionary Ethics, Eugenics, and Racism in Germany* (New York: Palgrave Macmillan, 2004), pp. 232-33.

[3]Darwin, *The Descent of Man, and Selection in Relation to Sex,* Works of Charles Darwin, vol. 21 (Princeton, NJ: Princeton University Press, 1981), p. 168.

[4]Darwin, *Descent of Man,* p. 169.

[5]Whereas the US Armed Forces allow for pacifists to be conscientious objectors (even though we now have an entirely volunteer army), the government wants to require doctors to perform abortions and prescribe abortive medication and businesses to pay for them, regardless of conscience. See the articles that address this on the United States Conference of Catholic Bishops website, accessed May 24, 2013: www.usccb.org/issues-and-action/religious-liberty/conscience-protection/. See also Mark R. Wicclair, *Conscientious Objection in Health Care: An Ethical Analysis* (Cambridge: Cambridge University Press, 2011); Benedict M. Ashley, Jean deBlois and Kevin D. O'Rourke, *Health Care Ethics: A Catholic Theological Analysis,* 5th ed. (Washington, DC: Georgetown University Press, 2007); and Robert George, *Conscience and Its Enemies* (Wilmington, DE: Intercollegiate Studies Institute, 2013).

[6]Hannah Arendt, *The Origins of Totalitarianism* (New York: Harcourt, Brace & World, 1968).

[7]See, for example, Watchman Nee, *The Spiritual Man* (1928; repr., New York: Christian Fellowship Publishers, 1968).

[8]Anne Hendershott, *The Politics of Abortion* (New York: Encounter Books, 2006); Erika Bachiochi, ed., *The Cost of Choice: Women Evaluate the Impact of Abortion* (San Francisco: Encounter Books, 2004); Theresa Burke with David C. Reardon, *Forbidden Grief: The Unspoken Pain of Abortion* (Springfield, IL: Acorn Books, 2007); Miriam Grossman, *Unprotected: A Campus Psychiatrist Reveals How Political Correctness in Her Profession Endangers Every Student* (New York: Penguin, 2007); Joe S. McIlhaney and Freda McKissic Bush with Stan Guthrie, *Girls Uncovered: New Research on What America's Sexual Culture Does to Young Women* (Chicago: Northfield, 2011); David M. Fergusson, L. John Horwood and Elizabeth M. Ridder, "Abortion in Young Women and Subsequent Mental Health," *Journal of Child Psychology and Psychiatry* 47, no. 1 (2006): 16-24; Willy Pedersen, "Abortion and Depression: A Population-Based Longitudinal Study of Young Women," *Scandinavian Journal of Public Health* 36, no. 4 (2008): 424-28; G. Kam Congleton and Lawrence G. Calhoun, "Post-Abortion Perceptions: A Comparison of Self-Identified Distress and Nondistress Populations," *International Journal of*

Social Psychiatry 39, no. 4 (1993): 255-65, http://isp.sagepub.com/content/39/4/255; and JoAnn Trybulski, "The Long-Term Phenomena of Women's Postabortion Experiences," *Western Journal of Nursing Research* 27, no. 5 (2005): 559-76.

[9] Eric Metaxas, "Gushing over the Royal Fetus," December 18, 2012, http://links.mkt3980.com/servlet/MailView?ms=NTMwMjM3NgS2&r=OTQoMjM1MzAoSo&j=NjExMTkyNTMS1&mt=1&rt=0.

[10] Abby Johnson, *Unplanned* (Colorado Springs, CO: Focus on the Family, 2010).

[11] Carol Swain, *Be the People: A Call to Reclaim America's Faith and Promise* (Nashville: Thomas Nelson, 2011); Hendershott, *The Politics of Abortion;* and Chuck Colson, "Fighting U.N. Abortion Culture: Pointing the Way from San José," *BreakPoint,* October 28, 2011, www.breakpoint.org/bpcommentaries /entry/13/18110; see the San Jose Articles: Abortion and the Unborn Child in International Law at www.sanjosearticles.com/.

[12] Ed O'Keefe, "Bill Banning 'Sex-Selective Abortions' Fails in the House," *WP Politics* (blog), May 31, 2012, www.washingtonpost.com/blogs/2chambers /post/bill-banning-sex-selective-abortions-fails-in-the-house/2012/05/31 /gJQAgCYn4U_blog.html.

[13] Mara Hvistendahl, *Unnatural Selection: Choosing Boys over Girls, and the Consequences of a World Full of Men* (Philadelphia: Perseus, 2012).

[14] Colson, "Worldview Blinders: 'Missing' Women and Abortion on Demand," *Break-Point,* July 18, 2011, www.breakpoint.org/bpcommentaries/entry/13/17480.

[15] Ming Wang et al., "Reduction in Corneal Haze and Apoptosis by Amniotic Membrane Matrix in Excimer Laser Photoablation in Rabbits," *Journal of Cataract & Refractive Surgery* 27, no. 2 (2001): 310-19, abstract at www.jcrs journal.org/article/S0886-3350(00)00467-3/abstract.

[16] Daniel Moynihan, "Defining Deviancy Down," *American Scholar* 62, no. 1 (1993): 17-30, www2.sunysuffolk.edu/formans/DefiningDeviancy.htm.

[17] Hendershott, *Politics of Abortion,* pp. 24-25.

[18] Sam Harris, *Free Will* (New York: Free Press, 2012); and idem, *The Moral Landscape: How Science Can Determine Human Values* (New York: Free Press, 2010).

[19] One such claim was debated at Stanford in 1994 between naturalist professor William Provine and Christian law professor Phillip Johnson, "Darwinism: Science or Naturalistic Philosophy?" April 30, 1994. See a video guide at www .arn.org/docs/guides/stan_gd1.htm; see films beginning with www.youtube .com/watch?v=AM-H6NxdCd4.

[20] Edward O. Wilson, *The Social Conquest of Earth* (New York: Norton, 2012), p. 288.

[21] Wilson, *Social Conquest of Earth,* pp. 292-93.

[22] "The Brights," who call themselves "the four horsemen of the anti-apocalypse" on their common atheist Facebook page, and other radical atheists bristle at

the suggestion that their worldview contains no safeguards to prevent abominations or even define "unprincipled actions." In reality there are no permanent moral principles in their worldview to inhibit the cruel applications of scientific knowledge and totalitarian power. A culture under material naturalism's grips is entirely dependent on particular elite and powerful naturalistically reasoned choices and their individual interpretations of what the Brights call "principled actions to bear on matters of civic importance." See a statement of the Brights' principles at "Is Your Worldview Naturalistic?" *The Brights,* accessed May 24, 2013, www.the-brights.net.

[23]Thomas Nagel, *The View from Nowhere* (Oxford: Oxford University Press, 1986), p. 79.

[24]Peter Singer, *Practical Ethics,* 2nd ed. (New York: Cambridge University Press, 1993); idem, *The Expanding Circle: Ethics, Evolution, and Moral Progress* (Princeton, NJ: Princeton University Press, 2011); idem, *Animal Liberation: The Definitive Classic of the Animal Movement,* updated ed. (New York: Ecco Book/Harper Perennial, 2009); and Mark Oppenheimer, "Who Lives? Who Dies? The Utility of Peter Singer," *Christian Century,* July 3-10, 2002, pp. 24-29, www.religion-online.org/showarticle.asp?title=2659.

[25]See, for example, "Noam Chomsky and Peter Singer on Abortion," taken from *Lake of Fire,* a 2006 documentary directed by Tony Kaye: www.youtube.com /watch?v=rzYoL2g1f64.

[26]Chris Gabbard, "A Life Beyond Reason," *Chronicle of Higher Education,* November 7, 2010.

[27]George Will, "Jon Will's Gift," *Washington Post,* May 2, 2012, www.washing tonpost.com/opinions/jon-will-40-years-and-going-with-down-syndrome /2012/05/02/gIQAdGiNxT_story.html.

[28]Caroline Mansfield, Suellen Hopfer and Theresa M. Marteau, "Termination Rates After Prenatal Diagnosis of Down Syndrome, Spina Bifida, Anencephaly, and Turner and Klinefelter Syndromes: A Systematic Literature Review, *Prenatal Diagnosis* 19, no. 9 (1999): 808-12; David W. Britt et al., "Determinants of Parental Decisions After the Prenatal Diagnosis of Down Syndrome: Bringing in Context," *American Journal of Medical Genetics* 93, no. 5 (1999): 410-16.

[29]Ellen Hsu, "The Day We Let Our Son Live," *Christianity Today,* November 2, 2009, www.christianitytoday.com/women/2009/november/day-we-let-our-son-live.html.

[30]*Stanford Encyclopedia of Philosophy,* ed. Edward N. Zalta, summer 2009 edition, s.v. "Jürgen Habermas," by James Bohman and William Rehg, http:// plato.stanford.edu/archives/sum2009/entries/habermas/.

[31]*Bureaucracy*—Max Weber's definition of the word refers to the process by which modes of precise calculation based on observation and reason increasingly dominate the social world.

[32]Milo Yiannopoulos, "WYD 2011: Pope Offers Challenges to Young Professors

and Religious," *Catholic Herald*, August 19, 2011.

[33]Alberto Giubilini and Francesca Minerva, "After-Birth Abortion: Why Should the Baby Live?" *Journal of Medical Ethics* 39, no. 5 (2012): 261-63; Julian Savulescu, *JME* editor, "Why Did the Journal Publish an Article Defending Infanticide?" *Practical Ethics: Ethics in the News* (blog), March 3, 2012, http://blog.practicalethics.ox.ac.uk/2012/03/why-did-the-journal-publish-an-article-defending-infanticide/.

[34] C. S. Lewis, *The Weight of Glory* (New York: HarperCollins, 2001), pp. 114-15.

Chapter 10: Countering God as Creator

[1]To see two videos of such experiments with NASA using the Hubble telescope, go to "Hubble Ultra Deep Field 3D: What Happens When You Point the Hubble Space Telescope to a Seemingly Blank Patch of Sky?" accessed May 24, 2013, www.flixxy.com/hubble-ultra-deep-field-3d.htm#.UWbybRwoQqk; and "How Many Galaxies Are There in the Universe? The Redder We Look, the More We See," *Discover* (The Crux blog), October 10, 2012, http://blogs.discovermag azine.com/crux/2012/10/10/how-many-galaxies-are-there-in-the-universe-the-redder-we-look-the-more-we-see/#.UXArAxwoQqk.

[2]John Lennox, *The Seven Days That Divide the World: The Beginning According to Genesis and Science* (Grand Rapids: Zondervan, 2011).

[3]Michael Ruse, *Science and Spirituality: Making Room for Faith in the Age of Secularism* (Cambridge: Cambridge University Press, 2010), p. 233.

Chapter 11: Man Makes Himself and His World

[1]"A Secular Humanist Declaration," Council for Secular Humanism, issued in 1980, www.secularhumanism.org/index.php?page=declaration &section=main.

[2]Hunter Baker, *The End of Secularism* (Wheaton, IL: Crossway, 2009), p. 108.

[3]See American Humanist Association, www.americanhumanist.org/AHA /Frequently_Asked_Questions.

[4]John Dewey, *A Common Faith* (New Haven, CT: Yale University Press, 1960).

[5]Signed by John Dewey and many Unitarian leaders. See "Humanist Manifesto I," American Humanist Association, 1933, 1973, accessed May 24, 2013, www .americanhumanist.org/Humanism/Humanist_Manifesto_I.

[6]Signed by Isaac Asimov, B. F. Skinner, Antony Flew, Francis Crick, Albert Ellis and many others, including a good number of professors of theology and religion. See "Humanist Manifesto II," American Humanist Association, 1973, accessed May 24, 2013, www.americanhumanist.org/Humanism/Humanist _Manifesto_II.

[7]Signed by E. O. Wilson, Kurt Vonnegut, Oliver Stone and others: "Humanism and Its Aspirations," American Humanist Association, accessed May 24, 2013, www .americanhumanist.org/Humanism/Humanist_Manifesto_III/Notable_Signers.

[8]Signed by B. F. Skinner, Albert Ellis, Francis Crick and Isaac Asimov.

[9]Mitchell Landsberg, "Religious Skeptics Disagree on How Aggressively to Challenge the Devout," *Los Angeles Times,* October 10, 2010, http://articles .latimes.com/2010/oct/10/local/la-me-humanists-20101010; and Mark Oppenheimer, "Atheists Debate How Pushy to Be," *New York Times,* October 15, 2010, www.nytimes.com/2010/10/16/us/16beliefs.html?_r=0.

[10]Paul Kurtz, "Apologia: Open Letter to Friends and Colleagues in the Center for Inquiry/Transnational movement," May 18, 2010, http://paulkurtz.net/apo logia.htm; "The Future of Secular Humanism," coverage of the Council for Secular Humanism conference, October 7-10, 2010, *SuperScholar,* www.su perscholar.org/the-future-of-secular-humanism/.

[11]Tom Flynn, "Secular Humanism Defined," Council for Secular Humanism, accessed May 24, 2013, www.secularhumanism.org/index.php?section=main &page=sh_defined5.

[12]"Amsterdam Declaration 2002," International Humanist and Ethical Union, submitted June 11, 2008, www.iheu.org/adamdecl.htm.

[13]David Bentley Hart, *Atheist Delusions: The Christian Revolution and Its Fashionable Enemies* (New Haven, CT: Yale University Press, 2009), p. 106.

[14]Salman Rushdie, "The Book Burning," *The New York Review of Books,* March 2, 1989, p. 26.

[15]Jean Bethke Elshtain, *Just War Against Terror: The Burden of American Power in a Violent World* (New York: Basic Books, 2003), p. 212.

[16]Philip Jenkins, *The Lost History of Christianity: The Thousand-Year Golden Age of the Church in the Middle East, Africa, and Asia—and How It Died* (New York: HarperCollins, 2009).

[17]Ibid. See also Rodney Stark, *God's Battalions: The Case for the Crusades* (New York: HarperCollins, 2009); Alan Wolfe, "The Reason for Everything," review of *The Victory of Reason: How Christianity Led to Freedom, Capitalism, and Western Success,* by Rodney Stark, *New Republic Online,* February 2, 2006, www.powells.com/review/2006_02_02.html; and Hart, *Atheist Delusions.*

[18]Hart, *Atheist Delusions,* p. 84.

[19]Ibid., esp. pp. 51-53.

[20]Ibid., p. 80.

[21]Ibid., pp. 72-78.

[22]C. S. Lewis, *Mere Christianity* (New York: HarperCollins, 2001), p. 14.

[23]Hart, *Atheist Delusions,* p. 9.

[24]Lewis, *Mere Christianity* (New York: Collier Books, 1960), p. 177, emphasis added.

[25]"Oxfam International Annual Report 2008-2009," Oxfam International, www .oxfam.org/sites/www.oxfam.org/files/oxfam-international-annual-report-2008-09.pdf.

[26]"Charity Review: United Way Worldwide," BBB Wise Giving Alliance, www .bbb.org/charity-reviews/national/human-services/united-way-worldwide -in-alexandria-va-1994.

[27]Tony Blair, "Debating Christopher Hitchens on Faith," *Washington Post*, November 29, 2010, http://onfaith.washingtonpost.com/onfaith/guest-voices/2010/11/tony_blair_on_religion.html.

[28]Vishal Mangalwadi, *The Book That Made Your World: How the Bible Created the Soul of Western Civilization* (Nashville: Thomas Nelson, 2011); and Thomas E. Woods Jr., *How the Catholic Church Built Western Civilization: Distinguishing Fact from Fiction About Catholicism* (Washington, DC: Regnery, 2005).

[29]"2011 Annual Review," *World Vision,* accessed May 2013, www.worldvision.org/content.nsf/about/ar-financials.

[30]Catholic Charities USA, accessed June 2012, www.catholiccharitiesusa.org/Document.Doc?id=2331.

[31]"The CRS 2010 Annual Report," Catholic Relief Services, http://crs.org/2010-annual-report/.

[32]"Financials," Christian Foundation for Children and Aging, accessed May 24, 2013, www.cfcausa.org/AboutUs/Financials.aspx.

[33]See the following resources: George Will, "Conservatives More Liberal Givers," *Real Clear Politics,* March 27, 2008, www.realclearpolitics.com/articles/2008/03/conservatives_more_liberal_giv.html; Arthur Brooks, *Who Really Cares: The Surprising Truth About Compassionate Conservatism* (New York: Basic Books, 2006); idem, "Religious Faith and Charitable Giving," Hoover Institution, Stanford University, October 1, 2003, www.hoover.org/publications/policy-review/article/6577; and Nicholas D. Kristof, "Bleeding Heart Tightwads," *New York Times,* December 20, 2008, www.nytimes.com/2008/12/21/opinion/21kristof.html.

[34]Emmanuel Sarpong Owusu-Ansah, "African Beggars on Strike," *Modern Ghana,* November 7, 2011, www.modernghana.com/news/359658/1/african-beggars-on-strike.html; "Gambia Says No to Aid Money Tied to Gay Rights," *VibeGhana.com,* April 24, 2012, http://vibeghana.com/2012/04/24/gambia-says-no-to-aid-money-tied-to-gay-rights/; "British PM Under Attack in Ghana, Zambia for Gay Rights Aid Cut Comments," *African Outlook,* 2011, www.africanoutlookonline.com/index.php?option=com_content&view=artic le&id=3177:british-pm-under-attack-in-ghana-zambia-for-gay-rights-aid-cut-comments; and Mfonobong Nsehe, "Obama Fights Nigerian Anti-Gay Bill, Threatens to Cut Off Aid," *Forbes,* December 9, 2011, www.forbes.com/sites/mfonobongnsehe/2011/12/09/obama-fights-nigerian-anti-gay-bill-threatens-to-cut-off-aid.

Chapter 12: Radical Individual Freedom

[1]"A Secular Humanist Declaration," Council for Secular Humanism, issued 1980, accessed May 24, 2013, www.secularhumanism.org/index.php?section=main&page=declaration; and Paul Kurtz, "In Defense of Eupraxsophy," *Hu-*

manism Today 6 (1991): 78-86, www.humanismtoday.org/vol6/kurtz.pdf.

[2]Jon Shields, *The Democratic Virtues of the Christian Right* (Princeton, NJ: Princeton University Press, 2009), p. 157.

[3]Steven Smith, *The Disenchantment of Secular Discourse* (Cambridge, MA: Harvard University Press, 2010), p. 27.

[4]Robert George, *Conscience and Its Enemies* (Wilmington, DE: Intercollegiate Studies Institute, 2013).

[5]"The Survey of Religious Hostility in America," Liberty Institute, http://liberty institute.org/pages/survey-of-religious-hostilities.

[6]George, *Conscience and Its Enemies*, p. 114.

[7]J. Budziszewski, *What We Can't Not Know*, rev. ed. (San Francisco: Ignatius Press, 2011), p. 19.

[8]Ibid., p. 26.

[9]"Archbishop Cardileone States Case Against Gay Marriage," Interview with *USA Today*, March 21, 2013, www.usatoday.com/story/news/nation /2013/03/21/archbishop-cordileone-gay-marriage-catholic-church /2001085.

[10]Rosaria Champagne Butterfield, *The Secret Thoughts of an Unlikely Convert: An English Professor's Journey into Christian Faith* (Pittsburgh, PA: Crown and Covenant Publications, 2012), pp. 8, 21, 25. See also Wesley Hill, *Washed and Waiting: Reflections on Christian Faithfulness and Homosexuality* (Grand Rapids: Zondervan, 2010).

[11]John Rawls, *A Theory of Justice* (1971; repr., Cambridge, MA: Harvard University, 2005), p. 388.

[12]Smith, *Disenchantment of Secular Discourse*, p. 6.

[13]Mary Ann Glendon, "Why the Bishops Are Suing the U.S. Government," *Wall Street Journal*, May 21, 2012, http://online.wsj.com/article/SB10001424052 702303610504577418201554329764.html.

[14]Mary Ann Glendon, responding to *The Naked Public Square*, by Richard John Neuhaus, in *First Things*, November 2004, www.firstthings.com/article /2009/02/001-the-naked-public-44. See also Glendon, *How the West Really Lost God* (West Conshohocken, PA: Templeton Press, 2013).

[15]George Will, "Conformity for Diversity's Sake," *Washington Post*, November 2, 2011, www.washingtonpost.com/opinions/conformity-for-diversitys-sake /2011/11/01/gIQAUBOmgM_print.html.

[16]R. R. Reno, "Religion and Public Life in America," Speech at Hillsdale College, *Imprimis*, April 2013. See also John Stonestreet, "Wake-Up Calls: Defending Our Religious Freedoms," *Breakpoint*, June 13, 2013, www.breakpoint.org /bpcommentaries/entry/13/22502.

[17]Similar efforts to quell religious expression had already taken place at Hastings Law School (UC) and Tufts, Arizona State, San Diego State, Southern Illinois, Rutgers and Montana State University, to name only a few. The University of

Texas and a few others have allowed for exemptions; their policy states: "An organization created primarily for religious purposes may restrict the right to vote or hold office to persons who subscribe to the organization's statement of faith." The following are just a few cases, many of which have seriously limited Christian student organizations' religious freedoms. All articles are from *The Chronicle of Higher Education*: Peter Schmidt, "Supreme Court Appears Split Over Law and Facts in Case Involving Christian Student Group," April 20, 2010; Thomas Bartlett, "Law School Can Deny Recognition to Christian Group That Bans Gay and Lesbian Students, Judge Rules," May 5, 2006; Beckie Supiano, "A Group for Secular Students Finds Its Way on a Christian Campus," February 27, 2011; Thomas Bartlett, "Southern Ill. Settles With Christian Group," June 1, 2007; Josh Keller, "Federal Appeals Court Ends Christian Student Group's Suit Against Law School," November 17, 2010; Sara Lipka, "Arizona State U. Allows Christian Group to Bar Gay Members," September 16, 2005; Peter Schmidt, "Christian Legal Society and Montana Law School Settle Dispute," August 11, 2011; Eric Kelderman, "Appeals Court Upholds San Diego State's Nondiscrimination Policy for Student Groups," August 2, 2011; Thomas Bartlett, "University Must Recognize Christian Group Pending Outcome of Lawsuit, Appeals Court Rules," July 21, 2006; "Not All Students Can Be Leaders in Religious Groups," March 4, 2005; Thomas Bartlett, "Christian Student Group Prevails in Dispute with Southern Illinois U. at Carbondale," May 24, 2007; Megan Rooney, "Rutgers Settles Lawsuit With Christian-Student Group," April 3, 2003.

[18]Syllabus, Supreme Court of the United States, Christian Legal Society Chapter of the University of California, *Hastings College of Law v. Martinez et al.* (2010), www.supremecourt.gov/opinions/09pdf/08-1371.pdf.

[19]Carol Swain's Testimony to the Civil Rights Commission on March 22, 2013.

[20]Carol Swain, *Be the People: A Call to Reclaim America's Faith and Promise* (Nashville: Thomas Nelson, 2011), p. 10.

[21]Miriam Grossman, *Unprotected* (New York: Penguin, 2007); and Frederica Mathewes-Green, *Real Choices: Listening to Women; Looking for Alternatives to Abortion* (Ben Lomond, CA: Conciliar Press, 1997).

[22]Nathan Harden, *Sex and God at Yale* (New York: St. Martin's Press), p. 285.

[23]Marcello Pera, *Why We Should Call Ourselves Christian: The Religious Roots of Free Societies* (New York: Encounter Books, 2011). For a review, see Michael Novak, "A Western Blueprint: An Atheist Defends the Judeo-Christian Ethic," *Weekly Standard*, October 24, 2011, www.weeklystandard.com/author /michael-novak. See also Jürgen Habermas, *Time of Transitions* (Cambridge: Polity, 2006), part 7; and David Berlinski, *The Devil's Delusion: Atheism and Its Scientific Pretensions* (New York: Basic Books, 2009).

[24]Edward Gibbon, *The History of the Decline and Fall of the Roman Empire, Selections* (London: Penguin, 2000), p. 35.

²⁵Will Durant, *Our Oriental Heritage*, vol. 1 of *The Story of Civilization* (New York: MJF Books, 1997), p. 71.

²⁶Robert Putnam and David E. Campbell with Shaylyn Romney Garrett, *American Grace: How Religion Divides and Unites Us* (New York: Simon & Schuster, 2010).

²⁷Smith, *Disenchantment of Secular Discourse,* p. 116.

²⁸Martin Luther King Jr., "Letter from a Birmingham Jail [King, Jr.]," African Studies Center, University of Pennsylvania, April 16, 1963, www.africa.upenn .edu/Articles_Gen/Letter_Birmingham.html.

²⁹Richard Wurmbrand, *Tortured for Christ* (1967; repr., Bartlesville, OK: Living Sacrifice Book, 1993).

³⁰*Rationalization* "is a habit of thought that replaces tradition, emotion, and values as motivators of human conduct. Bureaucracy is a particular case of rationalization applied to human social organization." Definition from *Social Science Dictionary,* http://sociology.socialsciencedictionary.com/Sociology-Dictionary/rationalization.

³¹Aleksandr Solzhenitsyn, *Gulag Archipelago*, vol. 1 (New York: Harper Perennial Reissue, 2002), p. 312.

³²See 1 John 1:9.

Chapter 13: Varieties of Secular Humanism

¹*Dictionary of Philosophy,* ed. Antony Flew, rev. 2nd ed. (New York: St. Martin's Press, 1984), s.v. "Romanticism," p. 307.

²Jean-Jacques Rousseau, *Emile: or, On Education,* with introduction and translation by Allan Bloom (New York: Basic Books, 1979).

³*Stanford Encyclopedia of Philosophy,* ed. Edward N. Zalta, summer 2011 edition, s.v. "Karl Marx," by Jonathan Wolff, http://plato.stanford.edu/archives /sum2011/entries/marx, section 2.3, Economic and Philosophic Manuscripts.

⁴James W. Sire, *The Universe Next Door: A Basic Worldview Catalog,* 5th ed. (Downers Grove, IL: InterVarsity Press, 2009); Donald De Marco and Benjamin D. Wiker, *Architects of the Culture of Death* (San Francisco: Ignatius Press, 2004); and Flew, *Dictionary of Philosophy.*

⁵Sara Murray, "Nearly Half of U.S. Lives in Household Receiving Government Benefit," Real Time Economics (blog), *Wall Street Journal,* October 5, 2011, http://blogs.wsj.com/economics/2011/10/05/nearly-half-of-households-receive-some-government-benefit/.

⁶Michael Novak, *Business as a Calling: Work and the Examined Life* (New York: Free Press, 1996), p. 81.

⁷Novak, "An Apology for Democratic Capitalism," *First Things,* January 2009, www.firstthings.com/article/2008/12/004-an-apology-for-democratic-capitalism-2. See Novak's classic work, *The Spirit of Democractic Capitalism* (Aurora, CO: Madison Books, 1990).

[8]Katherine Magnuson and Jane Waldfogel, *Steady Gains and Stalled Progress* (New York: Russell Sage Foundation, 2011); Amanda Pawlson, "Achievement Gaps Narrowing in US Schools since NCLB," *Christian Science Monitor,* October 1, 2009; and Matthew Springer, "The Influence of NCLB Accountability Plan on the Distribution of Student Test Score Gains," *Economics of Education Review,* 2008, www.vanderbilt.edu/schoolchoice/documents /influence_nclbaccountability.pdf.

[9]"Mary Poplin Interview," *SuperScholar,* www.superscholar.org/interviews/ mary-poplin/.

[10]John-Paul Sartre, *Nausea,* trans. Lloyd Alexander (New York: New Directions Press, 1959), p. 79.

[11]Friedrich Nietzsche, *The Portable Nietzsche,* ed. Walter Kaufmann (New York: Penguin, 1977), pp. 46-47.

[12]Sire, *Universe Next Door,* p. 95.

[13]Ibid., p. 101.

[14]Paul Spears and Steven Loomis, *Education for Human Flourishing: A Christian Perspective* (Downers Grove, IL: InterVarsity Press, 2009); Douglas Wilson, *The Case for Classical Education* (Wheaton, IL: Crossway Books, 2003).

[15]Anne Hendershott, *The Politics of Deviance* (San Francisco: Encounter Books, 2002), p. 153.

[16]Christopher Hitchens, "Why Orwell Matters," *Mesoamérica Foundation,* February 2, 2009, http://mesoamerica-foundation.org/february2reading.html.

[17]Elizabeth Shakman Hurd, *The Politics of Secularism in International Relations* (Princeton, NJ: Princeton University Press, 2008), pp. 1, 6.

Chapter 14: Principles of Secular and Christian Psychology

[1]"Quote: Carl Jung . . . I Know God Exists," *YouTube* video, uploaded November 8, 2008, www.youtube.com/watch?v=WJ25Ai__FYU&feature=related; and "Face to Face with Carl Jung—Part 4 of 4," *YouTube* video, uploaded December 3, 2007, www.youtube.com/watch?v=90VXHjQREDM&feature=related.

[2]Carl Jung, *Memories, Dreams, Reflections,* ed. Aniela Jaffé, trans. Richard and Clara Winston, rev. ed. (New York: Vintage Books, 1963, 1989), p. 140.

[3]C. S. Lewis, *The Abolition of Man* (New York: HarperCollins, 1974), see appendix.

[4]B. F. Skinner, *Skinner for the Classroom: Selected Papers,* ed. Robert Epstein (Champaign, IL: Research Press, 1982), see esp. chap. 6, "Freedom and the Control of Men," pp. 135-52.

[5]Ryan Howes, "Seven Questions for Donald Meichenbaum," In Therapy (blog), *Psychology Today,* December 3, 2008, www.psychologytoday.com/blog/in -therapy/200812/seven-questions-donald-meichenbaum.

[6]See The Albert Ellis Institute, http://albertellis.org/.

[7]Aaron Beck, *Depression: Causes and Treatments* (Philadelphia: University of Pennsylvania Press, 1972).

[8]Martin Seligman and Mihaly Csikszentmihalyi, "Positive Psychology: An Introduction," *American Psychologist* 55 (2000): 5-14.

[9]Tom Bartlett, "Soldiers of Optimism," *Chronicle of Higher Education*, October 30, 2011.

[10]John Hogan, "Are Psychiatric Medications Making Us Sicker?" *The Chronicle of Higher Education*, September 18, 2011.

[11]Paul Vitz, introduction to *The Self Beyond the Postmodern Crisis*, ed. Paul Vitz and Susan Felch (Wilmington, DE: Intercollegiate Studies Institute, 2006), pp. xi-xii; Vitz, *Psychology as Religion: The Cult of Self-Worship* (Grand Rapids: Eerdmans, 1994).

[12]Harold G. Koenig and Harvey Jay Cohen, eds., *The Link Between Religion and Health: Psychoneuroimmunology and the Faith Factor* (New York: Oxford University Press, 2002), see chap. 1 for summary.

[13]Neil Krause and Christopher Ellison, "Forgiveness by God, Forgiveness of Others, and Psychological Well-Being in Late Life," *Journal for the Scientific Study of Religion* 42 (2003): 89.

[14]Ibid., p. 90.

[15]Ibid., p. 89.

[16]Ibid., p. 90.

[17]Dallas Willard, *Knowing Christ Today: Why We Can Trust Spiritual Knowledge* (New York: HarperOne, 2009), p. 132.

[18]Christopher Hitchens, *The Missionary Position: Mother Teresa in Theory and Practice* (New York: Verso, 1995).

[19]Elizabeth Fox-Genovese, "Abortion: A War on Women," in *The Cost of Choice: Women Evaluate the Impact of Abortion,* ed. Ericka Bachiochi (San Francisco: Encounter Books, 2004), pp. 52-53.

[20]Hobart Mowrer, "Sin, the Lesser of Two Evils," *American Psychologist* 15 (1960): 301-4.

Chapter 15: Finding Moral Truth in Human Dialogue

[1]*Stanford Encyclopedia of Philosophy*, ed. Edward N. Zalta, summer 2009 edition, s.v. "Jürgen Habermas," by James Bohman and William Rehg, http://plato.stanford.edu/archives/sum2009/entries/habermas/.

[2]Marcello Pera, *Why We Should Call Ourselves Christian: The Religious Roots of Free Societies*, trans. L. B. Lappin (New York: Encounter Books, 2011), p. 210.

[3]Jürgen Habermas, *The Theory of Communicative Action Volume One: Reason and the Rationalization of Society,* trans. Thomas A. McCarthy (Boston: Beacon Press, 1984); idem, *The Theory of Communicative Action Volume Two: Liveworld and System; A Critique of Functionalist Reason,* trans. Thomas A. McCarthy (Boston: Beacon Press, 1987); Jürgen Habermas and

Joseph Ratzinger, *Dialectics of Secularization,* ed. Florian Schuller, trans. Brian McNeil (San Francisco: Ignatius Press, 2006); Jürgen Habermas, *Time and Transitions,* ed. and trans. Ciaran Cronin and Max Pensky (Cambridge: Polity Press, 2006); idem, "A 'Post-Secular' Society—What Does That Mean?" *Reset.doc,* September 16, 2008, www.resetdoc.org/story/00000000926; and idem, *An Awareness of What Is Missing: Faith and Reason in a Post-secular Age,* trans. Ciaran Cronin (Malden, MA: Polity, 2011).

[4]Steven Smith, *The Disenchantment of Secular Discourse* (Cambridge, MA: Harvard University Press, 2010), pp. 154, 184.

[5]Jonathan Sacks, "Reversing the Decay of London Undone," *Wall Street Journal,* August 20, 2011.

[6]Smith, *Disenchantment of Secular Discourse,* p. 198.

[7]Pera, *Why We Should Call Ourselves Christian,* p. 137.

[8]See Michael Novak, "A Western Blueprint: An Atheist Defends the Judeo-Christian Ethic," review of *Why We Should Call Ourselves Christian,* by Marcello Pera, *Weekly Standard,* October 24, 2011, www.weeklystandard.com /author/michael-novak.

[9]David Bentley Hart, *Atheist Delusions: The Christian Revolution and Its Fashionable Enemies* (New Haven, CT: Yale University Press, 2009), p. 106.

[10]Pera, *Why We Should Call Ourselves Christian,* pp. 160-61.

Chapter 16: Exorcising Sin

[1]C. S. Lewis, *Mere Christianity* (New York: HarperCollins, 2001), pp. 42-45. Also see Lewis's *Screwtape Letters,* one of the most revealing books written on the workings and influence of evil in our day-to-day lives.

[2]Aldous Huxley, *Ends and Means: An Inquiry into the Nature of Ideals and into Methods Employed for Their Realization* (New York: Greenwood Press, 1937), p. 316. As quoted in D. A. Carson, *Scandalous: The Cross and the Resurrection of Jesus* (Wheaton, IL: Crossway), p. 145.

[3]*Choosing the Creator's Path,* Indian Life Ministries, P.O. Box 3765, RPO Redwood Centre, Winnipeg, Canada R2W 3R6. 1-800-665-9275.

[4]I believe this is what Paul is talking about in 2 Corinthians 10:3-6: when we have "take[n] every thought captive to obey Christ," with his grace, we are "ready to punish every disobedience, when [our] obedience is complete." Punishing the disobedience that operated in him happened via my testimony to the power and grace of God.

Chapter 17: Contesting Jesus as Divine

[1]Fritz Stevens, Edward Tabash, Tom Hill, Mary Ellen Sikes and Tom Flynn, "What Is Secular Humanism?" www.secularhumanism.org/index.php?page= what&section=main.

[2]Robert Reich, "Bush's God," *American Prospect,* June 17, 2004.

[3]Thomas Nagel, *The Last Word* (New York: Oxford University Press, 1997), pp. 130-31.

[4]Phil Zuckerman, *Society Without God: What the Least Religious Nations Can Tell Us About Contentment* (New York: New York University Press, 2008).

[5]Per Henrik Hansen, "Denmark: A Case Study in Social Democracy," Ludwig von Mises Institute, July 22, 2003, http://mises.org/daily/1274/Denmark-A-Case-Study-in-Social-Democracy.

[6]Kjell Lejon and Marcus Agnafors, Review of *Society Without God: What the Least Religious Nations Can Tell Us About Contentment,* by Phil Zuckerman; Kjell O. Lejon, Review of *Society Without God: What the Least Religious Nations Can Tell Us About Contentment,* by Phil Zuckerman, *Kyrkohistorisk Årsskrift* (2010): 304-6; and Kjell Lejon and Marcus Agnafors, "Less Religion, Better Society? On Religion, Secularity, and Prosperity in Scandinavia," *Dialog: A Journal of Theology* 50 (Fall 2011): 297-307.

[7]C. S. Lewis, *Mere Christianity* (New York: HarperCollins, 2001), pp. 40-41.

Chapter 18: Immanence—The Spirit Within Us

[1]*Stanford Encyclopedia of Philosophy,* ed. Edward N. Zalta, spring 2012 edition, s.v. "Pantheism," by Michael Levine, http://plato.stanford.edu/archives/spr2012/entries/pantheism/. See also Huston Smith's books on world religions, such as *The World's Religions* (New York: HarperCollins, 1989).

[2]C. S. Lewis, *The Abolition of Man* (New York: HarperCollins, 1971), appendix.

[3]J. Budziszewski, *Written on the Heart* (Downers Grove, IL; InterVarsity Press, 1997); and idem, *What We Can't Not Know: A Guide* (Dallas: Spence, 2003).

[4]"Christianity and Buddhism, 10 Virtues of Buddhism," accessed May 24, 2013, http://hhdl.dharmakara.net/hhdlquotes2.html. The website is a collection of quotations from Dalai Lama XIV, *Beyond Dogma: The Challenge of the Modern World,* trans. Alison Anderson and Marianne Dresser (Berkeley, CA: North Atlantic Books, 1996). Also see "Dalai Lama—Conflicting Philosophies of World Religions," *YouTube* video, uploaded April 4, 2010, www.youtube.com/watch?v=9yQud-ckpJM&feature=related. Here the Dalai Lama explains that the differences between religious philosophies accomodate different mental dispositions and personalities of a wide variety of people. Religion then is not a search for truth but a choice of one or the other. Different philosophies satisfy different types of people.

[5]Dalai Lama, *The Universe in a Single Atom: The Convergence of Science and Spirituality* (New York: Broadway Books, 2005), p. 109.

Chapter 19: To Eliminate Suffering, Jettison Desire

[1]*Stanford Encyclopedia of Philosophy,* ed. Edward N. Zalta, fall 2010 edition, s.v. "Mind in Indian Buddhist Philosophy," by Christian Coseru, http://plato.stanford.edu/archives/fall2010/entries/mind-indian-buddhism/.

[2]See the excellent early biography of Mother Teresa by Eileen Egan, *Such a Vision of the Streets: Mother Teresa* (New York: Doubleday, 1986).

[3]Vishal Mangalwadi, *The Book That Made Your World: How the Bible Created the Soul of Western Civilization* (Nashville: Thomas Nelson, 2011). See also Ravi Zacharias, *The Lotus and the Cross* (Multnomah Books, 2010); idem, *Jesus Among Other Gods* (Nashville: W. Publishing Group, 2002).

Chapter 20: Pantheism's Many Faces

[1]I highly recommend James W. Sire, *The Universe Next Door: A Basic Worldview Catalog,* 5th ed. (Downers Grove, IL: InterVarsity Press, 2009), chaps. 7 and 8, for a more detailed exposition of these.

[2]Robert N. Bellah and Hans Joas, eds., *The Axial Age and Its Consequences* (Cambridge, MA: Belknap Press of Harvard University Press, 2012).

[3]Ibid., p. 10.

[4]Ibid., p. 443. This is a quote from Charles Taylor, *A Secular Age,* p. 739.

[5]Bellah and Joas, *Axial Age,* p. 443.

[6]"Major Religions of the World Ranked by Number of Adherents," August 2007, www.adherents.com/Religions_By_Adherents.html.

[7]His Holiness the 14th Dalai Lama of Tibet, official website, www.dalailama .com; Amy Yee, "Seeing Science Through a Spiritual Lens, with the Smithson-ian's Help," His Holiness the 14th Dalai Lama of Tibet, December 20, 2010 (originally published in *Washington Post,* December 18, 2010), www .dalailama.com/news/post/632-seeing-science-through-a-spiritual-lens-with-the-smithsonians-help; Pankaj Mishra, "Holy Man: What Does the Dalai Lama Actually Stand For?" *New Yorker,* March 31, 2008, www.newyorker.com /arts/critics/books/2008/03/31/080331crbo_books_mishra?printable=true.

[8]*Merriam-Webster's Encyclopedia of World Religions* (Springfield, MA: Mer-riam-Webster, 1999), s.v. "Buddhism," pp. 147-68; Sire, *Universe Next Door.*

[9]Herman Hesse, *Siddhartha* (New York: Bantam Classics, 1981), p. 16.

[10]Sire, *Universe Next Door,* pp. 144-65, esp. p. 153.

[11]*Stanford Encyclopedia of Philosophy,* ed. Edward N. Zalta, spring 2012 edition, s.v. "Taoism," by Chad Hansen, http://plato.stanford.edu/archives /spr2012/entries/taoism/. Also see "Taoism," *BBC: Religions,* accessed May 24, 2013, www.bbc.co.uk/religion/religions/taoism/.

[12]*Stanford Encyclopedia of Philosophy,* ed. Edward N. Zalta, spring 2011 edition, s.v. "Confucius," by Jeffrey Riegel, http://plato.stanford.edu/archives /spr2011/entries/confucius/.

[13]His Holiness the Dalai Lama, *The Universe in a Single Atom: The Convergence of Science and Spirituality* (New York: Morgan Road Books, 2005).

[14]See Dalai Lama, "Buddhism: The Last Honest Religion? Entertaining Q&A with Dalai Lama," *YouTube* video, accessed May 24, 2013, www.youtube.com /watch?v=eIRmpQbebQk.

[15]Dalai Lama, *Universe in a Single Atom*, p. 115.

Chapter 21: Western Pantheism—Spiritual, Not Religious

[1]"Profile of the 'Spiritual but Not Religious,'" in "'Nones' on the Rise: One-in-Five Adults Have No Religious Affiliation," *Pew Forum on Religion & Public Life,* October 9, 2012, www.pewforum.org/Unaffiliated/nones-on-the-rise-religion.aspx#profile.

[2]Michael King, L. Marston, S. McManus, T. Brugha, H. Meltzer and P. Bebbington, "Religion, Spirituality and Mental Health: Results from a National Study of English Households," *British Journal of Psychiatry* 202 (2013): 68-73. Summaries retrieved from Mark Vernon, "Spiritual, but Not Religious? A Dangerous Mix," *Guardian,* January 9, 2013, www.guardian.co.uk/commentisfree/belief/2013/jan/09/spiritual-but-not-religious-dangerous-mix; and Scott A. McGreal, "Troubled Souls: Spirituality as a Mental Health Hazard," *Psychology Today,* Unique—Like Everybody Else (blog), January 10, 2013, www.psychologytoday.com/blog/unique-everybody-else/201301/troubled-souls-spirituality-mental-health-hazard.

[3]See James W. Sire, *The Universe Next Door: A Basic Worldview Catalog,* 5th ed. (Downers Grove, IL: InterVarsity Press, 2009), chap. 8. See also Philip Jenkins, *Mystics and Messiahs: Cults and New Religions in American History* (New York: Oxford University Press, 2000).

[4]Stephen Batchelor, *Buddhism Without Beliefs: A Contemporary Guide to Awakening* (New York: Riverhead Books, 1997).

[5]1 Samuel 28; c. 1000 B.C.

[6]Rhonda Byrne, *The Secret* (New York: Atria Books, 2006), pp. 175-84.

[7]Helen Schucman, *A Course in Miracles: Combined Volume,* 3rd ed. (Mill Valley, CA: Foundation for Inner Peace, 2007); Eckhart Tolle, *A New Earth: Awakening to Your Life's Purpose* (New York: Dutton/Penguin Group, 2005); and Deepak Chopra, *The Ultimate Happiness Prescription: 7 Keys to Joy and Enlightenment* (New York: Harmony Books, 2009).

[8]The Chopra Center, www.chopra.com/programs.

[9]Herman Hesse, *Siddhartha* (New York: Bantam Classics, 1981), p. 7.

[10]The Theosophical Society in America, home page, www.theosophical.org.

[11]Unitarian Universalist Association of Congregations, home page, www.uua.org.

[12]The Transcendental Meditation Program, home page, www.tm.org; and "NIH Grants $1 Million to Study Whether Transcendental Meditation Can Prevent Future Heart Attacks in CHD patients," *NewsMedical,* November 7, 2009, www.news-medical.net/news/20091107/NIH-grants-241-million-to-study-whether-Transcendental-Meditation-can-prevent-future-heart-attacks-in-CHD-patients.aspx.

[13]Carlos Castaneda, *A Separate Reality* (New York: Washington Square Press, 1971); idem, *The Teachings of Don Juan: A Yaqui Way of Knowledge* (New

York: Washington Square Press, 1990); and idem, *Journey to Ixtlan: The Lessons of Don Juan* (New York: Washington Square Press, 1972). See also Robert Marshall, "The Dark Legacy of Carlos Castaneda," *Salon*, April 12, 2007, www.salon.com/2007/04/12/castaneda/; and Elaine Woo, "Margaret Runyan Castaneda Dies at 90; Ex-wife of Mystic Author," *Los Angeles Times*, January 30, 2012, http://articles.latimes.com/2012/jan/30/local/la-me-margaret-castaneda-20120130.

[14]Miguel Ruiz, *The Four Agreements: A Practical Guide to Personal Freedom* (San Rafael, CA: Amber-Allen, 1997); and idem, *The Fifth Agreement: A Practical Guide to Self-Mastery* (San Rafael, CA: Amber-Allen, 2012).

[15]Philip Jenkins, *Dream Catchers: How Mainstream America Discovered Native Spirituality* (New York: Oxford University Press, 2004), p. 211.

[16]See the Plum Village website, www.plumvillage.org/.

[17]Foundation for A Course in Miracles, www.facim.org; A Course in Miracles, www.acim.org; Marianne Williamson, *A Return to Love: Reflections on the Principles of "A Course in Miracles"* (San Francisco: HarperOne, 1996).

[18]Steven Hawking in his latest book, *The Grand Design*, suggests benevolence will be unlikely.

[19]Paul Zak, *The Moral Molecule: The Source of Love and Prosperity* (New York: Dutton, 2012); and Sam Harris, *The Moral Landscape: How Science Can Determine Human Values* (New York: Free Press, 2010). For an alternative view, see Mario Beauregard, *Brain Wars: The Scientific Battle over the Existence of the Mind and the Proof That Will Change the Way We Live Our Lives* (New York: HarperOne, 2012); and Mario Beauregard and Denyse O'Leary, *The Spiritual Brain: A Neuroscientist's Case for the Existence of the Soul* (New York: HarperOne, 2007).

[20]James Herrick, *Scientific Mythologies: How Science and Science Fiction Forge New Religious Beliefs* (Downers Grove, IL: InterVarsity Press, 2008); idem, *The Making of the New Spirituality: The Eclipse of the Western Religious Tradition* (Downers Grove, IL: InterVarsity Press, 2003); and idem, "Sci-Fi's Brave New World: How the Genre Draws Us to Its Own Views of Redemption," *Christianity Today*, February 2009, www.christianitytoday.com/ct/2009/february/16.20.html.

[21]Herrick summarizes his findings in a series of excellent interviews available on audio recordings at www.marshillaudio.org/resources/Segment.aspx?id=453054634, www.marshillaudio.org/resources/Segment.aspx?id=453054404.

[22]Ray Kurzweil has written three popular books: *The Age of Spiritual Machines: When Computers Exceed Human Intelligence* (New York: Penguin Group, 1999); *The Age of Intelligent Machines* (Cambridge, MA: MIT Press, 1990); and *The Singularity Is Near: When Humans Transcend Biology* (New York: Penguin Group, 2005).

[23]Kurzweil, *Singularity Is Near*. See also "Ray Kurzweil TED Talk—Singularity

University," *YouTube* video, uploaded June 9, 2009, www.youtube.com /watch?v=QJsHRltEVBc, and "The Six Epochs from the Singularity Is Near," *YouTube* video, uploaded June 7, 2009, www.youtube.com/watch?v =jOCoDBvhuaY, for summaries of these ideas.

[24]Sam Harris, *Free Will* (New York: Free Press, 2012); and idem, *The Moral Landscape: How Science Can Determine Human Values* (New York: Free Press, 2010).

[25]Richard Dawkins, *The God Delusion* (New York: Houghton Mifflin, 2008). p. 40.

[26]Starhawk, *The Spiral Dance: A Rebirth of the Ancient Religion of the Goddess,* 20th anniv. ed. (New York: HarperCollins, 1999); idem, *Dreaming the Dark: Magic, Sex, and Politics,* 15th anniv. ed. (Boston: Beacon Press, 1997); Margot Adler, *Drawing Down the Moon: Witches, Druids, Goddess Worshippers, and Other Pagans in America Today* (New York: Beacon Press, 1986).

[27]"A Quote by Eckhart Tolle on Divine Purpose, Eckhart Tolle, and Universe," *Giama Life,* Stream of Consciousness (blog), accessed May 24, 2013, http:/ /blog.gaiam.com/quotes/authors/eckhart-tolle.

[28]Krister Sairsingh, "Christ and Karma: A Hindu's Quest for the Holy," in *Finding God at Harvard,* ed. Kelly Monroe (Kullberg) (Grand Rapids: Zondervan, 1996), pp. 182, 185.

Chapter 22: Spiritual Transactions in People, Nature and Nations

[1]Tibetan Healing Mandala: For Healing and Protection in the Aftermath of September 11th, accessed May 24, 2013, www.asia.si.edu/exhibitions/online /mandala/default.htm; Jesse Rhodes, "The Spiritual Power of Sand Art," Around the Mall: Scenes and Sightings from the Smithsonian Museums and Beyond (blog), *Smithsonian.com,* March 11, 2010, http://blogs.smithson ianmag.com/aroundthemall/2010/03/the-spiritual-power-of-sand-art/; "Drawing a Line in the Sand: Where Art, Math, and Spirit Intersect," *misfits andheroes* (blog), November 14, 2011, http://misfitsandheroes.wordpress .com/tag/sand-mandala/; "Tibetan Buddhist Monks Construct Mandala sand painting at NDSU," *NDSU News,* North Dakota State University, accessed May 24, 2013, www.ndsu.edu/news/banner_stories/tibetanbuddhistmonkscreate sandpaintings/; G. Wayne Clough, "How Do Smithsonian Curators Decide What to Collect?" *Smithsonian.com,* January 2010, www.smithsonianmag .com/arts-culture/How-Do-Smithsonian-Curators-Decide-What-to-Collect .html; Deprung Loseling Monastery, Inc., Center for Tibetan Buddhist Studies, Practice & Culture, home page, www.drepung.org/Index.cfm; Drepung Loseling Monastery, *The Mystical Arts of Tibet,* home page, www.mysticalarts oftibet.org.

[2]"Tibetan Buddhist Monks Will Construct a Mandala Sand Painting and Perform Special Ceremonies at Aspen Chapel August 8-11, 2011," www.aspen

chapel.org/files/ac_-_Tibetan_Monk_Sand_Mandala.pdf (news release); "See Buddhist Monks Build a Sand Mandala," *Emory News Center*, February 7, 2012, http://news.emory.edu/stories/2012/02/er_take_note_buddhist _monks_mandala/campus.html.

³For a fuller explanation of the mandala, see especially Martin Braunen, *The Mandala: Sacred Circle in Tibetan Buddhism* (Boston: Shambhala, 1998).

⁴"About the Mandala," Tibetan Healing Mandala, www.asia.si.edu/exhibitions /online/mandala/mandala.htm.

⁵Jean Bethke Elshtain, *Just War Against Terror: The Burden of American Power in a Violent World* (New York: Basic Books, 2003).

⁶"Christianity and Buddhism, 10 Virtues of Buddhism," regarding choosing between Christianity and Buddhism, accessed May 24, 2013, http://hhdl.dhar makara.net/hhdlquotes2.html. The website is a collection of quotations from Dalai Lama XIV, *Beyond Dogma: The Challenge of the Modern World*, trans. Alison Anderson and Marianne Dresser (Berkeley, CA: North Atlantic Books, 1996).

⁷Philip Jenkins, *The Next Christendom: The Coming of Global Christianity* (New York: Oxford University Press, 2002); and Harvey Cox, *Fire from Heaven: The Rise of Pentecostal Spirituality and the Reshaping of Religion in the Twenty-First Century* (Cambridge, MA: Da Capo Press, 2001). See also Tim Stafford, "Miracles in Mozambique: How Mama Heidi Reaches the Abandoned," *Christianity Today* 56, no. 5 (2012): 18, www.christianitytoday.com /ct/2012/may/miracles-in-mozambique.html.

⁸For example, see Wagner Leadership Institute; Peter Wagner, *This Changes Everything* (Ventura, CA: Regal Books, 2013); idem, *On Earth as It Is in Heaven* (Ventura, CA: Regal Books, 2012); Peter Wagner, John Wimber, Neil Andersen and Charles Kraft, *Supernatural Forces in Spiritual Warfare* (Shippensburg, PA: Destiny Image, 2012); Charles Kraft, *Defeating Dark Angels: Breaking Demonic Oppression in the Believer's Life* (Ventura, CA: Regal Books, 1992); Charles Kraft and David DeBord, *Rules of Engagement: Understanding the Principles that Govern the Spiritual Battles in Our Lives* (Eugene, OR: Wipf & Stock, 2005); Ché Ahn, Rolland Baker and Heidi Baker, *When Heaven Comes Down* (Grand Rapids: Chosen Books, 2009); Ché Ahn, *Say Goodbye to Powerless Christianity* (Shippensburg, PA: Destiny Image Publishers, 2009); Ché Ahn and Peter Wagner, *Spirit Evangelism* (Bloomington, MN: Chosen Books, 2006); Bill Johnson, *When Heaven Invades Earth* (Shippensburg, PA: Destiny Image Publishers, 2003); idem, *The Supernatural Potential of a Transformed Mind* (Shippensburg, PA: Destiny Image Publishers, 2005); Kris Vallotton, *Basic Training in Prophetic Ministry* (Shippensburg, PA: Destiny Image Publishers, 2005); Kris Vallotton with Jason Vallotton, *Moral Revolution: The Naked Truth about Sexual Purity* (Ventura, CA: Regal Books, 2012); Kris Vallotton, Jason Vallotton and Bill Johnson, *Outrageous*

Courage: What God Can Do with Raw Obedience and Radical Faith (Bloomington, MN: Chosen Books, 2013).

[9]Pew Research Center's Forum on Religion & Public Life, *Global Christianity*, December 2011, p. 67; "Global Christianity: A Report on the Size and Distribution of the World's Christian Population," The Pew Forum on Religion & Public Life, December 19, 2011, www.pewforum.org/2011/12/19/global-christianity-exec/; Alessandra Nucci, "The Charismatic Renewal and the Catholic Church," *Catholic World Report,* May 18, 2013.

[10]Charles H. Kraft, *Defeating Dark Angels: Breaking Demonic Oppression in the Believer's Life* (Ventura, CA: Regal Books, 1992); and Charles H. Kraft and David M. DeBord, *Rules of Engagement: Understanding the Principles That Govern the Spiritual Battles in Our Lives* (Eugene, OR: Wipf & Stock, 2005).

[11]Steven J. Keillor, *God's Judgments: Interpreting History and the Christian Faith* (Downers Grove, IL: InterVarsity Press, 2007); and idem, *This Rebellious House: American History & the Truth of Christianity* (Downers Grove, IL: InterVarsity Press, 1996).

[12]William Koenig, *Eye to Eye: Facing the Consequences of Dividing Israel,* rev. ed. (n.p.: About Him, 2008). See also Sandra Teplinsky, *Why Care About Israel?* (Grand Rapids: Chosen Books, 2004).

[13]See "Israel Innovation" at www.youtube.com/watch?v=zHStBGk_D8Y.

[14]Nathan Schneider, "Nothing Is Ever Lost: An Interview with Robert Bellah," *The Immanent Frame,* September 14, 2011, http://blogs.ssrc.org/tif/2011/09/14/nothing-is-ever-lost.

Chapter 24: A Wider Rationality

[1]Lesslie Newbigin, *Foolishness to the Greeks: The Gospel and Western Culture* (Grand Rapids: Eerdmans, 1986), p. 54.

[2]C. S. Lewis, Appendix A: "On the Words 'Spirit' and 'Spiritual,'" in *The Complete C. S. Lewis Signature Classics* (San Francisco: HarperCollins, 2007), p. 305.

[3]Jesus taught that "the thief comes only to steal and kill and destroy. I came that they may have life and have it abundantly" (John 10:10).

[4]See for example an argument against hell: Rob Bell, *Love Wins* (New York: HarperOne, 2011). See also the response from Francis Chan and Preston Sprinkle, *Erasing Hell* (Colorado Springs, CO: David C. Cook, 2011).

[5]Newbigin, *Foolishness to the Greeks,* pp. 52-53.

[6]See Thomas Sowell, *Race and Culture* (New York: Basic Books, 1994); *Inside American Education* (New York: Free Press, 1993); Steven Smith, *Getting over Equality: A Critical Diagnosis of Religious Freedom in America* (New York: New York University, 2001).

[7]See James Conley, "America's Atheocracy," *First Things,* July 4, 2011, www.firstthings.com/onthesquare/2011/07/americarsquos-atheocracy.

[8]Stephen Jay Gould, "Nonoverlapping Magisteria," *Natural History* 106 (March 1997): 16-22, reprinted at The Unofficial Stephen Jay Gould Archive, www.stephenjaygould.org/library/gould_noma.html. The phrase *nonoverlapping magisteria* (NOMA) expresses the idea that different areas of study, such as religion and science, have separate domains of teaching authority and thus must be kept separate.

[9]J. Budziszeweski, *What We Can't Not Know,* revised and expanded ed. (San Francisco: Ignatius Press, 2011); and idem, *Written on the Heart: The Case for Natural Law* (1997; repr., Downers Grove, IL: InterVarsity Press, 2005).

[10]See, for example, Isaiah 24; 29:15-17; 32:9-30; 35:1-7.

Chapter 25: The Triune God

[1]Augustine, *Expositions of the Psalms,* quoted in George Howie, *Educational Theory and Practice in St. Augustine* (London: Routledge & Kegan Paul, 1969), p. 53.

[2]The idea of the tripart nature of man is not currently fashionable, but for me it makes more sense and is more scriptural than other explanations that use the terms *spirit* and *soul* interchangeably.

[3]Watchman Nee, *The Spiritual Man* (New York: Christian Fellowship Publishers, 1968). See also Oswald Chambers, *Biblical Psychology,* 1912 Lectures (Grand Rapids: Discovery House, 1995).

[4]These spirits may include spirits of soulishness (sloth, selfishness, anger, fear, pride, greed), addictive spirits (alcohol, drugs, pornography and sexual addictions) or those that are sheer evil (demonic spirits).

[5]The Nicene Creed, www.reformed.org/documents.

[6]*Believers* here indicates those who believe the orthodox principles of the faith spelled out in this creed. C. S. Lewis spelled it out in *Mere Christianity* (New York: HarperCollins, 2001); G. K. Chesterton in *Orthodoxy* (Chicago: Moody Publishers, 2009); and Dorothy L. Sayers in *Creed or Chaos? Why Christians Must Choose Either Dogma or Disaster* (Manchester, NH: Sophia Institute Press, 1995). Other apologetic authors include: Lee Strobel, Josh McDowell, Ravi Zacharias, Alister McGrath, John Lennox and various papal encyclicals.

[7]John Cobb and David Griffin, *Process Theology: An Introductory Exposition* (Philadelphia: Westminster Press, 1976); Norman Geisler and Peter Bocchino, *Unshakable Foundations: Contemporary Answers to Crucial Questions About the Christian Faith* (Minneapolis: Bethany House, 2001); and Eta Linnemann, *Historical Criticism of the Bible: Methodology or Ideology?* trans. Robert W. Yarbrough (1990; repr., Grand Rapids: Kregel, 1990).

[8]Wendy Griffith, "Israel's Messianic Jews: Some Call It a Miracle," *CBN News,* December 26, 2008, www.cbn.com/cbnnews/407139.aspx. See also Tony Carnes, "A Ministry Grows in Brooklyn," *Christianity Today,* September 2010, www.christianitytoday.com/ct/2010/september/28.19.html; and "What Is

Messianic Judaism?" Congregation Shema Yisrael, www.shema.com/mes sianic_judaism.php.

[9]International Alliance of Messianic Congregations and Synagogues (IAMCS), Havertown, PA (home page), www.iamcs.org/AboutUs.php; Messianic Jewish Alliance of America . . . for the Restoration of Israel, (MJAAroi), Springfield, PA (home page), www.mjaa.org/site/PageServer; Union of Messianic Jewish Congregations (UMJC), (home page), www.umjc.org; and Jews For Jesus (home page), www.jewsforjesus.org.

[10]See for example, "Who Are Messianic Believers?," Messianic.Org.UK, accessed May 24, 2013, http://messianic.org.uk/welcome/who-are-messianic-believers/.

[11]"A Brief List of Most Famous Messianic Jews," *Israel in Prophecy,* January 8, 2008, www.israelinprophecy.org/ENGLISH/live_site/brief_list-most _famous_messianic_jews.html.

[12]Various publications have begun to report, such as: "Who Is Jsa al Masih?— The Man in White?" *IsaalMasih.net,* accessed May 24, 2013, http://isaal masih.net/isa/dreamsofisa.html; J. Dudley Woodberry, Russell G. Shubin and G. Marks, "Why Muslims Follow Jesus," *Christianity Today* 51, no. 10 (October 2007); and Matthia Pankau and Uwe Siemon-Netto, "The Other Iranian Revolution," *Christianity Today* 56, no. 7 (July/August 2012): 44.

[13]Philip Jenkins, *The Next Christendom: The Coming of Global Christianity,* 3rd ed. (New York: Oxford University Press, 2011).

[14]"Global Christianity: A Report on the Size and Distribution of the World's Christian Population," The Pew Forum on Religion and Public Life, December 19, 2011, www.pewforum.org/Christian/Global-Christianity-exec.aspx.

[15]There are some denominations that do hold to pacifism, such as the Quakers, Amish and Mennonites.

[16]John 19:10-11.

[17]Jean Bethke Elshtain, *Just War Against Terror: The Burden of American Power in a Violent World* (New York: Basic Books, 2003); and *Stanford Encyclopedia of Philosophy,* ed. Edward N. Zalta, fall 2008 edition, s.v. "War," by Briand Orend, http://plato.stanford.edu/archives/fall2008/entries/war/.

[18]"The Future of Global Muslim Population: Projections for 2010-2030," *The Pew Forum on Religion and Public Life,* January 27, 2011, www.pewforum .org/future-of-the-global-muslim-population-muslim-majority.aspx.

Chapter 26: Jesus, Redeemer of Man and the World

[1]G. K. Chesteron, *Orthodoxy* (Chicago: Moody Publishers, 2009), pp. 127-28.

[2]C. S. Lewis, *Mere Christianity* (New York: HarperCollins, 2001), p. 205.

[3]Graham Cooke, *The Art of Thinking Brilliantly* (Vacaville, CA: Brilliant Book House, 2011), CD series.

[4]C. S. Lewis, *The Problem of Pain* (New York: HarperOne, 2007), p. 604.

[5]C. S. Lewis, *God in the Dock* (Grand Rapids: Eerdmans, 1972), p. 58.

[6]See Gregory Boyd, *God at War* (Downers Grove, IL: InterVarsity Press, 1997); idem, *Satan and the Problem of Evil* (Downers Grove, IL: InterVarsity Press, 2001); idem, *Is God to Blame?* (Downers Grove, IL: InterVarsity Press, 2003).

[7]Note also that in Revelation 8, a third of the trees burn up, a third of the seas turn to blood, a third of the earth is scorched, a third of the sea creatures die, a third of the ships are destroyed, a third of the water becomes bitter, and a third of the sun and moon are darkened increasing darkness on earth and a third of mankind dies.

[8]Note the relationship between the righteousness of human beings and the health of the earth.

[9]Jean-Claude Larchet, *The Theology of Illness*, trans. John and Michael Breck (Crestwood, NY: St. Vladimir's Seminary Press, 2002), p. 12.

[10]Ibid., pp. 12, 15.

[11]Catholics believe the bread and wine actually become the body and blood via transubstantiation; Protestants believe they represent his body and blood.

[12]George P. Landow, "The Light of the World," in *Replete with Meaning: William Holman Hunt and Typological Symbolism* (New Haven, CT: Yale University Press, 1979). See electronic version: www.victorianweb.org/painting/whh /replete/light.html.

[13]See Newbigin's chapter "The Word and the World," in *Foolishness to the Greeks: The Gospel and Western Culture* (Grand Rapids: Eerdmans, 1986).

[14]*Catholic Encyclopedia,* vol. 5 (New York: Appleton, 1912), s.v. "Tower of Babel," by A. Maas, www.newadvent.org/cathen/15005b.htm; and John H. Walton, "Tower of Babel," *Biblical Research* 5 (1995): 155-75, www.christian answers.net/q-abr/abr-a021.html.

[15]Martin Luther King Jr., Claybourne Carson and Peter Halloran, eds., *A Knock at Midnight: Inspiration from the Great Sermons of Reverend Martin Luther King, Jr.* (New York: Grand Central, 1998), p. 126.

[16]This booklet goes more deeply into the various objections: John P. Bowen, *Jesus the Only Way? Why Christians Seem Arrogant* (Toronto: InterVarsity Christian Fellowship of Canada, 1998). It is currently available online from Wycliff College Institute of Evangelism at www.institute.wycliffecollege .ca/1997/03/jesus-the-only-way-why-christians-seem-arrogant/.

[17]Lewis, *Mere Christianity*, p. 36.

[18]Ibid., pp. 40-41.

[19]Chesterton, *Orthodoxy*, p. 207.

[20]Dallas Willard, plenary address at Biola University Apologetics Series for Christian Faculty, November 2011.

Chapter 27: Signposts of Reality

[1]I am indebted to Francis Chan, author with Danae Yankoski of *Crazy Love: Overwhelmed by a Relentless God* (Colorado Springs, CO: David C. Cook,

2008), for this insight. Also see N. D. Wilson's *Notes from the Tilt-a-Whirl: Wide-Eyed Wonder in God's Spoken World* (Nashville: Thomas Nelson, 2009), and DVD of the same name.

[2]Arthur Holly Compton, *The Human Meaning of Science* (Chapel Hill: University of North Carolina Press, 1940), p. 69. Pierre-Simon Laplace was one of the first to try to replace the God hypothesis with physical laws (naturalism); he seemed to vacillate between deism and agnosticism or even atheism. Auguste Comte was a French philosopher in the 1800s who was active in the development of secular humanism, positing that social evolution had made God unnecessary.

[3]Michael Novak, *On Two Wings: Humble Faith and Common Sense at the American Founding* (San Francisco: Encounter Books, 2003).

[4]Derek Prince, *Shaping History Through Prayer and Fasting* (Charlotte, NC: Derek Prince Ministries, 1973); and Steven Keillor, *This Rebellious House: American History and the Truth of Christianity* (Downers Grove, IL: InterVarsity Press, 1996).

[5]Os Guinness, *A Free People's Suicide* (Downers Grove, IL: InterVarsity Press, 2012). See also Charles Murray, *Coming Apart: The State of White America* (New York: Crown Forum, 2013), p. 199.

[6]Robert E. Buswell and Timothy S. Lee, eds., *Christianity in Korea* (Honolulu: University of Hawai'i Press, 2007); Steve de Gruchy, Nico Koopman and Sytse Strijibox, eds., *From Our Side: Emerging Perspectives on Development and Ethics* (Amsterdam: Roszenberg, 2008); Lawrence Harrison and Samuel Huntington, eds., *Culture Matters: How Values Shape Human Progress* (New York: Basic Books, 2000), chaps. 9, 22; Donald Clark, "Christianity in Modern Korea," *Education About Asia* 11, no. 3 (2006): 35-39; Kirsteen Kim, "Christianity and Modernization in Twentieth-Century Korea," unpublished paper, University of Birmingham, England, 2007; and Scott M. Thomas, *The Global Resurgence of Religion and the Transformation of International Relations* (New York: Palgrave Macmillan, 2005). See also commentaries by Jonathan Sacks: "Rediscovering Religious Values in the Market Economy," *Huff Post, The Blog*, December 12, 2011, www.huffingtonpost.com/chief-rabbi-lord-sacks/religious-values-market-economy_b_1144469.html; Zhao Xiao, "Market Economies with Churches and Market Economies Without Churches," www.danwei.org/business/churches_and_the_market_econom.php.

[7]Marcello Pera, *Why We Should Call Ourselves Christians: The Religious Roots of Free Societies*, trans. L. B. Lappin (New York: Encounter Books, 2011); and Joseph Ratzinger and Marcello Pera, *Without Roots: The West, Relativism, Christianity, Islam*, trans. Michael F. Moore (New York: Basic Books, 2006).

[8]Billy Graham, "My Heart Aches for America," *Billy Graham Evangelistic Association*, open letter, July 24, 2012, www.billygraham.org/articlepage .asp?articleid=8813.

[9]Early church martyrs included Cecilia, Agnes, Felicia, Perpetua and Thecla. See Gail P.C. Streete, *Redeemed Bodies: Women Martyrs in Early Christianity* (Louisville, KY: Westminster John Knox, 2009).

[10]See, for example, English professor Rosaria Champagne Butterfield's conversion from radical feminist and a lesbian lifestyle, *The Secret Thoughts of an Unlikely Convert* (Pittsburgh, PA: Crown and Covenant Publications, 2012); political scientist Carol Swain, *Be the People* (Nashville: Thomas Nelson, 2011).

[11]Elizabeth Fox-Genovese, *Feminism Without Illusions: A Critique of Individualism* (Chapel Hill: University of North Carolina Press, 1991); idem, *Feminism Is Not the Story of My Life* (New York: Bantam, 1996); Lorraine V. Murray, *Confessions of an Ex-Feminist* (San Francisco: Ignatius Press, 2008); and Joan Ball, *Flirting with Faith* (New York: Howard Books, 2010).

[12]C. S. Lewis, *Mere Christianity,* in *The Complete C. S. Lewis Signature Classics* (New York: HarperOne, 2001), pp. 112-14.

[13]Jason DeParle, "Two Classes, Divided by 'I Do,'" *New York Times,* July 14, 2012, www.nytimes.com/2012/07/15/us/two-classes-in-america-divided-by-i-do.html?pagewanted=all4111744&CNT=100&HIST=1&_r=0; and Elizabeth Oltmans Ananat, "The Real Cost of Divorce (Hint: It's Not Welfare)," *Duke Today,* Office of News and Communication, April 27, 2008, http://today.duke.edu/2008/05/single_parent.html. See also Murray, *Coming Apart.*

[14]Adelle M. Banks, "Christians Question Divorce Statistics," *StarTribune* (Minneapolis), March 16, 2011, www.startribune.com/lifestyle/118101934.html?source=error; Glenn T. Stanton, "First-Person: The Christian Divorce Rate Myth," *Baptist Press,* February 15, 2011, www.bpnews.net/bpnews.asp?id=34656; Joe Carter, "The Christian Divorce Myth," *First Things,* February 22, 2011.

[15]William Jeynes, *Divorce, Family Structure, and Academic Success of Children* (New York: Haworth Press, 2002).

[16]Nancy Pearcey, *Saving Leonardo: A Call to Resist the Secular Assault on Mind, Morals, and Meaning* (Nashville: B & H Books, 2010).

[17]George Weigel, *The Cube and the Cathedral: Europe, America, and Politics Without God* (New York: Basic Books, 2005).

[18]William H. Jeynes, *American Educational History: School, Society, and the Common Good* (Thousand Oaks, CA: Sage, 2007).

[19]Douglas Wilson, *The Case for Classical Christian Education* (Wheaton, IL: Crossway, 2003); idem, *Recovering the Lost Tools of Learning: An Approach to Distinctively Christian Education* (Wheaton, IL: Crossway, 1991); Susan Wise Bauer and Jessie Wise, *A Well-Trained Mind: A Guide to Classical Education at Home,* 3rd ed. (New York: Norton, 2009); Susan Wise Bauer, *The Well-Educated Mind: A Guide to the Classical Education You Never Had* (New York: Norton, 2003).

[20]Lawrence Rudner, "Achievement and Demographics of Home School Students in 1998," *Education Policy Analysis Archives* 7, no. 8 (1999), http://epaa.asu .edu/ojs/article/view/543/666; Ignacio Higareda, Shane Martin, Jose Chavez and Daren Holyk-Casey, "Los Angeles Catholic Schools: A Research Report" (Los Angeles: Loyola Marymount University, June 2011).

[21]William Jeynes, *Religion, Education, and Academic Success* (Charlotte, NC: Information Age Press, 2003); and William Jeynes and Enedina Martinez, eds., *Christianity, Education, and Modern Society* (Charlotte, NC: Information Age Press, 2007). See also Nicole Baker Fulgham, *Educating All God's Children* (Grand Rapids: Brazos Press, 2013).

[22]Nancy Pearcey, *Saving Leonardo*; and Norman Geisler and Peter Bocchino, *Unshakable Foundations: Contemporary Answers to Crucial Questions About the Christian Faith* (Minneapolis: Bethany House, 2001).

[23]Geisler and Bocchino, *Unshakable Foundations*, p. 258.

[24]James Herrick, *The Making of the New Spirituality* (Downers Grove, IL: InterVarsity Press, 2003); idem, *Scientific Mythologies* (Downers Grove, IL: InterVarsity Press, 2008); and James Hogan, *Reel Parables: Life Lessons from Popular Films* (New York: Paulist Press, 2008).

[25]I am not suggesting that these characters truly reflect Christ. Rather, these films reflect the basic metanarrative of good, evil and a savior, one that is very similar around the world and over the ages.

[26]Lewis, *The Screwtape Letters*, in *The Complete C. S. Lewis Signature Classics* (New York: HarperOne, 2001).

[27]For example, Kelly Monroe Kullberg, *Finding God at Harvard* (Downers Grove, IL: InterVarsity Press, 2007); Dallas Willard, *A Place for Truth* (Downers Grove, IL: InterVarsity Press, 2010).

[28]John Ruth, *Forgiveness: Legacy of the Amish* (Scottdale, PA: Herald Press, 2007).

[29]Excerpted from Corrie ten Boom, "I'm Still Learning to Forgive," *Guideposts*, 1972, accessed May 24, 2013, www.familylifeeducation.org/gilliland/procgroup/CorrieTenBoom.htm.

[30]Johnson, *More God, Less Crime*, p. xii. Chuck Colson's work in prisons has been well known for decades. See Charles Colson, *Justice That Restores* (Carol Stream, IL: Tyndale House, 2001).

[31]G. K. Chesterton, *St. Francis of Assisi* (New York: Empire Books, 2012), p. 6.

Name Index

Subject Index

VERITAS·Books DISCARDED
FROM INTERVARSITY PRESS

As a partnership between The Veritas Forum and InterVarsity Press, Veritas Books connect the pursuit of knowledge with the deepest questions of life and truth. Established and emerging Christian thinkers grapple with challenging issues, offering academically rigorous and responsible scholarship that contributes to current and ongoing discussions in the university world. Veritas Books are written in the spirit of genuine dialogue, addressing particular academic disciplines as well as topics of broad interest for the intellectually curious and inquiring. In embodying the values, purposes and mission of The Veritas Forum, Veritas Books provide thoughtful, confessional Christian engagement with world-shaping ideas, making the case for an integrated Christian worldview and moving readers toward a clearer understanding of ultimate truth.

www.veritas.org/books

Finding God at Harvard: Spiritual Journeys of Thinking Christians
edited by Kelly Monroe Kullberg

Finding God Beyond Harvard: The Quest for Veritas
by Kelly Monroe Kullberg

*The Dawkins Delusion?: Atheist Fundamentalism
and the Denial of the Divine*
by Alister McGrath and Joanna Collicutt McGrath

*Finding Calcutta: What Mother Teresa Taught Me About
Meaningful Work and Service*
by Mary Poplin

*Did the Resurrection Happen? A Conversation with
Gary Habermas and Antony Flew*
edited by David Baggett

A Place for Truth: Leading Thinkers Explore Life's Hardest Questions
edited by Dallas Willard